Editor
Walter Kelly, M.A.

Managing Editor
Ina Massler Levin, M.A.

Editor-in-Chief
Sharon Coan, M.S. Ed.

Illustrator
Sue Fullam

Cover Artist
Denise Bauer

Art Coordinator
Kevin Barnes

Art Director
CJae Froshay

Imaging
Alfred Lau
James Edward Grace

Product Manager
Phil Garcia

Publisher
Mary D. Smith, M.S. Ed.

WRITER'S CRAFT
Models, Lessons, and More

Grades 3–5

- Rubrics
- Writing Samples
- Stationery
- Literature Links

Author

RuthAnn Billingsley Shauf, M.A.

Teacher Created Resources, Inc.
6421 Industry Way
Westminster, CA 92683
www.teachercreated.com

ISBN-0-7439-3060-6
©2004 Teacher Created Resources, Inc.
Reprinted, 2006
Made in U.S.A.

Table of Contents

Introduction

The Process

Writing is a process. It is strengthened by moms, dads, and teachers who read to their kids daily and by the discussions before, during, and afterwards. The process is complex, but it's how we learn to communicate our thoughts and ideas in today's world. For students, this becomes exciting and easier when teachers who understand the writing process break it down into small chunks for them. Teachers wishing to learn more about the writing process can prepare themselves by learning from the masters— Graves, Murray, Calkins, Routman, Harwayne, Wood Ray, Lane, Spandel, Fletcher, Thomason and York. Read them all! Absorb their teachings into the very pores of your body, letting them guide you as you struggle to make decisions about the young writers in your classroom. They won't let you down.

The Journey

With solid instruction and high expectations, teachers everywhere prepare their students for a journey of self-discovery that lasts a lifetime. No state test or formula should be your guide. The road map should be that we teach our students to write like the authors they read. It seems so simple, but there are lots of potholes in that road that we travel.

The Good Teacher: Guiding, Assessing, Savoring the Moment

Before writing the first word, writers need to consider their audience and purpose. And in order for their ideas to be easily understood, student writers need to organize what they say. No doubling back or detours are needed if their writing is clear and concise. A good teacher keeps them on track and doesn't let them miss a single important stop on the journey of learning to express their ideas in writing. Teachers guide while considering the range of experiences their writers have. They assess what their writers already know, and teach them to savor their extraordinary childhood adventures filled with quiet and memorable moments. They also demonstrate how writers make the language do good work for them without the comfortable tendency of teaching them to cram their ideas into a preconceived formula. Moreover, teachers need to match their instruction to the rate that enables students to demonstrate what they have learned.

The Goal: Courage, Confidence, Fluency

Our goal is to encourage our young writers to say what they think and to instill courage and confidence as they develop fluency in writing. As teachers, we should rejoice in the individual voice of each and every student, teaching them to craft well so that they feel competent and eager to express themselves. It is our reward when our time with these students has ended. Let us use that time well.

The Writing Process

If you want to improve the quality of students' writing, use the writing process. Remember that the process is recursive in nature—that is, you don't go through the stages in lock-step fashion. Rather, you move in and out of the stages, returning to previous stages and often skipping ahead to others as you draft. During drafting, you might get a better idea, so you return to prewriting. When you return to drafting, you might begin to revise—even before the piece progresses very far. As you reread the revisions, you might notice convention errors and correct them. While you edit, you might see a need to revise again. Then, you might draft some more, and before you write many words, you are weaving back into other stages of the process again. See, it is recursive! Teach students the process and the vocabulary so that as a community of writers you can discuss their writing in the context of the process.

Prewriting

In the prewriting stage, the big ideas are conceived and jotted down. Brainstorming begins with ideas flowing through the brain. As the writer thinks about the audience and purpose, he or she makes decisions about focus and how the piece should be organized. Professional writers use many ways to plan their writing, so teach your students many strategies to save their ideas during prewriting.

Drafting

Drafting is the stage where the actual writing takes place. It is messy, too. The writer is thinking hard while struggling to translate ideas from the plan into flowing text that shows. The writer must reread and craft more with the goal of the reader understanding the essence of meaning. Some young writers struggle with letter formation and spelling during this part of the process. This struggle takes up precious cognitive space needed for actual composition. So when you notice students struggling, support them by teaching one on one—use that "teachable moment." During drafting, teachers teach but also learn specific issues that cause their writers to struggle. Note them. Then address them because drafting is where writers discover much about themselves.

Revision

Revision is the stage where changes to actual composition occur. The intent is to make the content of the piece stronger. Sparsely developed ideas are revisited for additions. Often, writers rearrange or restructure sentences for a stronger connection to their intent or cut unclear, repetitive text. Consideration is given to word choice, searching for the precise word that conveys the idea. Structural changes are made during this stage so that the content of the piece is significantly improved.

Editing

The editing stage allows the writer to clean up mistakes made in the conventions of the piece. This stage is a courtesy to the reader. Misspelled words, punctuation, and capitalization errors are reviewed and made right. Think of editing as the clean-up phase for the reader.

Publishing

Publishing is the reason we write and the reward for doing so. It is the place where we show off our hard work. When we publish, we understand why the writing process is so vital to us. We understand why we must master the rules and grammar of the English language. We write so others will read our work and celebrate our effort. That makes us want to write again. Publishing is the culmination of all our effort.

Where to Begin?

Assessment

Regardless of the state rubric you are using, before the first lesson is taught you need to assess your students' writing to see what they can already do well. Ask them to write about anything in their lives. If they have trouble thinking of a topic, tell them to write about something they know—things they can do, people they know, places they've been, or things that they wonder or think about.

Strengths and Weaknesses

When assessing students' work, look for the strengths in their writing. Identify the strengths, and your task won't seem so impossible. Let their writing guide you in planning your next lesson. To do that, you also need to identify and prioritize the weaknesses. The guiding question in your mind should be "What is the biggest weakness in their writing that keeps it from being more effective?"

Elements of Effective Writing

Use the Elements of Effective Writing class assessment chart that follows this section to assess your students' writing. Laminate it so that you can reuse it each time you formally assess writing. As you read each student's piece, write the student's name with a marker underneath the element of effective writing where a weakness is located. After doing this, you'll be able to see where most of the class needs instruction. This assessment chart is organized around the elements of effective writing: *focus*, *organization*, *support*, and *conventions*. So, whether you are a writing teacher from Kansas, Tennessee, or Alaska . . . good writing always contains these four common elements.

Focus

Focus refers to the content of the piece.

- Is all the writing about the topic?
- Further, does the writer know what he or she wants to say in the piece?
- Can you put your finger on the place where the writer lingered longer or delved deeper into a particular part of it?

These questions help us understand what focus means.

Organization

Organization refers to the structure of the piece.

- Does it have a beginning, middle, and ending?
- Are the ideas presented clearly and logically so that the reader can retell them?
- Is there evidence that the writer planned for his or her audience and purpose?
- Does it move smoothly from idea to idea?

Without transitions, the writing won't flow gracefully, and the reader will struggle and feel disconnected from it.

Elements of Effective Writing *(cont.)*

Support

Support is all about providing enough rich, precise detail so that the reader is right there with the writer. When assessing for support, look for all the strategies that writers use to paint vivid pictures: *sensory development, facts, examples, definitions, anecdotes, dialogue, word choice such as specific nouns and verbs,* and *all the techniques of figurative language.* Our favorite writers *show* rather than *tell,* and they do it in their own distinctive voices. When assessing for support, consider these questions:

- Is the writer attempting support?
- If so, what support strategies is he or she using or not using?
- Do you see evidence of movement from weaker support to stronger support from piece to piece?
- When conferencing with the student writer, can you tell if the writer is making conscious decisions to show his or her ideas?

These strategies of supporting one's writing are used by the best writers when they write memorable pieces.

Conventions

Conventions are the writer's courtesies to the reader—those punctuation marks that help us read the writer's ideas as they were intended. The commas and dashes are placed appropriately to clarify, or an ellipse or a question is used to draw us in and force us to interact with the text. Our ability to use periods to stop the reader cold or exclamation marks to emphasize our feelings helps readers comprehend our thoughts. And to avoid monotony, we need variety in our sentence structure:

- Did the writer manipulate words or phrases to form a variety of sentence patterns?
- Are there short, medium, and long sentences in the piece?
- And did the writer use different types of sentences?

Also included in conventions is the use of capital letters and spelling. Readers need to be able to read each word so that the writer's ideas are clearly communicated. Conventions help the writer convey those ideas more precisely.

> Focus, organization, support, and conventions—these are the elements that tie the writing together and help us identify what we need to model for our students.

Class Assessment:
Elements of Effective Writing

Focus: ▬▬▬▬▬▬▬▬▬▬▬

Organization: ▬▬▬▬▬▬▬▬▬▬

Support: ▬▬▬▬▬▬▬▬▬▬▬

Conventions: ▬▬▬▬▬▬▬▬▬▬

Sample Assessment

Read the fourth-grader's piece below and review the assessment process.

> When the weather was bad I played my ninetendo sixty-four. Then I got tired of losing. so I played with my pitbull mixed with child. puppy. I Fead it an hamburger patie and took it an bath in an bucket. when it got out I dryed it withe the hair dryer. Then put it to bed in it comfortable crait. Then I got Jack and the bean stalk from my dresser and read it and Fasted my self to sleep.

Strengths

One of the many strengths of the piece is that it has a beginning, middle, and ending. Within the middle, there are events that happen. This child has ideas to write about and has organized them chronologically. Further, he shows that he is beginning to understand the difference between general and specific support. He demonstrates this when he writes, "Then I got my Jack and the bean stalk from my dresser and read it and fasted my self to sleep." A less fluent writer might write, "Then I got my book and went asleep." Also, he knows that a sentence begins with a capital letter and ends with a punctuation mark. Further, spelling does not impede the writing.

Weaknesses

Now for the weaknesses which become possible teaching points. This paper lacks focus. Yes, all of the writing is on topic, but where did the writer go deeper, delving into any aspect of it? It's a bed-to-bed piece that is common with inexperienced, less fluent writers. His piece is about what he does when the weather is bad, but do we as readers truly know what he specifically wants to tell us? What parts do we want to know more about? Looking at the plan below, we see that nothing is listed for specific support of his ideas.

> played game
> played with pupy
> read a book

Sample Assessment *(cont.)*

Perhaps using a timeline of the events would help this writer realize where he could slow his writing down to develop it more effectively. The weakness is *focus*, but it is also *support*. He has given equal attention to each part of the story. We want him to consider what he wants to explore more. Therefore, we need to teach some lessons on how to do those things. Write his name underneath "Focus" and again underneath "Support" on the chart. Then continue assessing the entire class in this same manner. You may conclude that everyone would benefit from some lessons that show them how to find the focus in their writing and also how to specifically support their ideas by *lingering longer on appropriate points*.

Writing that intrigues us always contains these elements: *focus, organization, support,* and *conventions.* These elements are common threads that separate good writing from bad. All state rubrics include these four elements within the basic framework of their rubrics. The words and organization of the rubric may be somewhat different from state to state, but when you look closely, you will see these common threads throughout. Why? Because, simply put, . . . good writing is simply good writing. That's why assessing your students' writing according to these common elements makes sense.

The teacher's job now is framed by these questions:

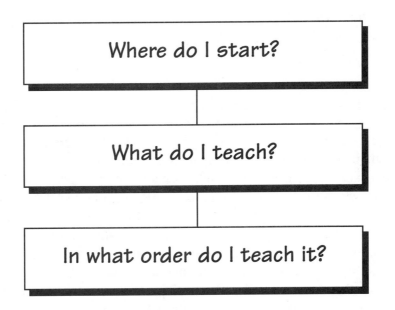

Where do I start?

What do I teach?

In what order do I teach it?

The answers to those questions lie in those writing weaknesses and your ability to select and prioritize them.

What's Inside the Book and How to Use It

This book is written from the perspective that children can and will write like the authors they read (or have read aloud to them) if we point them in that direction. What a novel ideal—the best children's authors become the example! You, the teacher, are the key. Your expectations, your experience, and your judgment are what counts.

From the pacing of the lesson to the quality of instruction, it is *you* who make the difference. You are the expert. Your decisions are critical and count. These craft lessons give you a clear picture of how each lesson unfolds. Every lesson follows the format of writer's workshop and is easy to follow.

For the teacher, these elements are included:

- strategies for assessment with analysis of strengths and weaknesses of a piece
- the lesson, including the literature link with all the procedures to follow
- a listing and samples of all materials to prepare
- samples of modeled or shared writing from the lesson
- samples of actual student writing from the lesson
- ideas for sharing and publishing

For the students, these elements are included:

- reference materials needed for the lesson
- stationery for planning
- stationery for writing
- rubrics to help students reflect on their writing

This book contains craft lessons based on specific teaching points. Students practice each specific teaching point in a small chunk of writing, rather than in a full piece. The reasons for this are that it's easier and the students are more successful. Students need time to practice and become proficient writers of small pieces where they can focus on a particular crafting technique. They are more successful at demonstrating your teaching point when you limit what you ask them to juggle. Direct your class to practice together in groups and individually until successful. Then you invite them to write full pieces, reminding them of the crafting techniques they have learned. Tell them that writers have choices and do things for reasons. The more they learn about what real writers do, the more choices they have when they write. So, direct them to practice small chunks in groups, small chunks individually, then full pieces in groups, and again full pieces individually. Turn the class into a writing community where all students contribute to one another's learning and where everyone celebrates one another's ideas.

Some of the best books in children's literature are featured as the launch for the lessons in this book. The crafting techniques presented in the lessons support any genre. No matter what the genre may be, specific support, voice, and sentence variety are important to the piece.

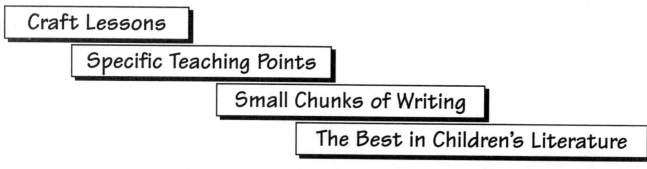

Craft Lessons

Specific Teaching Points

Small Chunks of Writing

The Best in Children's Literature

Writer's Workshop

All the experts in writing pay tribute to "writer's workshop," a teaching strategy that supports both the teacher and the students. But writer's workshop is more than just a strategy; it is a time that teachers set aside in their day that is both predictable and procedural in nature and is devoted to the goal of kids learning to write. It's a time when we directly instruct kids about some aspect of writer's craft needed to improve their writing. In the best classrooms, workshop is a safe environment with everyone involved in some part of the writing process, working towards building fluency and confidence, and you orchestrate it. Your goal is to build an atmosphere where students feel comfortable asking questions, exchanging ideas, and contributing to each other's pieces—even yours! How you handle their questions and contributions sets the stage for how they will handle each other's. Consider their suggestions carefully and thank them for helping you, for the exchange of ideas is vital to the success of writer's workshop and is what writing teachers crave.

Structure your writer's workshop so that the *students practice the teaching point*. Give them no choice about that. After all, if it's worth teaching, it's worth requiring your students to try it out. They need to learn how to do it so that it becomes a part of their own writer's craft, for only then does it truly become a strategy and a choice for them. *So state your teaching point; explain why they need to learn it; then require them to try it out.*

After assessing the weaknesses in your students' writing, select a book or passage to read aloud. The read-aloud selection should be a stellar example of the craft you want to teach in order to change student weaknesses into student strengths. For example, if your students write with bare ideas such as "My friend is funny," read aloud a selection that explicitly shows specific support, a piece so rich with description that we're right there with the writer. And remember to choose the read-aloud selections from a variety of genres too. After all, specific support is specific support, whether it's found in a poem, informational text, a story, or even a piece written by students.

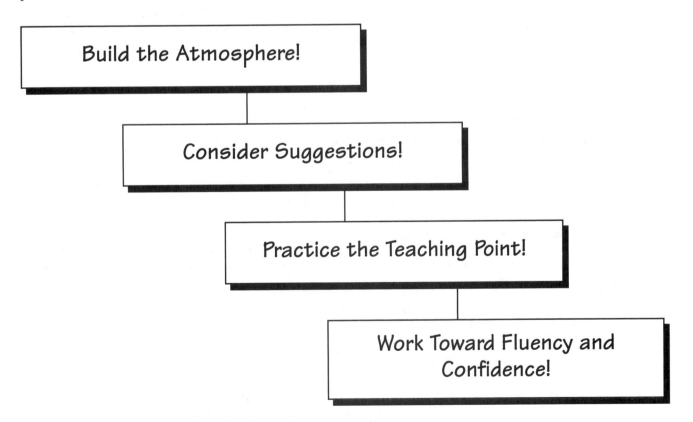

Build the Atmosphere!

Consider Suggestions!

Practice the Teaching Point!

Work Toward Fluency and Confidence!

Writer's Workshop *(cont.)*

The goal is to teach our children writer's craft found in all genres. You might ask, why begin a writing lesson with a read-aloud selection? Because it provides the direction for the lesson. It's the first opportunity that our students have to understand our lesson's focus. Tell them what to listen for as you read, and then check to see if they can identify the craft in the selection just read. Being explicit about the goal of the lesson helps them clearly understand what is expected and also teaches them that we want them to write like the writers we read to them.

Your read-aloud selection needs to be only long enough to illustrate your teaching point. When you can zero in on a small selection containing your teaching point, it makes it much easier for your students to concentrate. Since you can only keep their attention for so long, think about ways to maximize that attention as you build the lesson. Sometimes it's necessary to read an entire story, but most of the time it is not. Five to ten minutes for the read-aloud selection is often enough. It's all the time needed to set the stage and point the students in the direction you want them to go.

No writer's workshop is complete without a proficient writer demonstrating how to writers who are just learning. They need to see us do it right before their eyes. There is nothing so beneficial. So model, model, model—that's the ticket! Whether we show them through *modeled* writing (*teacher verbalizes and writes her/his own thoughts and ideas, without input from the students*) or *shared* writing, (*teacher contributes but also elicits ideas from the students and then records the piece for all to see*), we model for our students. Our kids need to see us struggle as we write, and we need to experience what our kids experience when we ask them to write. Better teaching. Better learning. It's a win-win situation when we model daily in our classrooms. Again, think about the kids' attention span as you model. Five to ten minutes, depending on your grade level, is about the right amount of time for modeled writing. Since our students are engaged in helping with the writing, we can usually keep their attention a little longer—10 to 15 minutes—for shared writing. But how do teachers decide which one to use—modeled or shared? Use modeled writing when you are demonstrating something new or writing about something only you have experienced. Use shared writing to refine and stretch a technique or idea you've previously presented. Whether modeled or shared, *always show!*

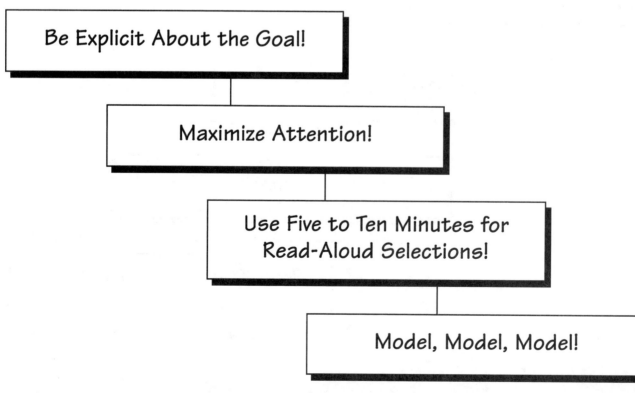

Be Explicit About the Goal!

Maximize Attention!

Use Five to Ten Minutes for Read-Aloud Selections!

Model, Model, Model!

Writer's Workshop *(cont.)*

Guided writing is the time in writer's workshop that is devoted to the students writing. It's the longest stretch of time in workshop, 25 to 30 minutes, depending on the age of your students. It is a time when your students are busy in groups or individually writing. During this time they are trying out the teaching point of the lesson and are also using writer's craft they've previously learned. They're thinking hard as they struggle getting the words down, and right about this point they are realizing that it is certainly harder to apply the teaching point of the lesson in their own writing. That's when they need our support and encouragement. Teachers work the room and support each writer, ever alert for frustration. Smiles and words of encouragement are offered. Over time we learn to recognize the writer who just wants to be left alone to write and the student who needs personal support before getting started. We also learn to recognize that confused look on some of their faces, so we pull out a focus group and reinforce the teaching point with them.

Now is the time for a sharing session, the part of workshop where we celebrate what we've written. Kids need someone other than their teacher to hear their ideas and applaud their efforts. In the most successful classrooms where there is an established writing community, children listen to one another share their pieces and coach each other. They tell the writers what they did well, and also tell them what they would like to know more about by asking questions. Sometimes the writer makes changes in the piece, other times not. It is the writer's decision whether to use suggestions provided; after all, it is that person's piece. Ten minutes spent in the sharing session makes our students realize the value of their ideas and efforts. It provides one big reason for their caring about the quality of their own writing and gives value to each person as an individual.

To plan the components for an effective writing lesson, use the lesson plan frame that follows. Grow this book by including lessons of your own that work well with your students.

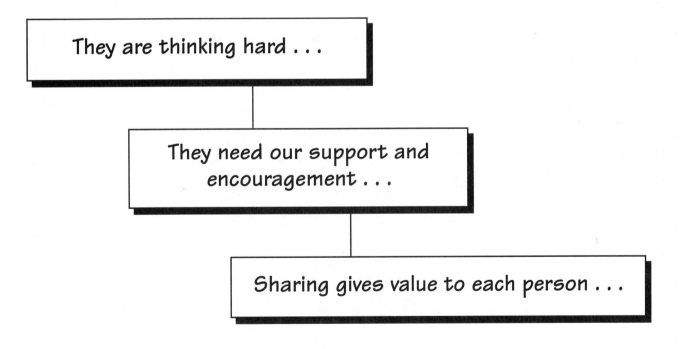

They are thinking hard . . .

They need our support and encouragement . . .

Sharing gives value to each person . . .

Writer's Workshop Lesson Plan

Assessed Weakness:

Lesson Focus/Teaching Point:

State Standards:

Materials:

Read Aloud: *(List procedures.)*

Modeled, Shared, or Interactive Writing: *(Select one of these modes of presentation and write the procedures for lesson delivery.)*

Guided Writing: *(List procedures.)*

Sharing Session: *(Describe procedures.)*

Writer's Notebook

Breathing In, Breathing Out by Ralph Fletcher provides the guidance we need in order to implement writer's notebooks in our classrooms, but other professional writers extol their usefulness too. Why keep writer's notebooks? Because they can store the treasures of our thinking, showing who we are and what we value at particular moments in our lives. These notebooks become a resource and support for our students. Notebooks are places to record interesting facts, words that we find intriguing, quotes and anecdotes we want to remember, bits of dialogue overheard, quirky thoughts, and beautifully crafted sentences or pieces pulled from our reading. The content we build in a writer's notebook can be referred to again and again to support us as we write. The categories of information need to be individualized for the students you teach. But, the important thing about keeping a writer's notebook is that it stores those bits of information we hold dear. A good teacher will keep one, share small bits he or she wrote, and model how to include some bits of information from the notebook in the pieces that they write. That bridge between the notebook and the piece under construction is vital for our students, especially if we want them to value keeping and using their notebooks.

Writer's Notebook

Contents

- interesting facts
- intriguing words
- quotations
- anecdotes
- bits of dialogue
- quirky thoughts
- beautifully crafted sentences
- pieces pulled from our reading
- treasures of our thinking
- and more. . . .

Emphasizing the Middle with Specific Support

Imagine this. You sit at your desk and you're reading a book. The main character is a male, but you don't know his age or what he thinks, feels, or does. You are in a place, but you don't know what place or why you're there, and you can't see or hear what's around you. You're sure something is happening, but you don't know exactly what. After reading a small bit, you probably close the book and look for another more interesting book—one that is chock-full of very specific details, details so rich that you're right there with the main character. Now, I'm not a boy, and I've never been coon hunting in my life, but each year when I read *Summer of the Monkeys* by Wilson Rawls to my class, I'm right there in the Ozark Mountains. My kids are there too. We're riveted to the edges of our seats waiting for the next thing to happen, or we're holding our stomachs rolling on the floor with laughter, or we're fighting unsuccessfully to hold back our tears. Why is that so? Simply, we're there with the writer because of the specific description. We know Jay Berry. We know Rowdy, his dog. We know where they are, what they are thinking and feeling, and what matters to them. We know this because Wilson Rawls understands the difference between specific and general support.

How can we teach our children to become writers like the best in children's literature? Books are the key. Our children need to understand what good writing sounds like and looks like. We need to immerse them in words that stream into sentences, and sentences that flow into paragraphs, and paragraphs that merge into entire pieces—pieces that demand our attention and keep us engaged until they end. We need to talk about the writing too. We need to analyze and examine it word by word, line by line, and we need to do it in small bite-size pieces so that our kids can learn to do it too. The teacher is the key. We need to know *what to teach, when to teach it,* and *how to present it.* If we are learning to write with specific details, why do we need to write an entire piece? Is it effective to have students juggle with writing a beginning and an ending, when they need to concentrate on mastering specificity? *The best lessons are those lessons where the teacher assesses the students' writing and targets a weakness that will move the writing.* Very often, such weaknesses are located directly in the middle of the piece. That's the place where most of the work is needed—that middle. It needs to be developed so that it tantalizes the readers. It should be so specific that our ideas are as clear as a bell. It requires precise nouns and verbs and descriptive phrases. It sounds easy but requires solid, frequent instruction and practice. A teacher never can have enough lessons on specific support. This book includes eighteen such lessons to provide powerful help to your writing instruction.

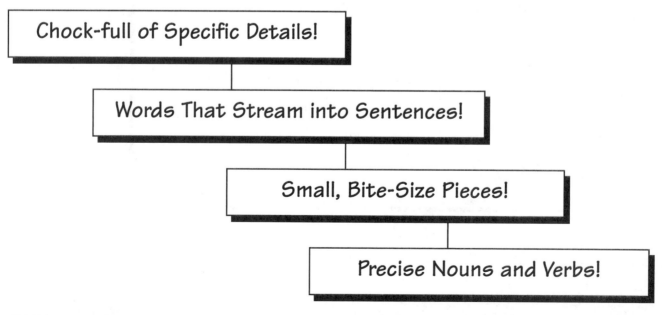

Chock-full of Specific Details!

Words That Stream into Sentences!

Small, Bite-Size Pieces!

Precise Nouns and Verbs!

So Many Memories

Materials

Teacher Materials You Need to Supply:

- read-aloud selection: *The Memory String* by Eve Bunting (alternate read aloud: *Dear Levi Letters from the Overland Trail* by Elvira Woodruff, pages 22–23. Begin with, "Now about Reuben's coat . . . ." End with, ". . . and his coat keeps changing with every new button he adds.")
- overhead projector, transparency markers, pencils
- transparencies of read-aloud T-chart (page 19), planning T-chart (page 22), stationery (page 23)
- 2-3 small personal objects (e.g., a rabbit's foot, friendship pin, and a carved peach-pit monkey)

Teacher Materials Included in the Lesson:

- sample modeled planning and modeled writing (pages 20 and 21)
- sample student writing (pages 24 and 25)

Student Materials Included in the Lesson:

- For each student, you will need to prepare packets containing copies of T-chart for planning (page 22), writing stationery (page 23), and the rubric (page 18).

Read Aloud

1. Build background by talking about the meaning of the word *memory*. Elicit some memories that students have. Probe for why the memory is important to them.
2. Tell students that the main character, Laura, in *The Memory String* holds her memories with a string of buttons.
3. Direct students to listen to the story, especially the specific details Laura gives about each button on her memory string. At the end of the book, we should be able to tell why Laura chose each item on the string.
4. Display overhead transparency of the characters T-chart (page 19). Elicit the special significance of each button on Laura's string: great-grandmother (*first grown-up dress*), great-aunt (*quilting party*), second cousin (*spelling bee*), mom (*two buttons—prom dress and wedding dress*), Laura (*two buttons—christening dress and fifth-birthday party dress.*)

Modeled Writing

1. Explain that readers want to know what matters to us and why things are important to us.
2. Display the blank planning transparency (page 22) and hold up the small items you brought. Talk briefly about each item, telling why they might be included on your memory string. Select one to write about and explain why you chose it.
3. On the overhead transparency, plan your piece, noting places where you want to slow your writing down to describe well.
4. On the overhead transparency for writing, model writing your piece, remembering to explain your thoughts as you write. Reread each sentence and then write another. Continue this reread-write pattern as you complete your writing.
5. As you write, focus on the spelling and grammar issues from your students' last writing sample. Refer to your word wall for those words that are difficult for students.

So Many Memories *(cont.)*

Guided Writing

1. Distribute to each student the prepared writing packets containing the T-chart for planning, stationery for writing their piece, and the rubric to help them think about their writing.

2. Direct students to list on their planning sheet three items of special significance in their lives.

3. Tell them to turn to a nearby partner and talk about the three items that they would put on a memory string. Instruct them to tell why they chose each item.

4. Direct students to choose one item to write about and then to generate their ideas on the planning stationery.

5. Direct students to write their piece, using the stationery for writing. Direct them to focus on memory and why it is important to them.

6. Remind students to think about their writing by completing the enclosed rubric. Encourage them to revise if necessary.

Sharing Session

Direct each student to read his or her piece to another person. Direct the listener to tell the writer what he or she did well in the piece. Then direct the writer to ask the listener what he or she wanted to know more about. Encourage all writers to consider the merit of their partner's ideas and to decide whether or not to include them in the piece.

Rubric for My Piece

Lesson Focus: Specific Support (*The Memory String* by Eve Bunting)

- I wrote about my object using the following descriptive attributes:

  color___   size___   shape___   texture___

  smell___   taste___   special features___

- I included how I felt about my object and why I wanted to keep it on my memory string when I wrote _____ .

- I s-l-o-w-e-d down my writing to show my memory .____

- I remembered to check my punctuation, capitalization, and spelling.____

- I am proud of this piece.____

- Today I learned _____

  _____ .

Read Aloud T-Chart

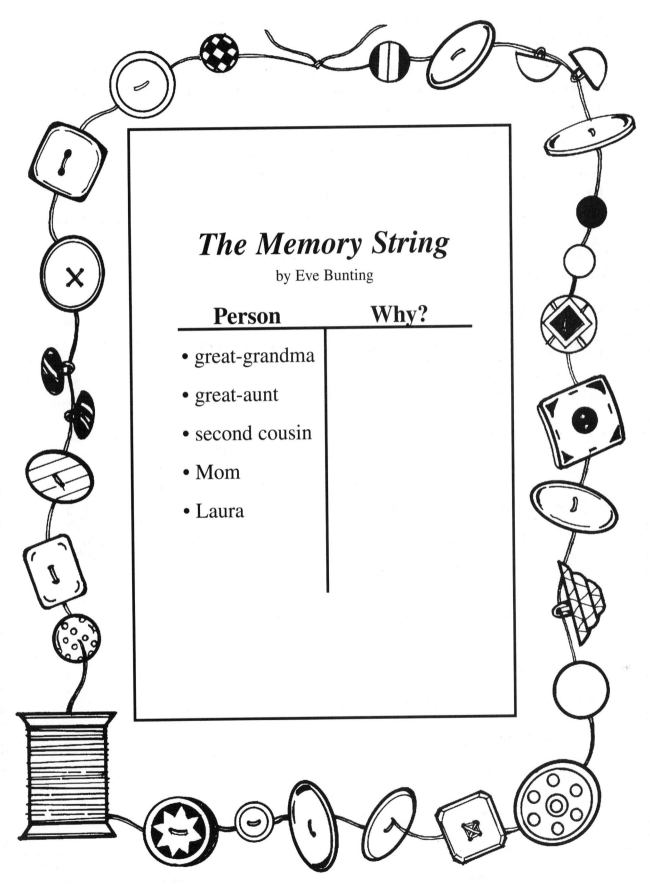

The Memory String
by Eve Bunting

Person	Why?
• great-grandma	
• great-aunt	
• second cousin	
• Mom	
• Laura	

Modeled Planning

The Memory String by Eve Bunting

Person

Pete

How I Feel

Pete—brother-in-law

Slow down writing here! ⟶

Why?

Focus: Love

- 35, callused hands

- listens and explains

- peach-pit monkey face:

  −eyes

  −nose

  −legs

Modeled Writing

Small things in our lives hold wonderful memories for us. It doesn't have to be something fancy or expensive either. A peach-pit monkey carved by Pete, my sister's husband, captures a wonderful moment for me. When I look at it, I relive the day he made it for me.

A pigtailed ten-year-old and a bearded man of 35 lean against an oak tree just behind the house. I'm talking. He's listening. Patiently, he answers each question as he rolls the peach-pit around in his big, callused hands. "How do you know where his face will be?" I ask.

"I look for a part that sticks out. That will become the nose on the monkey," Pete answers.

"Well, then what do you do?"

"I cut away the pit to make the sides of the nose stick out. Like this," Pete answers as he makes his two neat cuts into the pit.

"Where will the eyes be?"

He pointed above the nose to two places. Round and round he ground the knife, and when he stopped, he had two round holes.

"I see his face!" I shouted.

"Now for the legs. This monkey will be sitting. Let's pretend that he is high in a tree. Can you see him? I have to chop away two oval-shaped holes above and below each side."

On and on, he patiently listened and answered every question I asked. Never once did he say, "Go play," or "RuthAnn, you ask too many questions." I was important. What I thought was important. Pete made me feel like I mattered. Every time I look at my monkey, I remember—oak tree, two people—one big and one small, just enjoying being together. Yes, this would definitely go on my memory string.

Name: _____

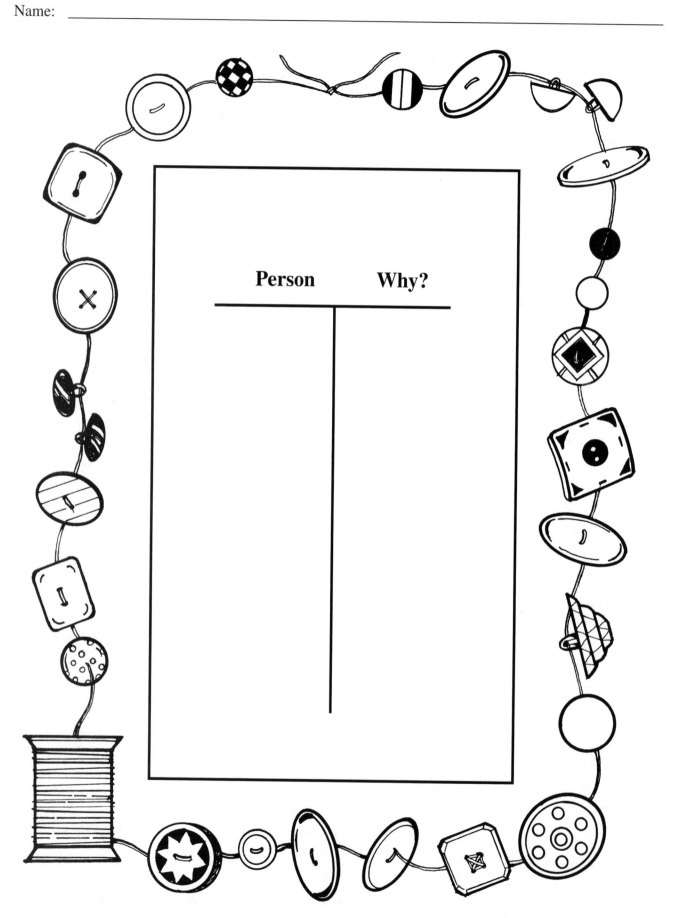

Person   **Why?**

Name: _____

Sample Student Writing

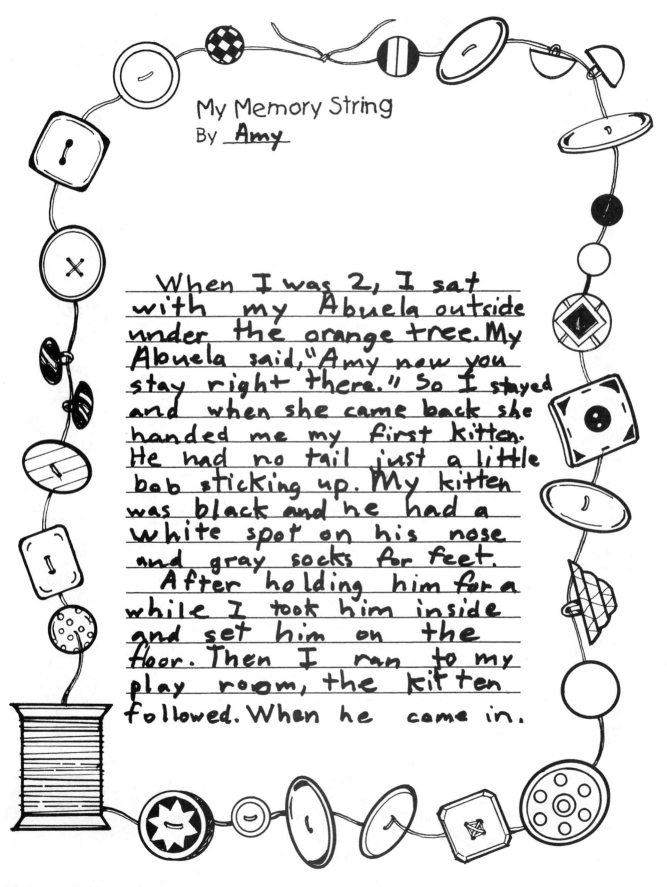

My Memory String
By <u>Amy</u>

When I was 2, I sat
with my Abuela outside
under the orange tree. My
Abuela said,"Amy now you
stay right there." So I stayed
and when she came back she
handed me my first kitten.
He had no tail just a little
bob sticking up. My kitten
was black and he had a
white spot on his nose
and gray socks for feet.
    After holding him for a
while I took him inside
and set him on the
floor. Then I ran to my
play room, the kitten
followed. When he came in.

Sample Student Writing (cont.)

Theresa my older sister who was 12 brought the little litter box and set it down next to me so I put him in, when he came out, I got a pillow, a blanket and a bottle for him. My mom put the kitten formela in the bottle and changed the nipol to a kitten sized one. After she fastoned the pink top, I feed the kitten formula to Mylow. Then I rokked him to sleep. Mylow lived 5 years. When I was 7 he died.

When Mylow was 4, I took a picture and a little chunk of fur. I put the fur and the picture in a glass box and I stilll have that picture. Even now 3 years later I have that picture and fur. Every time I look at it, it brakes my heart. My glass box holds a memory sting story for me.

Try It Using One

Materials

Teacher Materials You Need to Supply:

- read-aloud selection: *Ramona the Pest* by Beverly Cleary (alternate read aloud: *House on Mango Street* by Sandra Cisneros, pages 7–8, "Hairs.")
- overhead projector, transparency markers, book jacket of *Something Beautiful* by Sharon Dennis Wyeth, illustrated by Chris K. Soentpiet, overhead transparencies of stationery for planning (page 29) and stationery for writing (page 30), and pencils
- five or six children's books with large pictures of people (optional: use of magazine pictures of people instead of pictures from picture books)

Teacher Materials Included in the Lesson:

- sample shared planning and shared writing (page 28)
- sample student planning and writing (pages 31 and 32)

Student Materials Included in the Lesson:

- For each group of two to three students, you will need to prepare packets containing copies of stationery for planning (page 29), stationery for writing (page 30), and the rubric for thinking about their writing (page 27).

Read Aloud

1. Before reading *Ramona the Pest* by Beverly Cleary, build background by eliciting description. Ask questions about some people they have seen. "Who has seen someone with beautiful hair? Describe it. Who has seen someone wearing an unusual hat? Describe it. How about someone who has a weird nose? Describe it."

2. Tell students that Beverly Cleary wrote about a girl named Susan who had beautiful hair. Tell them to listen carefully to the description she provided about Susan's hair. Read pages 18 and 19 in *Ramona the Pest* by Beverly Cleary.

3. After reading, elicit the description of Susan's hair.

Shared Writing

1. Tell the students that we are going to write like Beverly Cleary. Display the book jacket of *Something Beautiful* by Sharon Dennis Wyeth, illustrated by Chris K. Soentpiet, or use a magazine picture.

2. Display the overhead transparency for planning (page 29). Quickly sketch the picture in the box provided. (You may wish to sketch the picture before the lesson to save time.) Elicit description of the picture, and then identify one part of the picture to write about—for example, the girl's hair. Record ideas on the overhead transparency for planning.

3. Using the overhead transparency of the stationery for writing (page 30), together write your piece. Remind them that the first sentence in the piece needs to tell the reader what you are writing about. Circle the word *hair*. Tell them that now the reader knows that all of our sentences will be about the girl's hair. When you model, try to incorporate sound in your piece. Remind them that Beverly Cleary wrote "Boing! . . . springy boing, boing hair." Include the sound as the barrettes or bow knockers clang together.

4. As you write, focus on the spelling and grammar issues from your students' last writing sample. Refer to your word wall for those words that are difficult for the students.

Try It Using One *(cont.)*

Guided Independent Writing

1. Establish groups of two to three students. Allow each group to select a picture to write about. Direct them to look and talk about the picture first. Tell them to sketch their picture in the box on their planning stationery so they can remember all the details to include in their writing. Then direct them to list their ideas. Again, encourage them to incorporate a sense other than sight. (Cleary used sound.)

2. After four or five minutes, direct them to write their piece on the stationery for writing (page 30). Remind them to include the feature they are writing about in the first sentence. Direct them to write their piece. Encourage them to say more so that they have a truly elaborated piece, and the reader can see what they are writing about.

Sharing Session

Collect the pictures from each group and display them on the chalkboard or whiteboard ledge so that all the students can see. Allow each group to read their piece to another group in the class. Then have the listeners share some things that they liked about the piece. Then see if the readers can match the writing to the pictures.

Follow-up: Revisit a previously written full piece of writing to revise for specific support.

Rubric for Our Piece

Lesson Focus: Specific Support (*Ramona the Pest* by Beverly Cleary)

- We talked about our picture and decided what part to describe. _____

- We sketched our picture to help us notice what to write about. _____

- We made a list to hold our ideas. _____

- We remembered to stay with our idea long enough for the reader to see what we are describing. _____

- We wrote down what we thought when we looked at our picture. _____

- We wrote sentences to show our picture to the reader. _____

- The best part of our description was when we wrote_____.

- We reread and revised when we finished. _____

- We remembered to check our punctuation, capitalization, and spelling. _____

- We are proud of this piece because we _____

_____

_____.

Shared Planning

Beginning:

- trade hair

Middle:

- barrettes (bow knockers) clickety-clackety

- bars, butterflies, balls—gumballs

- brownish-black

- thick, tight braids—5

- red, white, and blue

- My friend Kayla hears her coming

Ending:

- want her tight braids

Shared Writing

The hair on Karen's head was truly something to see! When I look at her hair, I wish I could trade my straight, blond hair for hers. Karen's hair was brownish-black and braided into five thick, tight braids. A bow knocker secured the hair on the top and bottom of each braid. To hold her hair in place, she had plain bars, butterflies, and balls the size of the gumballs that you get out of the candy machines at the laundromat. They were so colorful—red, white, and blue, just like the American flag. When Karen walks in line at Lockhart Elementary School, we can hear the clickety-clackety of those bow knockers clicking together. My friend Kayla says, "You can always tell when Karen's coming because you can hear her before you see her." Oh, how I wish I could get my straight blond hair into those thick, tight braids!

Name(s): _____

Ideas for Our Piece

- _____
- _____
- _____
- _____
- _____
- _____
- _____
- _____
- _____
- _____
- _____
- _____
- _____
- _____

Name(s): _____

Sample Student Planning

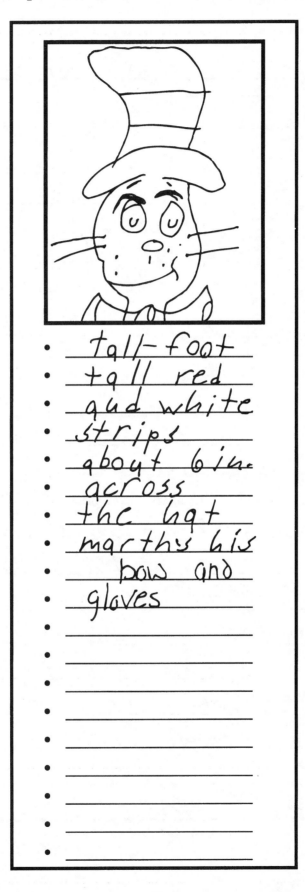

- tall-foot
- tall red
- and white
- strips
- about 6 in.
- across
- the hat
- marths his
-   bow and
- gloves
-
-
-
-
-
-
-
-
-
-

Sample Student Writing

Devin Dimiria

Hollycow! The cat and the hat have an awesome 12 in red and white striped hat. The white match's the gloves and the red match's this red tie bow. The white also reminds me of spegette without the sauce. The red reminds me of fire burning on charcko. When ever you see him his hat is never riakled. When we see him his hat always be clean. Every time you see him he would always have his hat on. His hat looks so cool it seams like you can fly it like a flying sasu. We wish we had a tall hat like that!

All in the Mood

Materials

Teacher Materials You Need to Supply:

- read-aloud selection: *Today I Feel Silly & Other Moods That Make My Day* by Jamie Lee Curtis (alternate read aloud: *Some Things Are Scary* by Florence Parry Heide)
- overhead projector, transparency markers, pencils, and crayons
- overhead transparencies of the planning stationery (page 37) and stationery for writing (page 38)

Teacher Materials Included in the Lesson:

- one set of emotion cards (page 35), enlarged and cut apart (If publishing a class book, add one paper plate for each group and ½ yard of ¼-inch ribbon for binding the book.)
- sample shared plan and shared writing (page 36)
- sample student planning and writing (pages 39 and 40)

Student Materials Included in the Lesson:

- For each group of four to five students, you need to prepare packets containing copies of stationery for planning (page 37), stationery for writing (page 38), and the rubric (page 34).

Read Aloud

1. Before reading, take a book-walk through two or three pages in *Today I Feel Silly & Other Moods That Make My Day*. Elicit from students the picture clues describing how the character feels.

2. Build background by eliciting what things students think might happen to cause the character to feel that way. Elicit also what their bodies might look like with those feelings.

3. Tell students to listen for the description as Curtis shows each emotion the character feels. Read *Today I Feel Silly & Other Moods That Make My Day*. Elicit description found in several pages of the book. Explain that we can tell the emotions that Ms. Curtis is writing about because of the specific support she used.

Shared Writing

1. Tell students that we are going to do the same thing that Ms. Curtis did in her book. Explain that we could even make our own book of our feelings (a book innovation).

2. Display the overhead transparency of the planning stationery. Model selecting an emotion. Using your planning transparency, elicit ideas for what happened to make you (the teacher) feel grumpy. Elicit three or four ideas, and then choose two to write about.

3. Next, tell students that you need them to describe how your body looks when grumpy. Tell them you will turn away from them and then reappear, showing them how your body looks when you feel grumpy. Direct them to watch closely so they can describe you. (Face away from the class and then turn around, showing a grumpy face and an aggravated stance.)

4. Elicit specific details from the students. List them on the transparency and add them to the drawing of your face. Referring to the plan for writing, write your piece together with the class, using the transparency for writing. Show "grumpy" without using the word grumpy. (Your writing should be so descriptive that students can guess the emotion without actually naming it in the piece—a hallmark of good descriptive writing.) Also, deliberately write a few general details and model revision by rereading and changing some general details to specific details. (example: "coffee" to *Folgers*, or "gas station" to *Texaco*.)

All in the Mood *(cont.)*

Guided Independent Writing

1. Establish groups of four to five students and distribute an emotion card to each group or allow each group to choose among two or three choices of emotion cards. Possible options are *lonely*, *scared*, *angry*, *thoughtful*, *confused*, *excited*, *surprised*, *sad*, and *happy*.

2. Distribute to each group the previously prepared student packets. Before writing, instruct them to talk about their emotion. Encourage students to quietly act out the emotion so other members can see what they look like. Remind them of what we did during shared writing.

3. Direct students to design a face with the crayons (in the space provided), which depicts the feeling they are to write about. Label it with the emotion. Direct them to use the planning stationery to list a few things that could happen to describe their mood. Also, direct them to describe what their bodies looked like when they felt the emotion.

4. Direct them to use their lists to write a piece on the stationery provided. Remind them that they must describe their feeling without naming it. Tell them that during sharing session, each group will read their piece, and the class will try to guess their mood.

5. Direct students to think about their writing by answering the questions on their rubrics.

Sharing Session

Collect the emotion cards. Shuffle. Draw an emotion card and allow that group to read their piece. Continue in this manner until all groups have read their pieces. Direct listeners to guess what mood the author wrote about. After guessing, the author should show the picture drawn. Elicit from the audience the specific ideas and words the writer used that enabled them to guess correctly (or incorrectly).

Follow-up Activity: Publish a book of student pieces. This will entail a lesson of organizing the pieces and writing a beginning and ending along with revising and editing the writing. One idea is to use paper plates with student-drawn faces on one side of the plate. Next, type the written text and glue it on the reverse side of the paper plate. Use ½ yard of ¼-inch ribbon to hold the pages in place.

Rubric for Our Piece

Lesson Focus: Specific Support (*Today I Feel Silly & Other Moods That Make My Day* by Jamie Lee Curtis)

- We remembered to draw our face with our feeling word underneath. _____

- We planned by listing "What Happened." _____

- We planned by listing "What Our Body Looked Like." _____

- We have specific details in our piece. We were specific when we wrote _____
  _____.

- We remembered to leave out our feeling word so the other kids can guess what our piece was about. _____

- We remembered to check our punctuation, capitalization, and spelling. _____

- We are proud of this piece. _____

Emotion Cards

Enlarge, copy on construction paper, and cut apart.

Shared Planning

Draw a face that shows your emotion here.

Today I Feel <u>*Grumpy*</u>!

<u>What Happened:</u>

Going to be late makes me feel grumpy!

- cat knocked coffee all over me
- car-gas on empty
- bumper-to-bumper traffic

<u>What My Body Looked Like:</u>

- wrinkled forehead
- sideways mouth
- eyes-slits
- eyebrows furl down

Shared Writing

Draw a face that shows your emotion here.

Today I Feel <u>*Grumpy*</u>!

Today I feel $\overline{\text{grumpy!}}$ I got up this morning, grabbed a cup of Folger's Columbian coffee and plopped down in the Lazy Boy to watch Fox News. Just as I sat down, Poli, my 23-pound cat, jumped in my lap, knocking coffee all over my beige Liz Claiborne slacks and sweater set. As I looked at the coffee bleeding down my sweater and puddling in my lap, I thought, "Oh, no! I'm going to be late! Now I have to get redressed."

Finally I was again ready to go, but when I got in the car, I noticed that the gas gauge sat on "Empty"! Now I have to get gas at the Texaco on Fowler Avenue! All these things are making me feel $\overline{\text{grumpy!}}$ When I looked in the rearview mirror, I saw my face. My eyebrows furled down and slid down towards my half-closed slits-previously known as eyes. I had a sideways mouth too! Boy, today I sure feel $\overline{\text{grumpy!}}$

Name(s): _____

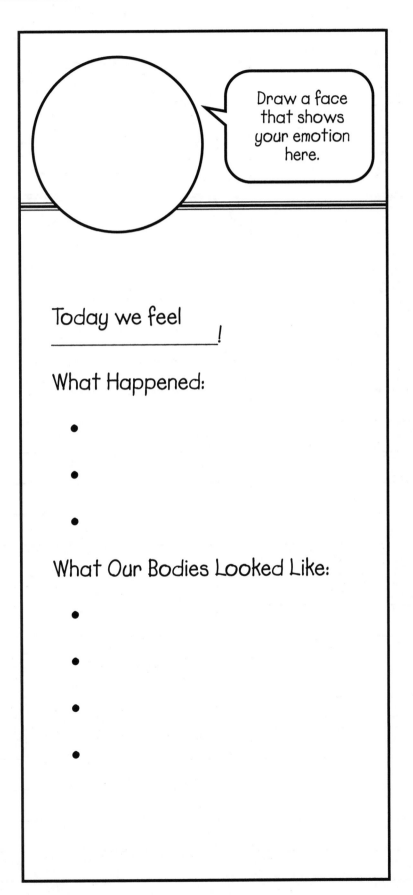

Name(s): _____

Draw a face that shows your emotion here.

Today We feel _____!

_____

_____

_____

_____

_____

_____

_____

_____

_____

_____

_____

_____

_____

_____

_____

_____

_____

_____

Sample Student Planning

Victoria, Kyle, and eurna

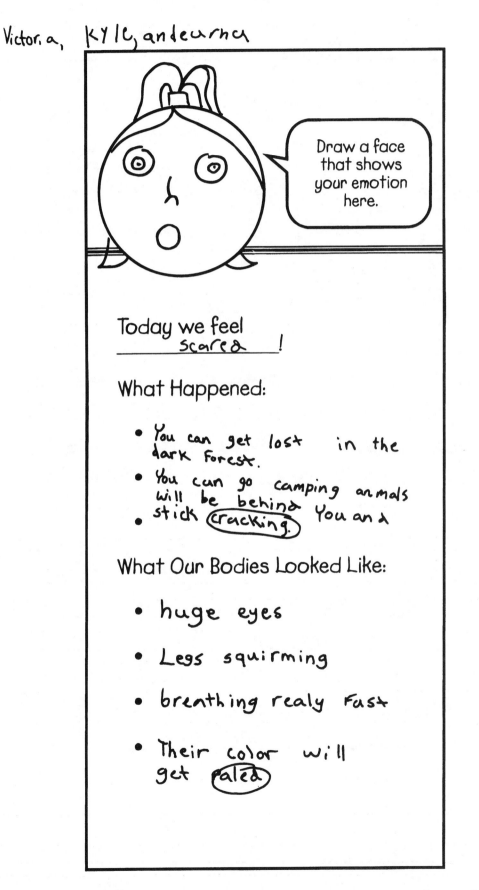

Draw a face that shows your emotion here.

Today we feel ___scared___!

What Happened:

- You can get lost in the dark forest.
- You can go camping animals will be behind You and
- stick (cracking.) You and

What Our Bodies Looked Like:

- huge eyes

- Legs squirming

- breathing realy Fast

- Their color will get (paled)

Sample Student Writing

victoria   kyle and eurha

Draw a face that shows your emotion here.

Today We feel ___Scared___!

Today we feel ——. Today we went camping in Deaths creak. We went for a two mile hike. We got lost at sunset and we started to hear sticks cracking. We saw a dark shado moveing throw Deaths-creak. We hera foot steps getting closer and closer. We was getting realy —— now. Our eyes were big as golf balls. We had (shizers) racing down our spienand our legs felt like jelly. Our breathing was hard to find. Our color _left_ our face. We started running. Boy we was ————.

Too Much Worry

Materials

Teacher Materials You Need to Supply:

- read-aloud selection: *Wemberly Worried* by Kevin Henkes
- overhead projector, transparency markers, and pencils (*optional if publishing a class book:* crayons or colored pencils and binding materials)
- items for modeled writing (e.g.—a picture of a relative, a picture of a pet, and a grocery list)
- overhead transparencies of stationery for planning (page 44) and stationery for writing (page 45)

Teacher Materials Included in the Lesson:

- sample modeled planning and modeled writing (page 43)
- sample student planning and writing (pages 46 and 47)

Student Materials Included in the Lesson:

- For each group of three to four students, you will need to prepare packets containing stationery for planning (page 44), stationery for writing (page 45), and the rubric for thinking about their writing (page 42)

Read Aloud

1. Before reading, ask the students if they ever worry about things. Tell them that you do, too. Build background by eliciting a few things that might cause them to worry.

2. Tell them that in the book a character named Wemberly also worried. Show them the book and tell them to listen to the specific things that caused Wemberly to worry. Read *Wemberly Worried* by Kevin Henkes.

3. Elicit several of the worries mentioned in the book. (Examples: a tree in the front yard, crack in the living room wall, noise the radiators made, chains on the swings, bolts on the slide, bars on the jungle gym, doll's ears, no one would come to her birthday party, whether there would be enough cake, etc.)

4. Tell them Kevin Henkes wrote so that we know exactly what caused Wemberly to worry. He didn't just say, "Wemberly worried," and leave it at that. He wrote about specific concerns so that we could understand what caused Wemberly to worry.

Modeled Writing

1. Display an item that you brought. Tell the students briefly why you worry about that item—e.g., a grocery list. Display your next item and again briefly talk about it—e.g., a picture of a relative. Display your third item and again talk about it—e.g., a picture of a dog.

2. Display the overhead transparency of the planning stationery. List those things that cause you to worry. Explain that these things are ideas for your writing today. Decide on one to write about and tell the students why you chose it. Circle it. Plan your piece by listing specific things that cause you to worry.

3. Display the overhead transparency of the stationery for writing and write your piece. Model referring back to your plan to retrieve your ideas.

4. Remember to model pulling words from your class word wall. Also, select two or three grammar issues and model using them correctly in your writing.

Too Much Worry *(cont.)*

Guided Writing

1. Establish groups of three to four students.

2. Distribute packets to each group containing list stationery for planning (page 44), stationery for writing (page 45), and the rubric for thinking about their writing (page 42).

3. Direct students to make a list of two or three things that cause them to worry. Have them circle the one they can say the most about. Then direct them to list specific things about that worry.

4. Direct students to write their piece, using the stationery for writing.

5. After they have written and reread their piece, direct students to think about their writing by completing the rubric. Have them make any changes necessary in their piece.

Sharing Session

Have students share their writing by topics. First, ask who wrote about people who caused them to worry (doctors, dentists, etc.). Direct those students to share. Next, ask who wrote about animals that caused them to worry (mean dogs, snakes, etc.). Direct those students to share. Finally, ask who wrote about a thing that caused them to worry (homework, tests, etc.). Direct those students to share.

Optional: Follow-up Activity: Publish a class book of worries modeled after *Wemberly Worried.* Write a simple beginning and ending modeled after the book or use others previously taught. Revise to make the piece stronger and then edit for conventions. Direct the students to add pictures to go with their text. (Bind and publish.)

Rubric for Our Piece

Lesson Focus: Specific Support (*Wemberly Worried* by Kevin Henkes)

- We wrote what we thought and felt. _____

- We s-l-o-w-e-d down our writing and described what we saw. _____

- When possible, we described what we heard or smelled. _____

- We were specific. (example: instead of "soda," *12 oz. Coke*; instead of "car", *silver Ford Explorer*). _____

- We compared one thing to another. (example: shaped like a cereal box) _____

- The reader can picture what we wrote. _____

- We remembered to check our punctuation, capitalization, and spelling. _____

- We are proud of this piece. _____

Modeled Planning

I worry about
Gingerbread.

- 14 years old

- golden retriever

- arthritis

- left front shoulder

- aspirin—morning/night

- hurts—hard to get up,
  hobbles, three legs

- medicine—won't work

Modeled Writing

I worry. I worry most of all about my golden retriever named Gingerbread. G-dog is 14 years old and has a hurt left front shoulder. The vet told me that she has arthritis, an illness that old people and animals sometimes get. He explained that there is no cure, but one yellow baby-aspirin at 6:00 a.m. and another again at 6 p.m. will help relieve the pain. Some days the medicine doesn't seem to work. She can barely get up, and when she does she hobbles three-legged. On those days, she looks at me as if to say, "Please make the ache in my shoulder go away." Oh! How I wish I could! I worry that she suffers too much and that the medicine she takes won't work any more. Worry. Worry. Worry. Too much worry about G-dog.

Name(s): _____

worry, worry, worry, worry, worry, worry, worry,

We worry about:

worry, worry, worry, worry, worry, worry, worry,

Name(s): ____

worry, worry, worry, worry, worry, worry, worry, worry, worry,

worry, worry, worry, worry, worry, worry, worry, worry, worry, worry, worry,

worry, worry, worry, worry, worry, worry, worry, worry, worry, worry, worry,

worry, worry, worry, worry, worry, worry, worry, worry, worry,

Sample Student Planning

Name(s): Devonte, Prince, Diamond

worry, worry, worry, worry, worry, worry, worry,

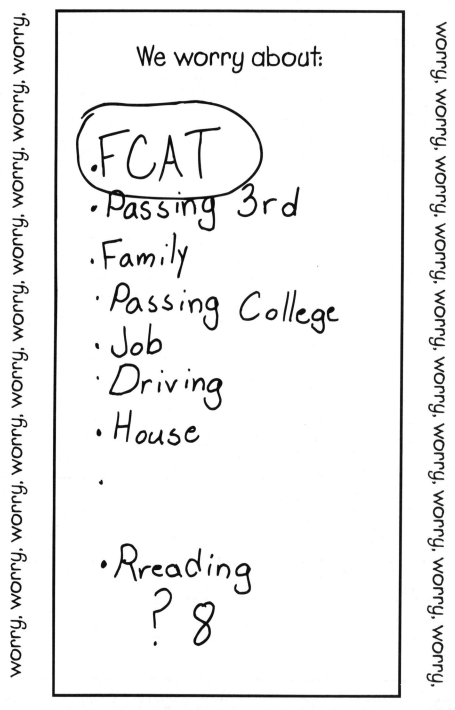

We worry about:
- (FCAT)
- Passing 3rd
- Family
- Passing College
- Job
- Driving
- House
-
- Rreading ? 8

worry, worry, worry, worry, worry, worry, worry,

Sample Student Writing

Name(s): Devonte, Prince, Diamond

worry, worry, worry, worry, worry, worry, worry, worry, worry,

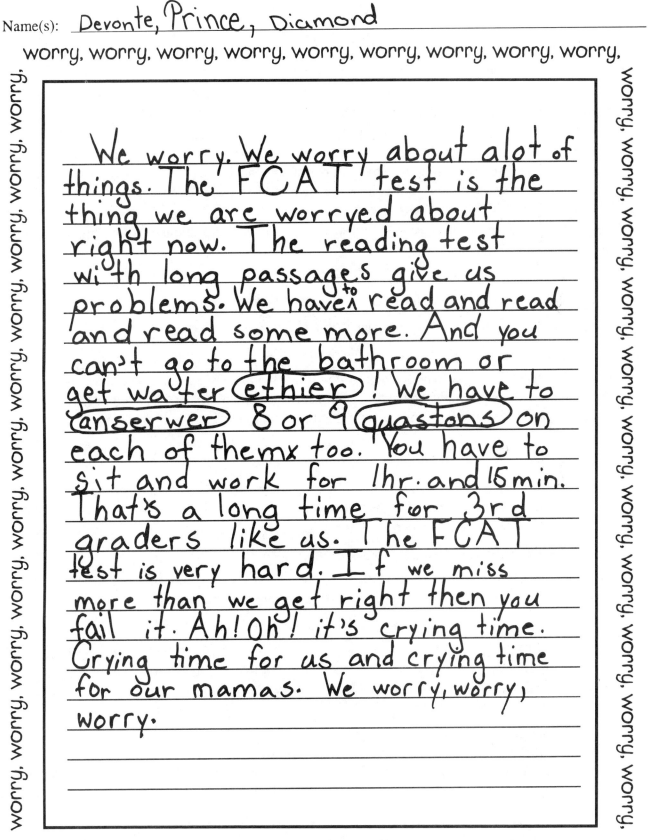

We worry. We worry about a lot of things. The FCAT test is the thing we are worryed about right now. The reading test with long passages give us problems. We have to read and read and read some more. And you can't go to the bathroom or get water ethier! We have to anserwer 8 or 9 quastons on each of themx too. You have to sit and work for 1hr. and 15min. That's a long time for 3rd graders like us. The FCAT test is very hard. If we miss more than we get right then you fail it. Ah! Oh! it's crying time. Crying time for us and crying time for our mamas. We worry, worry, worry.

worry, worry, worry, worry, worry, worry, worry, worry, worry,

It's Not Too Late, Leo

Materials

Teacher Materials You Need to Supply:

- read-aloud selection: *Leo, the Late Bloomer* by Robert Kraus
- overhead projector, transparency marker, pencils (optional if publishing a flip book: for each group of three to four students, crayons, colored pencils or markers, two 9" x 12" pieces of construction paper, and spiral bookbinding.)
- large index cards with the following sentences written on them: "Leo can't write." "Leo can't read." "Leo can't draw." (To reduce the number of students in each group, make two sets of cards of each sentence or add additional topics such as "Leo can't tie his shoes," "Leo can't ride his bike," "Leo can't brush his teeth," etc.)
- overhead transparencies of the stationery for planning (page 54), stationery for writing (page 55), and show-and-tell samples (page 51)

Teacher Materials Included in the Lesson:

- sample shared planning and shared writing (pages 52 and 53)
- sample student planning and writing (pages 56 and 57)

Student Materials Included in the Lesson:

- For each group of three to four students, you will need to prepare packets containing copies of show-and-tell writing samples (page 51), stationery for planning (page 54), stationery for writing (page 55), and the rubric for thinking about their writing (page 50).

Read Aloud

1. Before reading the show-and-tell samples, tell the students that since they are strong readers, they know a lot about good writing. Tell them that you want them to listen to two samples of writing to decide which of the two is better.

2. Read the show-and-tell sample for "The dog looked dirty."

3. Elicit why the show piece is better. (Possible answers: "We can picture the dog." "The writing was specific with many detail sentences to show us where the dog looked dirty.")

4. Repeat the process with the show-and-tell sample for "The kitchen was a mess."

5. Tell students that you are going to read a book called *Leo, the Late Bloomer* by Robert Kraus. Direct them to listen to the story. Explain that when you finish, you are going to reread some sentences from the story and ask them to decide if they are "telling" or "showing" sentences. Read *Leo, the Late Bloomer*.

6. Refer back to the text from *Leo, the Late Bloomer* to decide whether "Leo was a sloppy eater," "Leo can't write," "Leo can't read," and "Leo can't draw," are showing or telling sentences. Explain that Mr. Kraus wrote this book for very young children who are just learning to read and that we can expand his ideas by revising the text to include more specific details for older students.

It's Not Too Late, Leo *(cont.)*

Shared Writing

1. Display the overhead transparency for planning. Read the sentence "Leo was a sloppy eater." Remind students that the sentence tells rather than shows.

2. Explain that we are going to change this telling sentence into a showing sentence.

3. Using the overhead transparency for planning, elicit and list some phrases for demonstrating sloppy eating. Elicit and list four or five descriptive phrases to show what "sloppy" means by asking these questions: "What would Leo's face look like? What would Leo's hands look like? What sounds might Leo make? What would Leo's clothes look like if he ate sloppily?"

4. Using your overhead transparency for writing, together write your piece. As you compose, reread often to answer the question "Does this show . . . ?" Refer back to your plan to retrieve your ideas.

5. Remember to model pulling words from your class word wall and to also model class grammar issues in your shared piece.

Guided Writing

Group students into sets of three or four and then distribute the packets of materials for writing.

1. Explain that each group has a job to do. They are to write a piece to show whatever their sentence on the index card says. Read all the sentence choices aloud. Then tell them you will allow each group to select a sentence from the pile.

2. Direct students to read their sentence and then write it on the planning stationery. Tell them to reread the show-and-tell samples included in their packets. Direct them to revise their sentence so that it becomes show writing, just like the samples. Encourage them to talk about what their sentence looks like, sounds like, etc. Then direct them to list one or two words for each idea on their planning stationery.

3. Direct students to write their piece on their stationery for writing. Remind them that they may begin or end their piece with the sentence written on the index card. When finished, they should complete the rubric for thinking about their writing. Allow them to make any needed changes in their piece.

It's Not Too Late, Leo *(cont.)*

Sharing Session

Collect the sentence cards. Randomly choose groups to read their writing by selecting one of the sentence cards. Continue sharing in this manner until all students have read their pieces.

Optional Follow-up: Publish a class flip book. The following day, model revision of the shared writing. Then model editing it. Assist the students as they revise and edit their pieces. Then, provide each group of students with two 9" by 12" pieces of white construction paper. Fold one in half from top to bottom. Staple the under side of each corner to the bottom of the unfolded piece. (This creates a flip piece.) Students illustrate their sentence from the text (the "tell" sentence) on the top part of the page and write their tell sentence below the picture. Flip the page. On the second page, students write their "show" piece. To complete this easy-to-make flip book, add a title and a back page and then assemble with the spiral book binding.

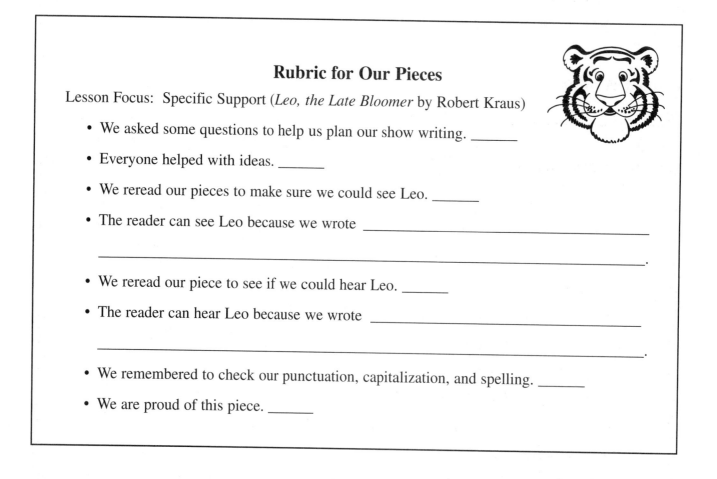

Rubric for Our Pieces

Lesson Focus: Specific Support (*Leo, the Late Bloomer* by Robert Kraus)

- We asked some questions to help us plan our show writing. _____

- Everyone helped with ideas. _____

- We reread our pieces to make sure we could see Leo. _____

- The reader can see Leo because we wrote _____

  _____.

- We reread our piece to see if we could hear Leo. _____

- The reader can hear Leo because we wrote _____

  _____.

- We remembered to check our punctuation, capitalization, and spelling. _____

- We are proud of this piece. _____

Show-and-Tell Writing

Tell Writing

The dog looked dirty.

Show Writing

Mud stuck to the golden retriever's ears, and clumps clung all down her back. The fur on her tail looked as if it had been dipped in black tar. I could see bits of lettuce and tomato dangling from her dog collar, and when I touched her, my hand came away with red clay all over it. I said, "Phew! Ginger, you need a bath!"

Tell Writing

The kitchen was a mess.

Show Writing

Pots and pans filled the sink and spilled over onto the counters. Some to the right. Some to the left. Last night's spaghetti stuck to the front of the stove, and red sauce stained the walls where it had dripped. Mom's red handprints decorated the kitchen towel, and mine painted the front of the refrigerator. When you walked on the floor, your feet stuck to it as if they had been Super-glued. I sure need Mr. Clean and a roll of Bounty paper towels!

Shared Planning

Tell Writing

Leo is a sloppy eater.

Show Writing

(Think of some other questions to help you show Leo.)

Some Phrases to Show Leo:

- Jaws poof out.
- Talks—food in his mouth
- Chews—mouth open—smacks
- No napkin
- Food dribbles down chin to shirt.
- Elbows on table
- Burps!

We show! We show! We show! We show!

Shared Writing

Tell Writing

Leo is a sloppy eater.

Show Writing

Leo is a sloppy eater. You should see that messy Leo gobble down his food. He chews with his mouth open, making smacking noises as he grinds his steak. And if he thinks of something to say, he just goes ahead and says it as he continues to chew his food. Food spills out as he talks, dribbles down his shirt, drops to his lap and even onto the floor. He fills his mouth so full that his cheeks poof out like those big balloons at the fair. When Leo eats, he props his elbows on the table and waves his knife and fork around in the air. "Burp!" That's Leo. He burps out loud and doesn't even say, "Excuse me!" Napkins? Leo has never heard of them! Leo! Leo! Leo! You need some manners when you eat.

We show! We show! We show! We show!

Name(s): _____

Tell Writing

Leo can't _____.

Show Writing

What does Leo look like?

What sounds would Leo make?

(Think of some other questions to help you show Leo.)

Some Phrases to Show Leo:

❑ _____

❑ _____

❑ _____

❑ _____

❑ _____

❑ _____

❑ _____

❑ _____

We show! We show! We show! We show!

Name(s): _____

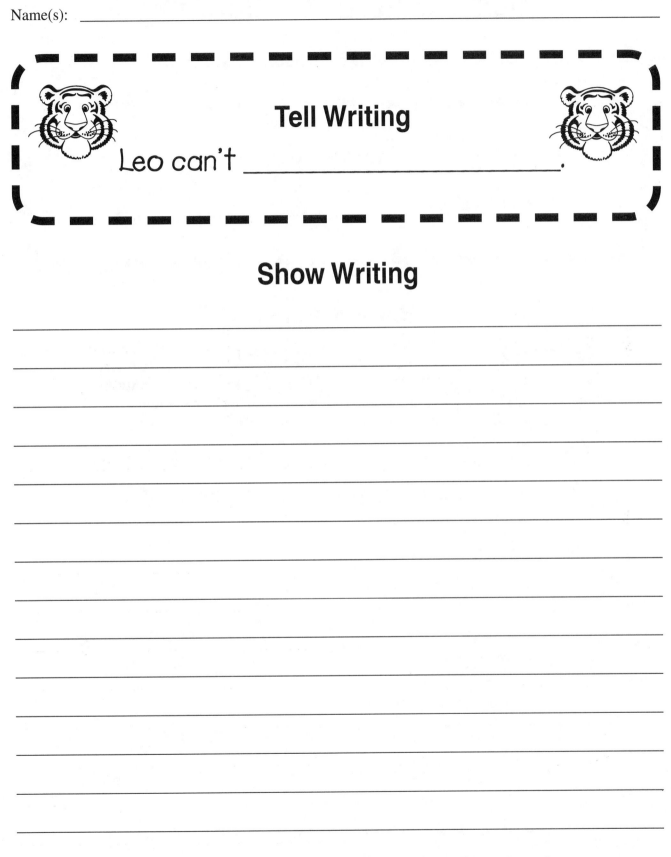

Tell Writing

Leo can't _____.

Show Writing

_____

_____

_____

_____

_____

_____

_____

_____

_____

_____

_____

We show! We show! We show! We show!

Sample Student Planning

Name(s): <u>Joyce, John, Javier, Yvette</u>

Tell Writing

Leo can't _____<u>read</u>_____.

Show Writing

What does Leo look like?

What sounds would Leo make?

(Think of some other questions to help you show Leo.)

Some Phrases to Show Leo:

· He would pretend to read right to left like chinesse.

· He would go around asking people to help him read.   whining.

· He's always bugging people to read his favorite books. <u>Are you my mother</u>

· His favorite books was <u>are you my mother.</u>

· He would even go under the table and read.

We show! We show! We show! We show!

Sample Student Writing

Name(s): Joyce, John, Javier, Yvette

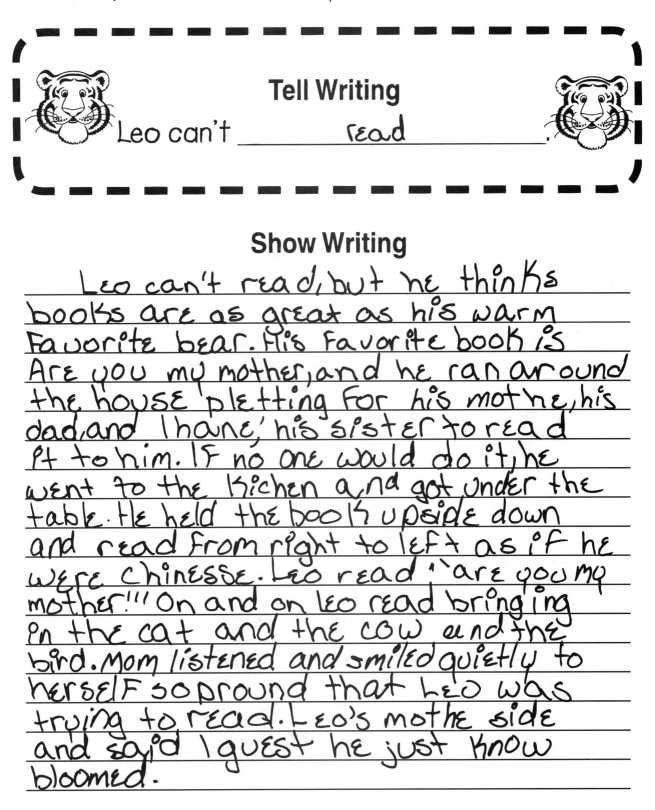

Tell Writing

Leo can't _____read_____.

Show Writing

Leo can't read, but he thinks
books are as great as his warm
favorite bear. His favorite book is
Are you my mother, and he ran around
the house pletting for his mothe, his
dad, and Ihane, his sister to read
it to him. If no one would do it, he
went to the kichen and got under the
table. He held the book upside down
and read from right to left as if he
were chinesse. Leo read "are you my
mother!!! On and on leo read bringing
in the cat and the cow and the
bird. Mom listened and smiled quietly to
herself so pround that Leo was
trying to read. Leo's mothe side
and sayd I guest he just know
bloomed.

We show! We show! We show! We show!

Write Small to Show

Materials

Teacher Materials You Need to Supply:

- read-aloud selection: *All the Places to Love* by Patricia MacLachlan (alternate read alouds: *Ruby Holler* by Sharon Creech, pages 131–132. Begin with: "A week later, a postcard came . . . ." and end with: ". . . she packed her bags and moved back to Ruby Holler." *The Relatives Came* by Cynthia Rylant.)
- overhead projector, transparency marker, and pencils for each student
- "Slow Down" writing signs (page 61), prepared for each student by copying on yellow construction paper. Laminate and attach with tape to wooden coffee stirrers or straws. (*optional:* 3" x 5" lined sticky-notes for the lesson follow-up, and a photograph of your special place)
- overhead transparencies for stationery for planning (page 64), stationery for writing (page 65), and a "slow down" writing sign (page 61)

Teacher Materials Included in the Lesson:

- sample modeled planning and modeled writing (pages 62 and 63)
- sample student writing (page 66)

Student Materials Included in the Lesson:

- For each student, you will need to prepare packets containing copies of planning stationery (page 64), stationery for writing (page 65), and the rubric for thinking about their writing (page 60). Also, distribute the "Slow Down" writing signs which are not included in the packet.

Read Aloud

1. Tell the students to listen to *All the Places to Love* for ideas. Direct them to pay particular attention to the extended description of the farm where the main character was born. Read five or six pages of the book.

2. Elicit some of the description used in the book. Focus on the numerous sentences the author crafted to build the picture of the specific place she described.

Modeled Writing

1. Display the photograph of your special place.

2. Explain that you are going to describe just the way Ms. MacLachlan did, but to do so you will have to plan carefully and find the part to slow down your writing to show great detail. Also, tell them that it is easier to write well when we write about something that we actually experienced, just as the writer of this book did.

3. If your students typically write about topics they think will impress adults, such as theme parks or expensive trips, model writing about an important memory in your life. You may find they will take the hint and write about the small experiences in their lives. Following is a sample experience to set the stage for the piece:

"I am the youngest of five children. During summer, if I wanted to avoid my mother handing out chores all day, I played outside in the yard. Since there were few girls who lived nearby and my youngest brother hated me tagging after him, I invented games to play. Using only my imagination and the things surrounding me in my yard, I entertained myself for hours."

Write Small to Show *(cont.)*

Modeled Writing *(cont.)*

4. Display the overhead transparency of the planning stationery. Quickly sketch the place. (You save time by having it previously done.) Continue telling the story, talking and jotting down your ideas on the parts of the picture you've drawn. After planning, find the place where you want to slow down the writing. Tell them where and why you want to describe that part well. Label the writing "Slow Down" at this point. Hold up your "Slow Down" writing sign. Tell them you made this to help you remember where to stay longer and say more.

5. Display the overhead transparency of the stationery for writing. (You save time if you have previously written the beginning of the piece. Remember that your lesson's teaching point is to demonstrate where and how to provide detailed support. Spend the bulk of your time focusing on that part of your piece.) Tell them that you began your piece by telling the reader where you are. Explain that it is important for the reader to know right away so that they don't have to read lots and lots trying to find out what you're writing about.

6. Write your piece, using the writing process. Reread and write more, going back to change parts of the text. As you write, use your class word wall for help with high frequency words that your students misspell. Refer to your plan often and stress slowing down the writing to say more. Close your eyes and picture yourself in the place. Describe orally what you see and feel. Then ask them if they think you should include it in the piece to help them see your place. Continue in this manner until your piece is completed, concentrating on the place where you need to slow down your writing. Hold up your "Slow Down" writing sign at the place where you've chosen to slow down. Model writing more to show.

7. Reread your text. Model checking to see if you remembered to use some of the things you've learned from previous lessons. Some ideas might be strong verbs, repetitions, and questions within the text to keep the reader actively involved with the writing. Model making changes to your text next to the places where you see a weakness.

Guided Independent Writing

1. Distribute the writing packets to each student. Direct them to think about a place that brings to mind a strong memory. Then, direct them to record the name of the place on their planning sheet.

2. Tell students to make a fast sketch of their place. To keep them focused on the text, tell them that a sketch means only a basic outline of the place—no coloring.

3. Remind them to plan their piece by jotting down their ideas within their sketch.

4. Circulate as students plan and distribute the "Slow Down" writing sign. When most students have ideas down, direct them to locate the place where they want to S-L-O-W down the writing to describe. You may support them further by saying, "Find the place where the reader needs to see." Tell them to label that place with the words "Slow Down." Remind them of your model.

5. Direct students to begin writing. Again remind them to tell the reader where they are so that the reader doesn't have to read volumes to find out.

6. Encourage students to continue writing. Circulate and support as needed. Invite them to point out where they are slowing down the writing. Tell them to display their "Slow Down" writing sign when they get to the place where they want to slow down. (This sign helps in two ways. It keeps them focused on the place to slow down, and it serves as a signal to you that they are attempting the strategy. Go to them and support them as needed.)

Write Small to Show (cont.)

Sharing Session

Have students pair off in groups of two. Direct group members to take turns reading their pieces to each other. Encourage the listener to hold up their "Slow Down" writing sign at the part where the writer slowed down and described.

Follow-up Activity (Day 2)

Find a read-aloud selection from one of your students. Read it and then revisit your model from the previous day. Locate the part where you slowed the writing to show more. Reread and make revisions. Direct the students to select a piece from their writing folder. Have them find the part where the writing needs to be slowed down to describe more. Tell them to circle it. Then direct them to revise that part. (optional: A lined 3" x 5" sticky-note can be very useful for revising small parts. Have them locate it next to the place where the revision belongs. Circulate and locate two or three students who demonstrated the strategy and mid-lesson, have them share.)

Rubric for My Piece

Lesson Focus: Specific Support (*All the Places to Love* by Patricia MacLachlan)

- I thought about a place I love and drew it on my planning stationery. _____

- I sketched my picture and labeled the parts with my ideas. _____

- I slowed down my writing and stayed with my idea long enough for the reader too see my place. _____

- I did this when I wrote this _____

  _____.

- I wrote about what I thought from my memories of the place. _____

- The best part of my description was when I wrote _____

  _____.

- I reread and revised when I finished. _____

- I remembered to check my punctuation, capitalization, and spelling. _____

- I am proud of this piece because I _____

  _____.

Modeled Planning: Special Place

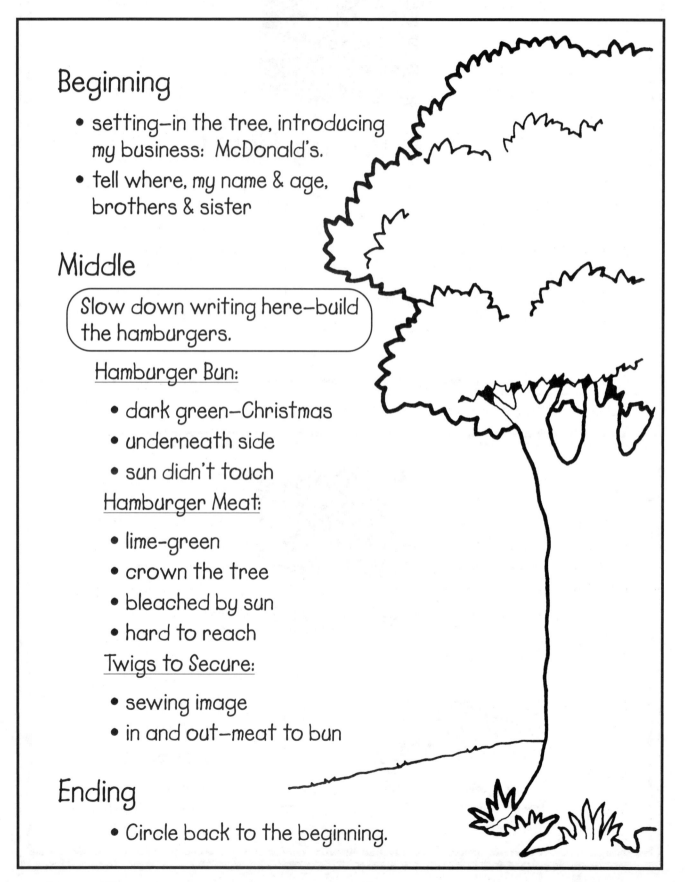

Beginning

- setting—in the tree, introducing my business: McDonald's.
- tell where, my name & age, brothers & sister

Middle

Slow down writing here—build the hamburgers.

Hamburger Bun:

- dark green—Christmas
- underneath side
- sun didn't touch

Hamburger Meat:

- lime-green
- crown the tree
- bleached by sun
- hard to reach

Twigs to Secure:

- sewing image
- in and out—meat to bun

Ending

- Circle back to the beginning.

Modeled Writing: Special Place

(prepared in advance of the lesson)

On the endless, hot, Tennessee days of summer, I'd wake up early and head right to the mulberry tree in my front yard. I'd shinny up the trunk and perch upon a limb that stretched far out over the road and skirted the edges of my world. Spraddled-legged over the branch, I'd sit with my legs dangling–swinging back and forth with the rhythm of the day. Then I'd start preparing the hamburgers that launched my McDonald Restaurant business, located on 304 Delawanna Terrace. Who's the proud owner you might ask? It's none other than RuthAnn Billingsley, the youngest sister to Marianela, Travis, Winfred, and Gary. I owned the only franchise for miles around where the hamburgers sold cheap and the service–well, none compared! When asked what was the secret of her business, RuthAnn responded, "It's all in the hamburgers which I personally prepare."

(written before the students)

Two dark Christmas-tree-colored leaves served as the buns for the burger. These leaves hung on the underneath side of the tree where the sun scarcely breathed on them. I piled up 50 or 60–one sitting on top of the other in readiness for the meat of the lemon-lime green ones. These leaves hid from me, ashamed of the bleach-job performed by the Clorox sun. To get them, I had to risk much, for they crowned the tip-top of the tree. Here the rays shot through the foliage in straight arrows that pierced my eyes. Reaching as far as my nine-year-old arms could stretch and balancing on the balls of my bare feet, I stole many and tucked them into the waistband of my shorts. I thought to myself, "These sure make me itch, but every customer deserves a hamburger made from U.S. 100% pure, homegrown leaves . . . Oops! I mean meat." Finally, "Old Mulberry" gave up the twigs that held each sandwich together. Carefully, I stitched bun to meat, meat to bun. In, bend . . . then out again, I poked the needle-sharp sticks, barely avoiding prickles to my fingers. And when the stack reached from the top of my legs to my waist, I opened my business. Here comes the first invisible customer. "Welcome to McDonald's! May I take your order please?"

Oh! . . . Those endless, hot, Tennessee days of summer! One nine-year-old girl and a mulberry tree. Sitting spraddled-legged, building burgers.

Name: _____

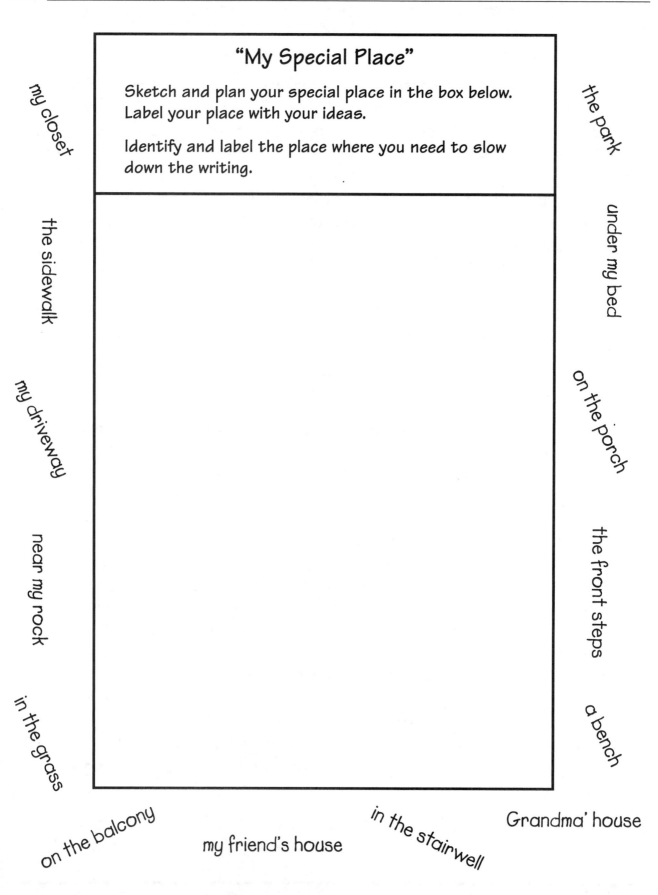

"My Special Place"

Sketch and plan your special place in the box below. Label your place with your ideas.

Identify and label the place where you need to slow down the writing.

my closet

the sidewalk

my driveway

near my rock

in the grass

on the balcony

my friend's house

in the stairwell

Grandma' house

the park

under my bed

on the porch

the front steps

a bench

Name: _____

my closet

the sidewalk

my driveway

near my rock

in the grass

on the balcony

my friend's house

in the stairwell

Grandma' house

the park

under my bed

on the porch

the front steps

a bench

Sample Student Writing

Name: <u>Matthew</u>

my closet

the sidewalk

my driveway

near my rock

in the grass

the park

under my bed

on the porch

the front steps

a bench

on the balcony

my friend's house

in the stairwell

Grandma' house

"My Special Place"

Sketch and plan your special place in the box below.
Label your place with your ideas.

Identify and label the place where you need to slow
down the writing.

atic room at
Gama's hows

My grama's hows has a big atic
that has alot of cool old antecs. It is
very dusty an when we walk in the atic litel
dots fall on the fenicher. Then It setels right back
down on the fencher where it came from. It
also has a very comefertubl fetherbed. When
you liey on it fels like sleping on air, It's
like back on a clowd. Thers also has a old
trunk full of motelaplans. Some have two
wings that are called a biplan. It also has
my granpa old balonies. He has his old clows
that has hols in it. I alwas go in the atic
with my granma. It has alot of coolold
antecs I alwas have fune in the atic.

You Gotta Eat!

(two- to three-day lesson)

Materials

Teacher Materials You Need to Supply:

- read-aloud selection: *Zak's Lunch* by Margie Palatini
- overhead projector, transparency markers, one piece of chart paper or whiteboard, four different colors of markers, and pencils for each group of four to five students
- overhead transparencies of planning stationery (page 73) and writing stationery (page 74). If continuing to days two and three, you will need additional pages of the overhead transparency of the writing stationery.

Teacher Materials Included in the Lesson:

- sample modeled planning and modeled writing (pages 71 and 72)
- sample student planning and writing (pages 75 and 76)

Student Materials Included in the Lesson:

- For each group of four to five students, you will need to prepare packets containing copies of stationery for planning and for writing (pages 73 and 74) and the rubric for thinking about their writing (page 70). (*Optional:* For day two and day three, each group of four to five students will need an additional piece of the stationery for writing.)

Read Aloud

1. Before reading, build background by saying, "Raise your hand if you always like what you get for lunch." Then ask, "What kind of food do you find boring and would not want to eat?"

2. After a few students have shared, explain that the main character in *Zak's Lunch* has exactly the same problem. He doesn't want to eat what his mother has prepared.

3. Before reading, direct your students to listen for the specific details furnished in the description of the food Zak conjures up in his imaginary restaurant. Read from pages 5–15. Just before reading, "Okay then. Here it goes . . . " (bottom of page 10), tell them to get ready for the specific detail about the hamburger. Also, (top of page 15) tell them to listen again for the specific details. "Hmmm . . . French fries . . . . "

4. Elicit the specific details Margie Palatini wrote about the hamburger and French fries.

You Gotta Eat! *(cont.)*

Shared/Modeled Writing

1. Generate a list of food preferences that your class would like for lunch. Record them on chart paper or a whiteboard.

2. Using a colored marker, circle all the drink items. Label them "drinks." Using a different colored marker, circle and label all the appetizers. Label them "appetizers." Using a third colored marker, circle and label all the entreés. Again, label them "entreés." Repeat this process with desserts. Explain that this helps writers to organize their ideas for writing. Clumping the items this way will help you choose the best one to write about.

3. Elicit the order of food items for the piece. (It really doesn't matter which you write about first, but probe their reasoning for choosing the order. We want them to think and make decisions when they write.) Choose one food from the list to write about.

4. Using the overhead transparency for planning, list specific details for that food item. (The modeled plan chooses a strawberry milkshake at the Hard Rock Café because we can give many specific details about how we want it made. Soda or milk might be difficult to support with specific details.)

5. Using the overhead stationery for writing (page 74), write your piece describing your food. Refer back to the plan often to model retrieving your specific ideas for your piece.

6. Remember to model pulling words from the class word wall and include any grammar issues troubling your students. Don't forget to reread and revise where you need to be more specific. (If continuing to days two and three, save your modeled writing.)

Guided Writing

1. Form groups of four to five students. Since you wrote a main idea on drinks, assign the remaining categories of appetizer, entrée, or dessert to each group. (You should have all the courses of a meal represented.)

2. Direct each group to talk about what they would like to have for lunch. Then, direct them to decide on one item that they can be the most specific about. Tell them to circle it.

3. Next, tell them to list specific details about their food on the stationery for planning. Remind them of the modeled writing and also the read aloud.

4. Direct them to write their piece on the stationery for writing, reminding them to refer back to their plan often to retrieve their ideas.

Sharing Session

Share writing by food topics. Ask each group of students to read their piece. Direct the audience to give thumbs up every time they hear a specific detail. (If continuing to days two and three, collect the pieces and save for the next day's lesson.)

You Gotta Eat! *(cont.)*

Day Two Teaching Points: Writing an ending and demonstrating how their pieces are main ideas in an expository text. (Return the previously written pieces to each group of four or five students.)

Read Aloud

Reread the beginning of your previously written piece and the main idea on drinks from modeled writing. Then, have all the groups read their previously written main ideas. Remind them of the goal— to write like Margie Palatini. Reread the description on the French fries from *Zak's Lunch*. Elicit the words that give the reader a picture. Read or paraphrase the rest of the story and then move to reading the ending. Point out how every piece needs an ending. Discuss how Margie Palatini ended her story. Tell them that this is only one way to end a piece and that writers have choices.

Shared Writing

Tell students that our piece needs an ending. Elicit some ending ideas. On the whiteboard, write up four or five ending strategies that you have studied. Connect writing to reading by reminding them of some of the shared endings you've read recently. Add those to your list. Using the overhead transparency of the stationery for writing, choose one ending and together write an ending to your piece.

Guided Writing

Direct students to write an ending to the piece, using a different ending strategy. Allow them to choose a type of ending from the list on the whiteboard and to write their ending on the additional piece of stationery for writing.

Sharing Session

Direct each group to share their ending. Have the class vote which ending they would like to use in the piece. (If publishing, collect and save for day three.)

Day Three Teaching Point (Revision)

Display the overhead transparency of the modeled writing. Read and then revise it to make structural improvements in the piece. Edit for conventions. Remind them to be specific. Direct each group to revise and edit their main idea. Tell them that writers always reread and make changes. Then, publish several versions of the piece, making sure that each group gets a copy with the main idea that they wrote. *Note:* The middle of this piece will contain all of your group's main ideas representing each food category. Make copies for all your students to include in their writing folders. (This piece could be referred back to as a model of effective writing and also become a powerful teaching tool for your students. Remember, you can also revise it again later to include any new techniques you learn.)

You Gotta Eat! *(cont.)*

Rubric for Our Piece

Lesson Focus: Specific Support (*Zak's Lunch* by Margie Palatini)

- We have *specific details* in our piece. _____ (Example: general = ice cream/*specific* = two scoops of Edy's vanilla ice cream)

- We were *specific* when we wrote _____

    _____

    _____.

- We used an *example* when we wrote _____

    _____

    _____.

- We used *facts* when we wrote _____

    _____

    _____.

- We included a *personal experience* when we wrote about _____

    _____

    _____.

- We remembered to check our punctuation, capitalization, and spelling. _____

- We are proud of our piece. _____

Modeled Planning

Check

For my <u>drink</u>, I will have a <u>strawberry</u> <u>milkshake</u>.

<u>Specific details</u> about my food are these:

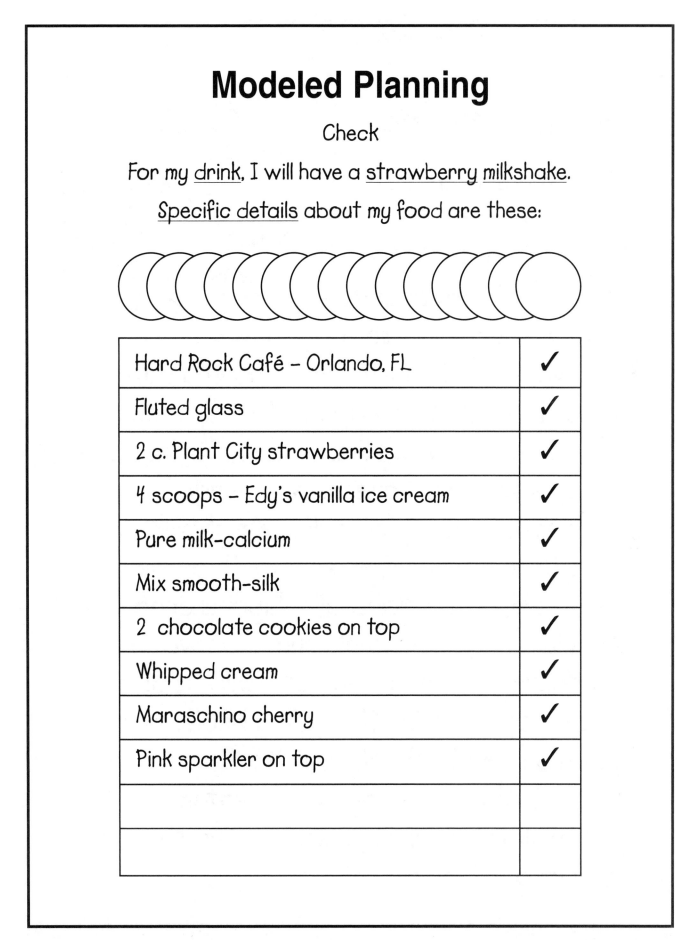

Hard Rock Café – Orlando, FL	✓
Fluted glass	✓
2 c. Plant City strawberries	✓
4 scoops – Edy's vanilla ice cream	✓
Pure milk-calcium	✓
Mix smooth-silk	✓
2 chocolate cookies on top	✓
Whipped cream	✓
Maraschino cherry	✓
Pink sparkler on top	✓

Modeled Writing

When the server from Hard Rock Café in Orlando, Florida, came over to take my order, I said, "Please bring me a strawberry milkshake served up in a fluted glass. Blend up two cups of freshly picked Plant City strawberries. Add in four scoops of Edy's vanilla ice cream (*No ice milk for me!*) along with one cup of calcium-rich milk. Mix everything up until it is as smooth as silk. Top it off with a cloud of whipped cream. Stick in a Maraschino cherry and two triangular-shaped chocolate chip cookies on the top. And for the grand finale, plop down a pink sparkler! Yum! Yum!" Just the thought of it makes *my* mouth water. But if you think the drink is great, just wait till you hear about the entrée!

_____ 's Lunch

(group member names)

Check

For our _____, I will have _____.

Specific details about our food are these: ✔

Name(s): _____

Sample Student Planning

_____ Thomas _____ 's Lunch

(group member names)

Check

For our __ Lunch __, I will have __ a hot dog __.

Specific details about our food are these: ✓

Daudurch foot-long hot dog	
Freshly baked bun – out of the oven	
Pickles – squirt	
Mound of chili – Oscar Myer	
Melted cheese – runs chin – elbows	
2 dabs of French's mustard	
Mel's Hot dog's – 22nd Ave	

Sample Student Writing

Name: _Thomas_

When I arrived at Mel's Hot dog's on 22nd east Ave right by the interstat, I went up to the counter. I waited my turn. When it was may turn I saw a man standing in front of me with a pointy hair due and a spoon in his left hand and fork in his right hand. I said, "may I have a foot-long hot dog called a Dauchuach with a freshly baked bun right out the oven with pickles that squirts when you bite the Daushuach and also a mound of greasy Oscar Myer's chili Bring it whith two dab's of frenches mustard, Please." Then the waiter Hollored to the cook behind him, "hay Fred, Gimme a parker-make that a foot Long with pickle's and all the dressings!" Now when I herd that order my mouth started watering and my stomach was grawling" moomm, I can't wait to gobble my Lunch.

Be a Maniac About It!

Materials

Teacher Materials You Need to Supply:

- read-aloud selection: *Maniac Magee* by Jerry Spinelli (alternate read alouds: *Holes* by Louis Sacher, pages 3 and 4. *Thunder Cake* by Patricia Polacco, page 1. Begin with: "On sultry summer days . . . ." End with: " . . . helped me overcome my fear of thunderstorms." *Charlie and the Chocolate Factory* by Roald Dahl, page 88. Begin with: "Charlie stared around the gigantic room . . . ." End with: " . . . and the whole place was filled with smoke and steam and delicious, rich smells.")

- overhead projector, transparency markers, chalkboard, chalk, and pencils for each group of three to four students. (*optional*: writer's notebooks for recording specific support found in *Maniac Magee*.)

- overhead transparencies of stationery for planning (page 81) and stationery for writing (page 82)

Teacher Materials Included in the Lesson:

- sample modeled planning and modeled writing (pages 79 and 80)
- sample student planning and writing (pages 84 and 85)

Student Materials Included in the Lesson:

- For each group of three to four students, you will need to prepare packets containing stationery for planning (page 81), stationery for writing (page 82), and the rubric for thinking about their writing (page 83).

Before the Lesson

Find a room in your school littered with interesting items that you can describe—e.g., a coach's equipment room. Sketch the room on the planning stationery overhead transparency. (The modeled writing for the lesson will be on this room.) Find a second room in your school to take your class to visit. Again, choose a room filled with interesting items—e.g., the lunchroom kitchen, office supply closet, team planning room, music equipment area, etc. Before the lesson, establish groups of three to four students and distribute the packets of writing materials. Then, take them to visit the room in order to sketch and record specific details on the planning stationery.

Read Aloud

1. Build background by asking the students to name and describe some of the items they saw in the room. Elicit why they found that item interesting. Elicit their thoughts by asking, "What did you think when you saw the item?"

2. Before reading *Maniac Magee*, tell the students to listen to Jerry Spinelli's description of a room inside an abandoned house. Tell them that he slows his writing down and shows us sections of the room, describing what he sees, thinks, feels, and smells.

3. Read pages 131–132 from *Maniac Magee*. Begin with the paragraph, "Maniac had seen some amazing things in his lifetime . . . ." End with the paragraph on the top of page 132. The last sentence reads, "They weren't raisins; they were roaches."

4. Generate a list of the details from the text and record them on the chalkboard. Label them "specific description from *Maniac Magee*." (*optional*: If your students have writer's notebooks, encourage them to record the description in their notebooks.)

Be a Maniac About It! *(cont.)*

Modeled Writing

1. Tell students that writers like Spinelli notice every physical detail—color, light, smells, sounds, and also include what they are thinking in their writing. Since a writer's job is to construct pictures for their readers, their brains have to become video cameras capturing everything on film. A writer then replays the video in their mind on slow speed, and records all the detail so that the readers can see it too.

2. Display the overhead transparency for planning. Tell them that this is your sketch of a room you decided to write about. Point to each item you drew and describe it. Tell them what you were thinking when you saw it. Model deciding what to leave out and what to write about. To avoid "listy" writing, choose two things to write about and explain why you chose them.

3. Using the overhead transparency for writing, write your piece, making sure to include specific details from your plan. Tell them the first sentence needs to tell the reader where you are. Make sure you stress slowing the writing to describe. Tell them that merely listing everything you saw in the room is not the objective. You want to describe the room so well that they can see what you saw and know what you were thinking.

4. Reread your piece focusing on the spelling and grammar issues found in your students' last writing sample. Refer to your word wall to check the spelling and usage of those words that are difficult for the students.

Guided Independent Writing

1. Reestablish your groups of three to four students. Tell them to pretend to do a slide show of their room in their brains. Remind them of the sketch and list of things on their planning stationery. Have them select two of the most interesting things to describe and circle the items on their plan.

2. Remind them to make additions to their plan by adding what they heard, smelled, touched, and thought. Tell them that readers want to peek inside their brains for a glimpse at their thinking.

3. Direct students to write their piece. Remind them of the way Spinelli began in *Maniac Magee*. Tell them that their first sentence should tell the reader where they are.

4. Encourage them to think about their writing by completing the rubric. Tell them that if they forgot to put something in their piece, to go back and do so.

Sharing Session

Direct the groups to pair and share their pieces. Collect and assess their pieces for evidence of specific support.

Follow-up Activity: The following day, do a revision lesson, revisiting a previous piece to insert description of the scene. Be sure to model where in the piece the description should occur. Understanding the place where description is needed is very important and the hardest for students. They know strong writing has description, but finding the most appropriate place is difficult for them. Again, stress that readers want to know what the characters think. Telling what characters think helps the reader know and connect with the characters.

Modeled Planning

Wherever Maniac Magee goes, he notices every detail.

Specific Details about My Room:

- bats, balls, gloves
- smell–Olympians
- smell–damp
- smell–Vlasic pickles
- touch–rough mortar
- walls–no paint
- red & yellow parachute hanging limp–hook

- cages of basketballs
- garbage–specific items
- stack of hula hoops
- bases–his footprints
- laundry basket–soft balls

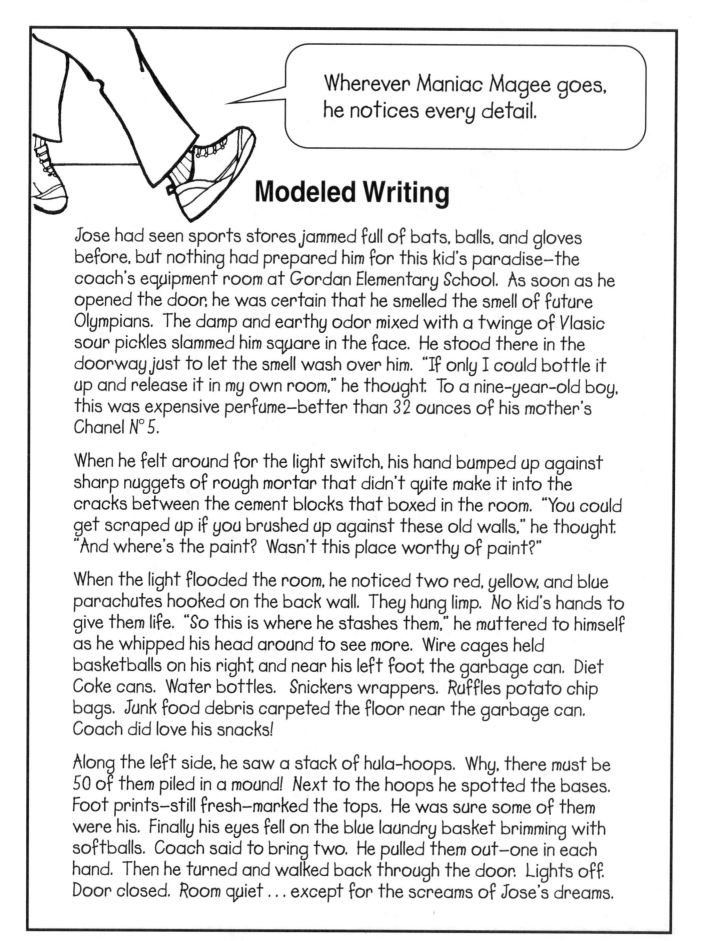

Wherever Maniac Magee goes, he notices every detail.

Modeled Writing

Jose had seen sports stores jammed full of bats, balls, and gloves before, but nothing had prepared him for this kid's paradise—the coach's equipment room at Gordan Elementary School. As soon as he opened the door, he was certain that he smelled the smell of future Olympians. The damp and earthy odor mixed with a twinge of Vlasic sour pickles slammed him square in the face. He stood there in the doorway just to let the smell wash over him. "If only I could bottle it up and release it in my own room," he thought. To a nine-year-old boy, this was expensive perfume—better than 32 ounces of his mother's Chanel N° 5.

When he felt around for the light switch, his hand bumped up against sharp nuggets of rough mortar that didn't quite make it into the cracks between the cement blocks that boxed in the room. "You could get scraped up if you brushed up against these old walls," he thought. "And where's the paint? Wasn't this place worthy of paint?"

When the light flooded the room, he noticed two red, yellow, and blue parachutes hooked on the back wall. They hung limp. No kid's hands to give them life. "So this is where he stashes them," he muttered to himself as he whipped his head around to see more. Wire cages held basketballs on his right, and near his left foot, the garbage can. Diet Coke cans. Water bottles. Snickers wrappers. Ruffles potato chip bags. Junk food debris carpeted the floor near the garbage can. Coach did love his snacks!

Along the left side, he saw a stack of hula-hoops. Why, there must be 50 of them piled in a mound! Next to the hoops he spotted the bases. Foot prints—still fresh—marked the tops. He was sure some of them were his. Finally his eyes fell on the blue laundry basket brimming with softballs. Coach said to bring two. He pulled them out—one in each hand. Then he turned and walked back through the door. Lights off. Door closed. Room quiet . . . except for the screams of Jose's dreams.

Name(s): _____

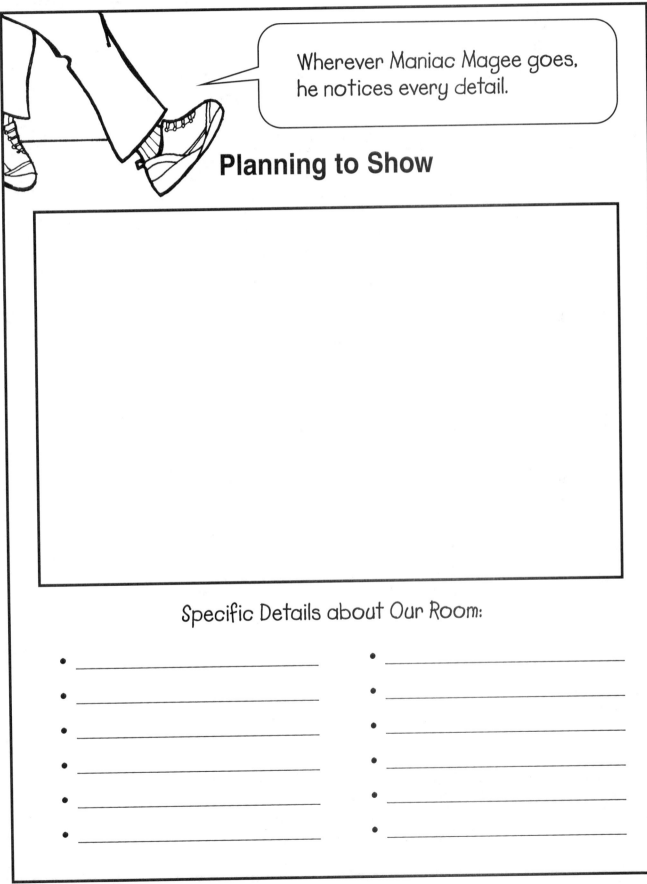

Wherever Maniac Magee goes, he notices every detail.

Planning to Show

Specific Details about Our Room:

- _____
- _____
- _____
- _____
- _____
- _____

- _____
- _____
- _____
- _____
- _____
- _____

Name(s): _____

Wherever Maniac Magee goes, he notices every detail.

_____

_____

_____

_____

_____

_____

_____

_____

_____

_____

_____

_____

_____

_____

_____

_____

_____

_____

_____

_____

_____

_____

Name(s): _____

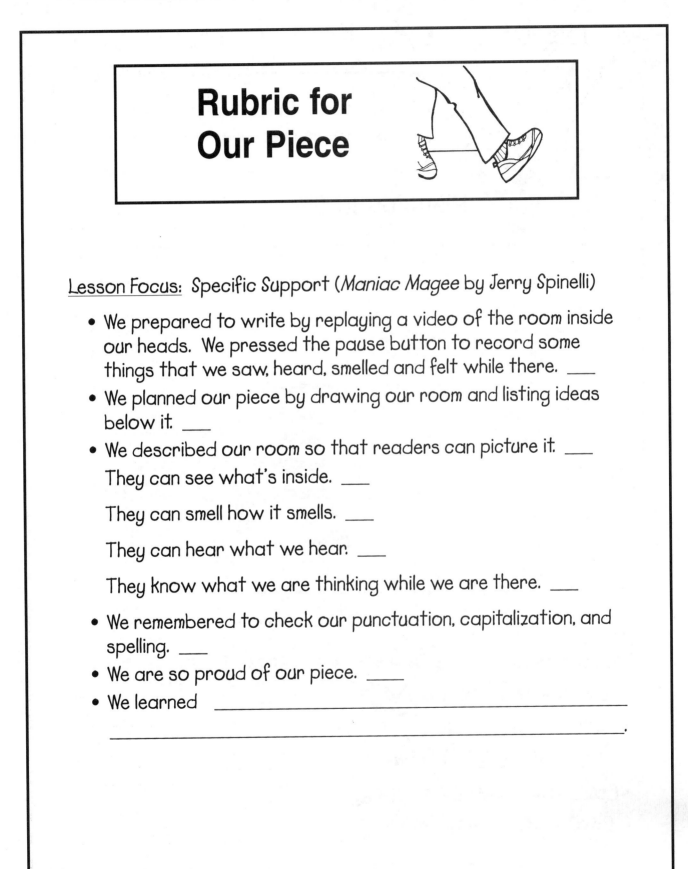

Rubric for Our Piece

<u>Lesson Focus:</u> Specific Support (*Maniac Magee* by Jerry Spinelli)

- We prepared to write by replaying a video of the room inside our heads. We pressed the pause button to record some things that we saw, heard, smelled and felt while there. ___
- We planned our piece by drawing our room and listing ideas below it. ___
- We described our room so that readers can picture it. ___

    They can see what's inside. ___

    They can smell how it smells. ___

    They can hear what we hear. ___

    They know what we are thinking while we are there. ___

- We remembered to check our punctuation, capitalization, and spelling. ___
- We are so proud of our piece. ___
- We learned _____
_____.

Sample Student Planning

Name(s): _Meghan , Randi, Reid, Michael,Alafi_

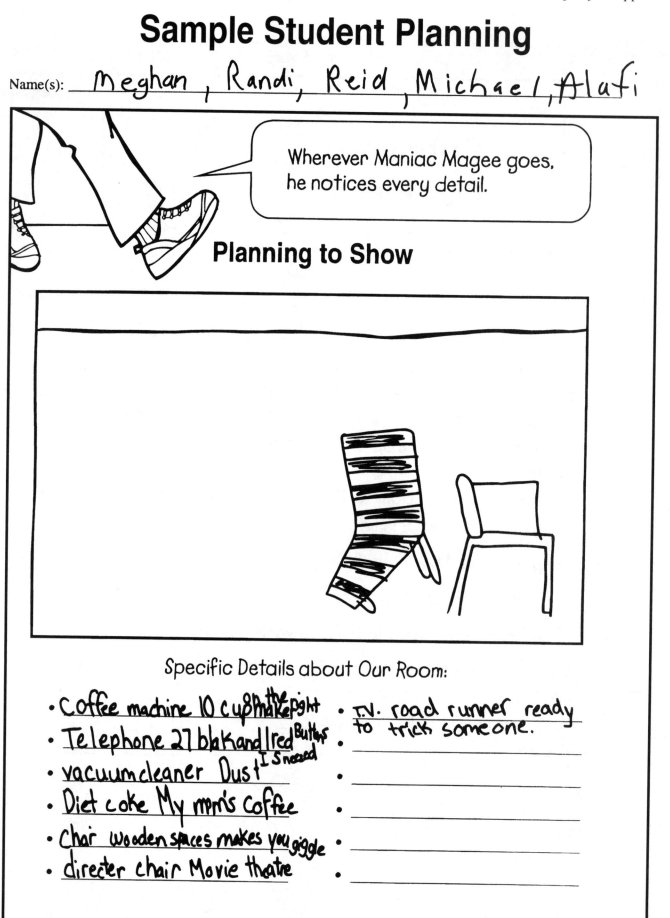

Wherever Maniac Magee goes, he notices every detail.

Planning to Show

Specific Details about Our Room:

- Coffee machine 10 cup Makes right on the
- Telephone 27 blk and lred Butters
- vacuumcleaner Dust I Sneezed
- Diet coke My mom's coffee
- Chair wooden spaces makes you giggle
- direcer chair Movie thatre

- T.V. road runner ready to trick someone.
- _____
- _____
- _____
- _____

Sample Student Writing

Name(s): Meghan, Randi, Reid, Michael, Alafia

Wherever Maniac Magee goes, he notices every detail.

David walked into the teacher's planning room in building 600 at. The first thing he did was smell and he smelled coffee. The coffee made 10 cups. The brand was Sunbeam. It was on the right of him.

He tried it and he spit it out. He thought it tasted like dirt that just got stepped on from a shoe that had bubble gum on the bottom of it. Ring, Ring, Ring!!! He looked to his left and saw an old fasion phone with 27 black buttons and 1 red button. "I wonder what this button does"? ah, ah, ah, achoo" He looked behind him and saw a dusty old vacuum cleaner! achoo" He opened the door and dun, dun, dun The pincipal face looked down at him. Am I in trouble?" He wondered.

Scarecrows That Paint

Materials

Teacher Materials You Need to Supply:

- read-aloud selection: *Scarecrow* by Cynthia Rylant

- overhead projector, transparency markers, pencils

- an overhead transparency of an everyday object such as fire hydrant, swings set, traffic light, bird bath, trampoline, mailbox, etc. (The sample shared writing uses a fire hydrant.)

- 12–15 laminated digital pictures of everyday objects for students to write about—e.g., water slides from a recreation center, telephone pole, soda machine, swing set, playground slide, etc.)

- overhead transparencies of stationery for planning (page 90) and stationery for writing (page 91) and point of view—first person, second person, third person (page 88)

Teacher Materials Included in the Lesson:

- sample shared planning and shared writing (page 89)

- sample student planning and writing (pages 93–96)

Student Materials Included in the Lesson:

- For each group of two to three students, you will need to prepare packets containing copies of point-of-view sheet (page 88), stationery for planning (page 90), stationery for writing (page 91), and rubric for thinking about their writing (page 92).

Read Aloud

1. Build background by asking the students to think about scarecrows. Elicit the details about them and also their purpose.

2. Before reading *Scarecrow* by Cynthia Rylant, tell the students to listen to the way the author describes the scarecrow. Listen for what he is made of, what he thinks about, and what he does all day. Read the story.

3. Reread page one. Tell students that the writer wrote her story using the pronoun *his—his hat, his suit, his eyes,* etc.

4. Display the overhead transparency of point of view. Review the options writers have when they tell their stories. Tell them that *Scarecrow* was written in third person. Elicit the words that let us know that—(*his, he*). Remind them of other third-person stories the class has previously read.

Scarecrows That Paint *(cont.)*

Shared Writing

1. Tell the students that you are going to write in the third person like Cynthia Rylant. Tell them that you took some pictures of everyday objects so that you could write about one of them.

2. Display the overhead transparency of your picture—e.g., a fire hydrant. Talk about the picture.

3. Display the overhead transparency of the plan. Elicit ideas for describing the fire hydrant. Elicit and record a description about the picture. Decide whether it will be a boy or girl. (Sample planning uses a boy.) Elicit ideas for what he might be thinking all day. What does he look like—his eyes, nose, mouth, etc.? Who might he see? Remind them that we will write our story in third person just like Cynthia Rylant.

4. Display the overhead transparency of the stationery for writing. Together, write your piece, referring back to the plan to retrieve your ideas. Reread the text from *Scarecrow* line by line. Structure your sentences similar to Rylant's sentences.

5. As you write, focus on the spelling and grammar issues from your students' last writing sample. Refer to your word wall for those words that are difficult for the students.

Guided Independent Writing

1. Establish groups of two or three students. Allow them to select one of your pictures to write about. (If you have extra pictures, each group can choose.)

2. Distribute to each group the packets for writing containing the point-of-view sheet, stationery for planning, stationery for writing, and the rubric for thinking about their writing.

3. Direct students to talk about their picture as we did during shared writing. Then direct them to list their ideas about their picture. Again, remind them of the process from shared writing. Remind them to use their picture to help them with their description and to write in third person (his/her).

Sharing Session

Collect the pictures and display for all the students to see. Randomly, select a picture and have the group read their piece. Encourage them to talk about the decisions they made before they wrote. Have each group share out. Remind them to jot down any new ideas they hear during sharing session on their planning stationery for later revisions. Celebrate their ideas and creativity.

Scarecrow by Cynthia Rylant

Point of View

1st person—my hat

2nd person—your hat

3rd person—his hat

Shared Planning

The Lone Fire Hydrant

Our Ideas for Writing like Cynthia Rylant's *Scarecrow*

- hat—blue
- body—neon yellow
- blunt nose
- no eyes
- best quality—patience
- hangs on side of the road—waiting
- solitude
- concern for people (name some)
- "necessary"
- gift—usefulness

Shared Writing

The Lone Fire Hydrant

His hat is painted blue, his body is painted neon yellow, even his arms are the same neon yellow as his body. And his eyes—probably somebody forgot to add them.

But a fire hydrant's life is all his own.

It takes patience hanging on the side of the road all day long. It takes a love of solitude and an appreciation for both sun and rain. A liking for waiting . . . and waiting. A concern for people and their things.

Yes, people. Cubans, Americans, Italians, Iranians, Indians. Ask them how they feel about fire hydrants, and they say, "Necessary." They ignore his blunt, yellow nose and the fact that he has no eyes, and they see the fire hydrant's best gift: his usefulness.

Name(s): _____

Ideas for Our piece

Name(s): _____

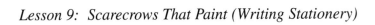

Name(s): _____

Rubric for Our Piece

<u>Lesson Focus:</u> Specific Support (*Scarecrow* by Cynthia Rylant)

- We selected a picture or drew one of our own. ___

- When we wrote, we wrote in 3rd person (his/her). ___

- We listed specific details about our picture. ___

- We used our imagination to figure out what could be the eyes, the nose, the mouth, etc. ___

- We wrote about what he/she thought. ___

- We decided on one of his or her attributes (example: usefulness) to write about. ___

- We remembered to check spelling, grammar, and punctuation.

  ___

- We are proud of our piece. ___

- From this lesson we learned _____

_____ .

Sample Student Planning

Name(s): **Roxanne**

Ideas for Our piece

Flag hat-blue
and white
Body cookie-
monster
Love
noise
kicking feet
hot long days
niceness
kid's Laughter

Pool Slide

Sample Student Writing

Name(s): ___Roxanne___

Her hat is a blue
and white flag, her
body is blue like
cookie monster,
even her two long
arms.And her legs
Were Probaly Stollen
from Some one's
stair well.
But a pools slide's
life is all her own.
It takes a lot of
love for kids, Stand-
ing in a pool of
water al day.
It takes a love

Sample Student Writing *(cont.)*

Name(s): _Roxanne_

of lound noises and
Kicking feet. A liking
for hot long days.
A friendlyness
to words children.
Yes, pool slides,
children, Adults, Teen-
agers, todlers. Ask
then how they feel
about a pool slides
and they'll say
happy. They ignore
her blue long arms
and her stolen
steps. And see
instead the pool

Sample Student Writing *(cont.)*

Name(s): _Roxanne_

Slides best gift: her niceness. They climb up her
Steps and slide all day.
She knows that she
isn't real. A pool slide
under stands that she
is plastick and maddle
Shaped to make some
One happy. But she
knows this too: that
life isn't always fair.
Water splashes around
her, and kids are
Shouting out, of
long arm's and fun and
laugter gos on for
ever.

Lights, Camera, and Action

(Note: *This is a great lesson to do before an open house since you will have a class book to display. If the open house is more formal, make overhead transparencies of each child's page and have the students perform their book. If technology is available, you can even scan each child's page and do a PowerPoint presentation.*)

Materials

Teacher Materials You Need to Supply:

- read-aloud selection: *Snapshots from the Wedding* by Gary Soto
- overhead projector, transparency markers, a picture of yourself (*Suggestion:* Use one of yourself at the same age of the children you are teaching. They love seeing their teacher as a young child. Make an overhead transparency of the picture if possible.), family album, and pencils for each student.
- Two or three days before this lesson, direct each of your students to bring in his or her picture. If possible, ask them to bring a school picture near their current age. (*Optional*: If you are publishing the student pieces in a book, you will need materials for the style of book you plan to publish.)
- overhead transparencies of stationery for planning (page 100) and stationery for writing (page 101)

Teacher Materials Included in the Lesson:

- sample modeled planning and writing (page 99)
- sample student planning and writing (pages 103–105)

Student Materials Included in the Lesson:

- For each student, you need to prepare packets containing copies of stationery for planning (page 100), stationery for writing (page 101), and the rubric for thinking about their writing (page 102).

Read Aloud

1. Build background by asking the students to tell about some pictures their family takes. Tell them that some people save those pictures in a book called an album.

2. Hold up your family album. Flip through several pages and show them a few pictures. Tell them that pictures and words help us remember special times in our lives.

3. Before reading *Snapshots from the Wedding* by Gary Soto, tell them that Mr. Soto wrote a book about the pictures taken at a wedding. Tell them that the pictures and the words tell all about the wedding and will hold that memory for him.

4. Read several pages from *Snapshots from the Wedding* by Gary Soto and then elicit the specific details about each picture.

Modeled Writing

1. Tell students that you want to remember this class—each and every one of them, so you would like to make a class book just like *Snapshots from the Wedding*. Tell them that you will call it "Snapshots from Ms./Mr. _____'s _____ Grade Class."

2. Display your picture. Tell them how old you were when this picture was taken. Think and write about what you liked and what you thought about at that age. Include in your piece who you were looking at and what you were thinking about when the photographer snapped the picture. End the piece with a sentence that will let the reader know that you are an adult now teaching this wonderful class.

Lights, Camera, and Action *(cont.)*

Modeled Writing *(cont.)*

3. Reread your piece to focus on the spelling and grammar issues from your students last writing sample. Refer to your word wall to check the spelling and usage of those words that are difficult for students.

Guided Independent Writing

1. Direct the students to take out their pictures. Tell them to think about the day it was taken. Tell them to tap into what they were thinking and to describe what was important to them at that moment in their life.

2. Distribute the packets containing stationery for planning, stationery for writing, and the rubric for thinking about their writing. Direct students to list ideas on the planning stationery. Remind them to write only one or two words to hold their ideas. Circulate and support them as they capture their ideas.

3. Direct students to write their pieces using the stationery for writing. At the appropriate time, tell them to end their piece by writing what they would like to do when they are grown up.

4. Remind them to think about their writing by completing the rubric. Tell them that if they forgot to put something in, to go back and do so. The rubric should guide and support them as they think about their writing.

Sharing Session

Direct the students to pair and share their pieces. Collect and assess their pieces.

Follow-up Activity (day two teaching points: revision and publishing)

During your next writer's workshop, begin by reading two or three different pages from *Snapshots from the Wedding* by Gary Soto. Elicit the specific detail found underneath each picture. Talk about your favorite entries and discuss why they are your favorites. Then, tell your students to listen again to what you wrote during modeled writing the previous day. Read your piece aloud. Ask them if you have given enough information. Ask them to tell you what they want to know more about. Revise your piece to include answers to their questions. Check your conventions. Make some changes so that they can see you, the proficient writer, modeling in your piece what you want them to do in theirs. Distribute their pieces and direct them to revisit them. In pairs, have them share their piece again—this time for revision purposes. Encourage them to borrow ideas from each other and to collaborate with their partner. Tell them that all their words must be spelled correctly, and the punctuation must be perfect—no mistakes! This will be a real book. Assure them that you will circulate to help them. (Suggestion: if you notice the same misspelled words by several students—make a temporary word wall just for this book. To do this, simply write the words on the chalkboard and label it "Word Wall for Snapshots from Ms./Mr. _____'s _____ Grade Class." If publishing a book, begin the process in the book publishing style you have chosen.

Modeled Planning

Snapshots All About Me!

Ideas About My Picture:

1. What am I thinking?

2. What's important to me?

3. What does my picture tell about me?

   - Wanted to wear–Brownie dress
   - tatting–watched her making it (s-l-o-w down writing)
   - man's words
   - ending–me as an adult: teacher

Modeled Writing

RuthAnn, Age 6

I'm in the Brownies, only I'm not wearing my uniform today. Today is Picture Day, and I'm wearing a dress handmade by my mother. Can you see the tatting on the collar? My mother tatted it, and I watched her make it especially for me. It took her hours, and I thought she'd never get done! In and out with the shuttle, over and under–fast as lightning her fingers flew. Now the man at Mountain Creek Elementary School wants to take my picture. He said, "Sweetheart, you look cuter than a speckled pup." And just like that–I smiled for him! Snap! He took the picture capturing a moment of a young child at school. Who would think that this girl would spend most of her life in schools? Blissfully content. Standing before both children and teachers, savoring each moment.

Name: _____

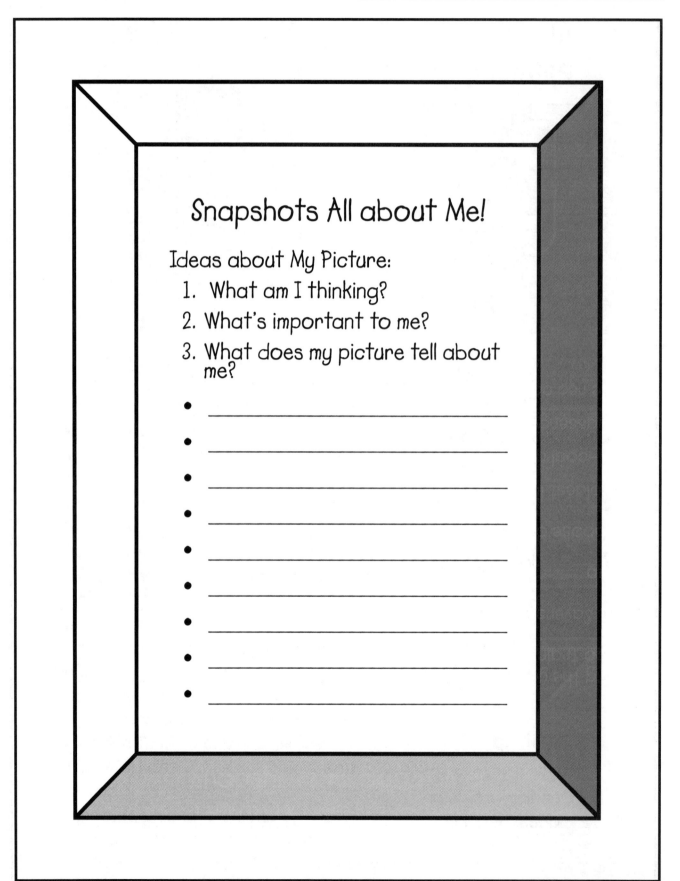

Snapshots All about Me!

Ideas about My Picture:

1. What am I thinking?
2. What's important to me?
3. What does my picture tell about me?

- _____
- _____
- _____
- _____
- _____
- _____
- _____
- _____
- _____

Name: _____

_____

_____

_____

_____

_____

_____

_____

_____

_____

_____

_____

_____

Name: _____

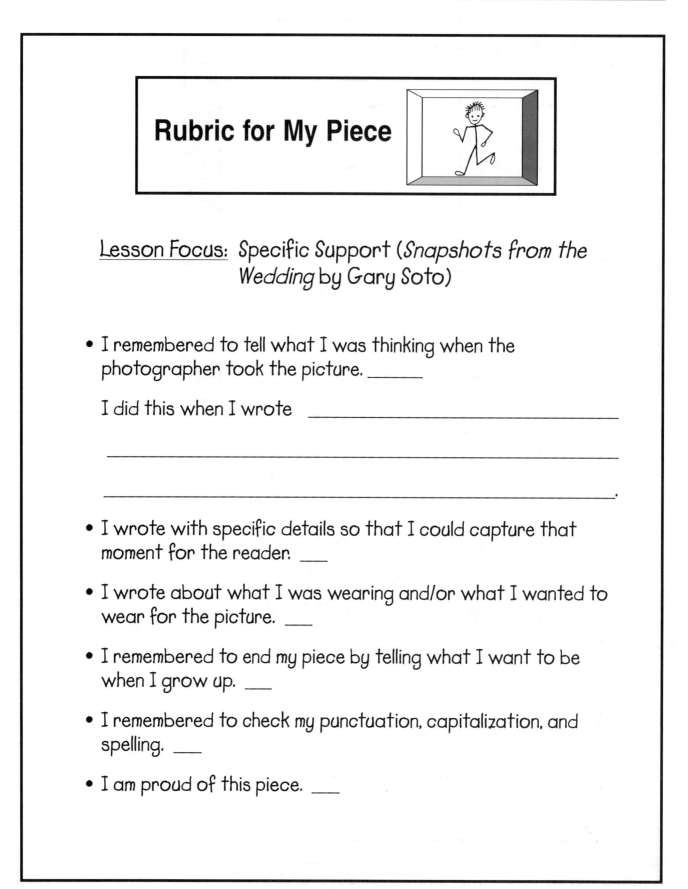

Rubric for My Piece

<u>Lesson Focus:</u> Specific Support (*Snapshots from the Wedding* by Gary Soto)

- I remembered to tell what I was thinking when the photographer took the picture. _____

  I did this when I wrote _____

  _____

  _____.

- I wrote with specific details so that I could capture that moment for the reader. ___

- I wrote about what I was wearing and/or what I wanted to wear for the picture. ___

- I remembered to end my piece by telling what I want to be when I grow up. ___

- I remembered to check my punctuation, capitalization, and spelling. ___

- I am proud of this piece. ___

Sample Student Planning

Name: Roxanna grade 4

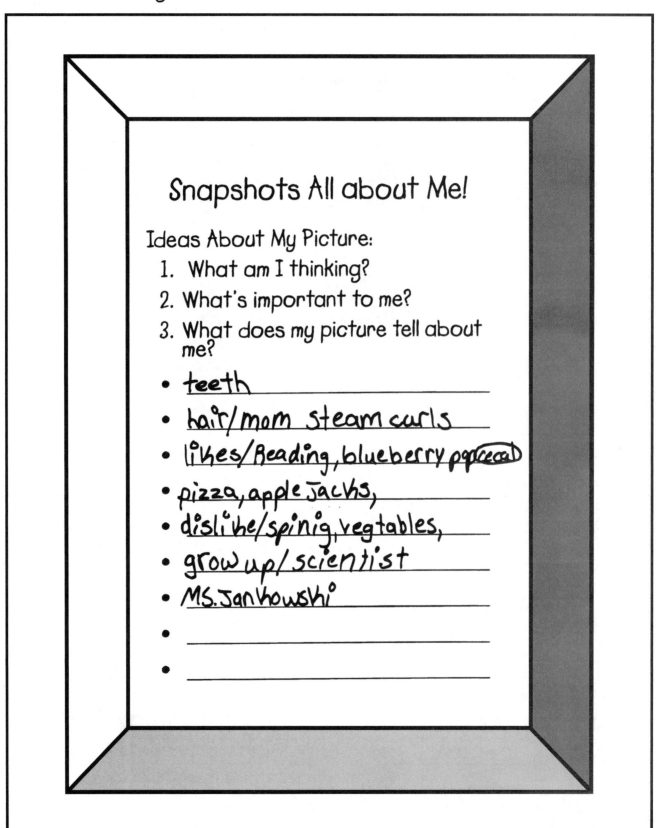

Snapshots All about Me!

Ideas About My Picture:

1. What am I thinking?
2. What's important to me?
3. What does *my* picture tell about me?

- teeth
- hair/mom steam curls
- likes/Reading, blueberry popcorn
- pizza, apple Jacks,
- dislike/spinig, vegtables,
- grow up/scientist
- MS.Jankowski
-
-

Sample Student Writing

Name: Roxanna grade 4

Thank goodness my teeth are not showing in this picture tacken outside Sulpher Spring Elem. School. Sometimes my teeth look like Bugs Bunnys. If I had known I was getting my picture tacken today I would have woren my hair down with steam curls all around my face. Curles that look and bounce just like my Slinky. I'm a kid who likes pizza- Pizza Hut with pepperonie, blueberry popcecals, and Apple Jacks cereal. I hate spinich on anything and when I grow up I want to be a scientist and find a cure for the common cold.

Sample Student Writing (cont.)

Name: Roxanna grade 4

I won't always be a kid in Ms.
Jankowski's 4th grade class. Someday
I'm going to grow up and go to
Collage-USF here in Tampa and
be Succesful in life. Someday
when the kids in my class look
back at my picture the'll remember
me as a good friend.

What's It Like?

Materials

Teacher Materials You Need to Supply:

- read-aloud selection: *Fig Pudding* by Ralph Fletcher
- overhead projector, pencils for each student, transparency markers, signs reading "Brothers Only," "Sisters Only," "Brothers and Sisters," and "Only Child"
- *Optional*: a photograph of you and your siblings to share with your students. If publishing a class book, you will need additional materials depending on the style of your book and an additional overhead transparency of the stationery for writing.
- transparencies of stationery for planning (page 111) and stationery for writing (page 112)

Teacher Materials Included in the Lesson:

- sample modeled planning (page 109) and sample modeled writing (page 110)
- sample student planning and writing (pages 113 and 114)

Student Materials Included in the Lesson:

- For each student, you need to prepare packets containing copies of stationery for planning (page 111), two pieces of stationery for writing (page 112), and the rubric for thinking about your writing (page 108).

Read Aloud

1. Before reading, build background by eliciting some information about the students in your class. Ask, "How many of you have brothers?" Direct them to indicate the number by holding up the appropriate number of fingers. Elicit information about their sisters and also those who are the only children in their family. In the same manner, elicit their position in their family. Ask, "Who are the oldest, middle, and youngest children in your family?"

2. Tell the students that in *Fig Pudding*, Ralph Fletcher writes about his family and what it feels like to be the oldest of nine children. Direct them to listen to the description Mr. Fletcher provides on how it feels to be the oldest child in the Fletcher family.

3. Read pages two and three in *Fig Pudding* by Ralph Fletcher. Begin with the paragraph: "Don't get me wrong . . . ." End with the sentence, "He's like the last blanket piled on my bed just before I fall asleep."

4. Elicit the specifics of how the author described what it's like to be the oldest child in his family. Make sure the students notice the comparison he used.

5. Tell the students that one way to help the reader clearly understand what we are writing about is to make comparisons to commonly known things that all readers know about.

What's It Like? *(cont.)*

Modeled Writing

1. *Optional:* If available, display the photograph of your family. Tell the students the names of your brothers and/or sisters and their position in the family.

2. Display the overhead transparency of the plan for writing. Using stick figures, draw your own brother(s) and/or sister(s) by age in the box provided at the top of the page. Label each figure with the person's name. As you draw, describe each person.

3. Tell them that you want to describe what it feels like to be the _____ child in the family, and to do that you are going to use a comparison just like Ralph Fletcher did so they can see what it is like to be the _____ child in your family.

4. Model brainstorming two or three ideas for your comparison—examples: taco, hamburger, one seed inside a pumpkin, the third hump in a caterpillar, etc. Then choose one and explain why you chose it. Model listing each element in the comparison and make clear the connection to the family member. When finished, go back and add a phrase to describe that sibling.

5. Using the overhead transparency for writing, model writing your piece, referring back to the plan that holds your ideas. Remember to use your class word wall to model spelling. Also, focus on modeling the correct usage of the conventions that trouble your students. Save your piece if publishing a class book.

Guided Independent Writing

1. Distribute the prepared packets to each student. Tell them to use stick figures to draw their family, starting from oldest to youngest, in the box on their planning stationery. Direct them to label each figure with the person's name. Remind them to include themselves.

2. Direct students to choose a comparison and list their ideas. Remind them of your model. (Redisplay yours if they need additional support.)

3. Direct students to write their piece on the stationery for writing provided.

4. When they are finished, tell students they should think about their writing by completing the rubric included in their packet. Encourage them to make any needed changes so that their writing is strong. While students are writing, hang your signs for sharing out in the four corners of the room.

What's It Like? *(cont.)*

Sharing Session

Calling one group at a time, direct them to the appropriately labeled corner. When the groups are established, direct them to read their piece to the members of their group. Circulate and listen in. (If publishing a book, collect pieces and save for tomorrow's lesson.)

Follow-up Activity: (day two teaching points: revision, editing, and publication)

If publishing a book, you will need to take your writing through the entire writing process. Begin by rereading the piece in *Fig Pudding* by Ralph Fletcher. Display the piece that you wrote. Model revision by adding or moving text, replacing words, etc. Then model editing by checking your spelling, punctuation, and grammar. Model checking the spelling of a word not on the word wall, by looking it up in a dictionary. Then draw your family members carefully and copy your piece over on a new overhead transparency. Tell students the piece can now be published because it has been through the entire writing process. Distribute their previously written pieces. Direct them to do the same with their piece. It may be helpful to have them work alone at first, then share at their tables and take suggestions from their friends. Of course, dictionaries should be close at hand. Publish their pieces by making a class book. All you need is a catchy title. Voila! They are real published writers!

Don't forget to celebrate your writing by sharing it with as many people as you can. This makes your students want to write again and again and again . . . and helps them see the purpose for writing!

Name: _____

Rubric for My Piece

Lesson Focus: Specific Support (*Fig Pudding* by Ralph Fletcher)

- I drew my family from the oldest to youngest child and labeled each person with his or her name. ____

- I decided to compare my position in my family to a(n) _____

    _____.

- I listed my ideas so that I can show what it is like to be the _____ child in my family. ____

- When I wrote, I mentioned the names of family members in my piece and described what it feels like to be who I am in my family. ____

- I remembered to check my punctuation, capitalization, and spelling. ____

- I am proud of this piece. ____

Modeled Planning

Draw stick figures of your family from the oldest to the youngest. Label each person with his or her name.

RuthAnn, the Youngest

My Ideas:

- Being the <u>youngest</u> is like being the <u>caboose on the Chattanooga Choo Choo train.</u>

- Life Savers

- Pizza

- Caboose on Chattanooga Choo Choo (I'm from Chattanooga, TN)

<u>Travis</u>—oldest, like the engine—always #1, Mom's favorite

<u>Winfred</u>—coal car, needed, charming, peacemaker

<u>Gary</u>—passenger car, magnet for friends and animals

<u>Me</u>—little red caboose, brings up the end, daddy's girl—spoiled

Modeled Writing

Travis   Winfred   Gary   Me (RuthAnn)

Draw stick figures of your family from the oldest to the
youngest. Label each person with his or her name.

RuthAnn, the Youngest

Being the youngest girl in the Billingsley family is not all that easy
because all your brothers think they're your bosses. If you're the
youngest with three older brothers, you are like the caboose on the
Chattanooga Choo Choo Train. Out front, Travis, the engine,
commands the train. And everybody knows engines are always first.
So is Travis. First in the brother-line. First in our mother's heart.
Next comes Winfred. He is the coal car. Without him, the train is
going nowhere! The family needs him to charm and encourage
(especially the youngest). The coal car makes the peace in our family.
He settles our fights and gets things moving. Next come the
passenger cars. Without the passenger cars, who would use the
train? Gary, brother #3, is a passenger car, for he drags in all sorts
of people. He charges the house—with friends and once even a
crow! (But that's another story.) I bring up the rear—the little red
caboose. The "odd girl out." RuthAnn. Some say spoiled. Some say
Daddy's favorite. But anyway you look at it, last, with those other
three cars chugging on before me. Demanding yet caring, they
forced me to stand up to them and hold my own place in this family!
And I did. And I still do. And I always will.

Name: _____

Draw stick figures of your family from the oldest to the youngest. Label each person with his or her name.

Being _____ is like_____.

Name: _____

Draw stick figures of your family from the oldest to the youngest. Label each person with his or her name.

_____

_____

_____

_____

_____

_____

_____

_____

_____

_____

_____

_____

_____

_____

Sample Student Planning

Lauren.L / Marissa / Sal

Draw stick figures of your family from the oldest to the
youngest. Label each person with his or her name.

Being ___*youngest*___ is like___*being Joe Hamilton*___.

LL = Glaciers (owners of Bucs) $ power

MM = Jon G. (coach of Bucs) Backup

Sal = Joe Hamilton (Q.B. of Bucs)
complete passes, follow
Oders

Sample Student Writing

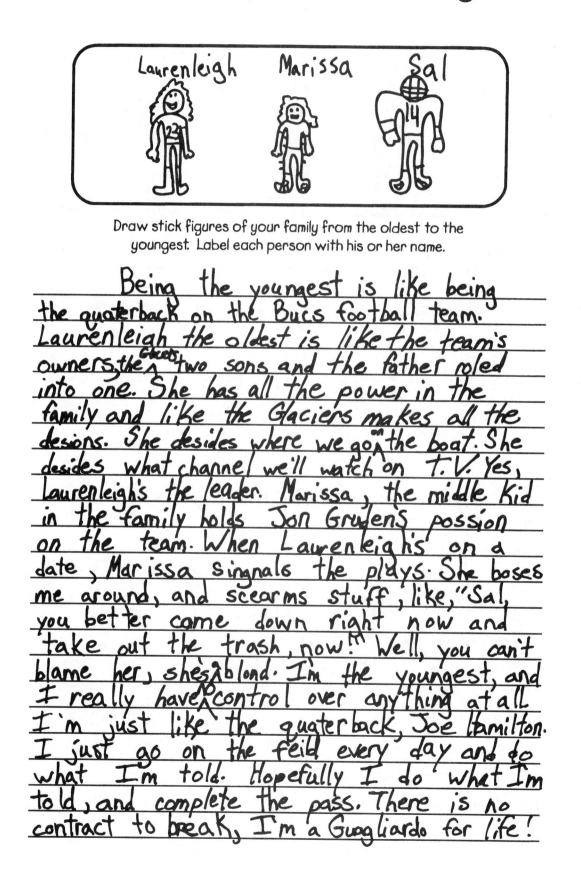

Draw stick figures of your family from the oldest to the youngest. Label each person with his or her name.

Being the youngest is like being the quaterback on the Bucs football team. Laurenleigh the oldest is like the team's owners, the two sons and the father roled into one. She has all the power in the family and like the Glaciers makes all the desions. She desides where we go on the boat. She desides what channel we'll watch on T.V. Yes, Laurenleigh's the leader. Marissa, the middle kid in the family holds Jon Gruden's possion on the team. When Laurenleigh's on a date, Marissa singnals the plays. She boses me around, and scearms stuff, like, "Sal, you better come down right now and take out the trash, now!" Well, you can't blame her, she's blond. I'm the youngest, and I really have control over anything at all I'm just like the quaterback, Joe Hamilton. I just go on the feild every day and do what I'm told. Hopefully I do what I'm told, and complete the pass. There is no contract to break, I'm a Guagliardo for life!

Make It Happen

Materials

Teacher Materials You Need to Supply:

- read-aloud selection: *Iktomi and the Boulder* by Paul Goble
- overhead projector, transparency marker, pencils for each group of four to five students, masking tape, dice or spinner, cards with the words "beginning," "middle," and "end," chalk, and chalkboard
- Optional: For the follow-up lesson (day two) you will need an overhead transparency of a previous class narrative piece (or save the one from today's lesson), along with strong group samples generated from this lesson. Also, each child will need colored pencils to revise his or her piece.
- overhead transparency of stationery for planning (page 118), two overhead transparencies of stationery for writing (page 119)

Teacher Materials Included in the Lesson:

- sample shared planning and shared writing (page 117)
- sample student planning and writing (pages 121 and 122)

Student Materials Included in the Lesson:

- For each of your groups of students, you will need to prepare packets containing copies of stationery for planning (page 118), stationery for writing (page 119), and the rubric for thinking about their writing (page 120).

Read Aloud

1. Using the masking tape, attach the word cards—"beginning," "middle," and "end"—to the chalkboard.

2. Before reading, explain that a fictional narrative has a beginning, middle, and end. (Point to each of the cards as you mention them.) Using a piece of chalk, write the word "problem" between the words "beginning" and "middle." Explain that in a good fictional narrative, there is usually a problem with events included. Explain that the character(s) try to solve the problem in the story.

3. To build some background, elicit the problem and events in a familiar fairy tale such as *The Three Little Pigs*.

4. Hold up the book *Iktomi and the Boulder* by Paul Goble. Read the title and discuss the meaning of the word *boulder*. (In some areas of the country, children might not understand that a boulder is a huge rock.)

5. Tell them to listen carefully to *Iktomi and the Boulder* by Paul Goble. Tell them to listen to find out how Iktomi tries to solve his problem.

6. Read *Iktomi and the Boulder* by Paul Goble.

Make It Happen *(cont.)*

Shared Writing

1. Elicit the problem followed by the events in the story. Record them on the overhead transparency for planning.

2. Tell them that we are going to take out one of Paul Goble's events and put in one of our own (this is known as a "book innovation"). Instead of the buffalo and prairie dogs trying to remove the boulder, we will make wild horses come to the aid of Iktomi.

3. Using the overhead transparency for planning, elicit several possibilities for wild horses removing the boulder. Tell them to think of ways wild horses might try to get a boulder off someone. (Examples: a stampede to break the boulder apart, kicking the boulder with their hooves, etc.) Continue the author's pattern in the book by eliciting possible insults that Iktomi might say to the horses in order to trick them into helping him. Record the insults.

4. Using the overhead transparency for writing, write your piece together, remembering to use the repetition of the insults. Remember to model using your class word wall. Stress one or two conventions that the students struggle with. Tell them that we are not going to rewrite the beginning or the ending of the book, only one event in the middle. (Start and end your piece with Iktomi lying in the prairie with a boulder on him. If continuing to day two, save your shared writing piece.)

Guided Writing

1. Establish six groups of students; assign numbers 1–6 to each group.

2. Distribute a packet of materials to each group containing the following: stationery for planning, stationery for writing, and a rubric for thinking about their writing. Designate a writer.

3. Direct them to work together to write an event for the story using the wind to get the boulder off Iktomi.

4. Direct them to brainstorm strong words to describe the wind. Remind them that they need to come up with insults that Iktomi could use to trick the wind into removing the boulder.

5. Since we are working on developing an event and not leads or conclusions, tell each group to begin with the following statement: "Iktomi is lying on his back in the middle of the prairie with a boulder sitting on top of his legs. He can't get it off. Far in the distance, Iktomi sees . . . ."

6. Direct the students to think about their writing by completing the rubric. Encourage them to make any changes necessary in their piece.

Sharing Session

Use a dice or spinner to select groups 1–6 to read their piece. Allow each group to share their writing.

Follow-up Activity (day two teaching point: revision)

For your read-aloud, read a few of the strong student pieces from day one. Point out the strong development of the events. Then, using a previously written class narrative, or yesterday's piece from shared writing, read and revise in order to improve the support to an event. Then, direct each child to select a previously written fictional narrative from his or her writing folders. Direct students to reread and revise an event (using their colored pencils) to make the support stronger.

Shared Planning

Remember to begin your event with Iktomi lying in the prairie with a boulder on top of him.

Wild horses—describe using strong verbs (How do they move? What do they do to try to remove the boulder?)

- stampeding across the prairie
- galloping up to the boulder
- stallion leads
- kicked and butted the boulder

Iktomi insults the wild horses

- looks like a stinky dog
- legs look like string beans

Shared Writing

Iktomi is lying down on his back in the middle of the prairie with a boulder sitting on top of his legs. He can't get it off. In the distance, Iktomi sees a herd of wild horses stampeding across the prairie. Suddenly they stop galloping because they notice an Indian man pinned underneath a huge boulder, yelling at the top of his lungs.

"Help! Help! Younger brothers!" Iktomi hollered as he tried to wiggle out from under the rock.

"Can you believe that I was walking across the prairie, minding my own business, when this nasty rock come out of nowhere and crashed down upon me? I've been here for days listening to this mean boulder talk about people. Do you know what he just said about you? He said that your legs look like string beans and you are as weak as a newborn kitten. He also taunted that you look just like an overgrown, stinky dog."

The fierce stallion replied, "Don't worry, brother. We can help you get this rude pebble off you."

So the horses kicked and butted up against the boulder, and although it moved a little bit, it did not roll off Iktomi's legs. After a long while, they finally gave up. Kicking their legs up towards the night sky, they raced off across the prairie.

Name(s): _____

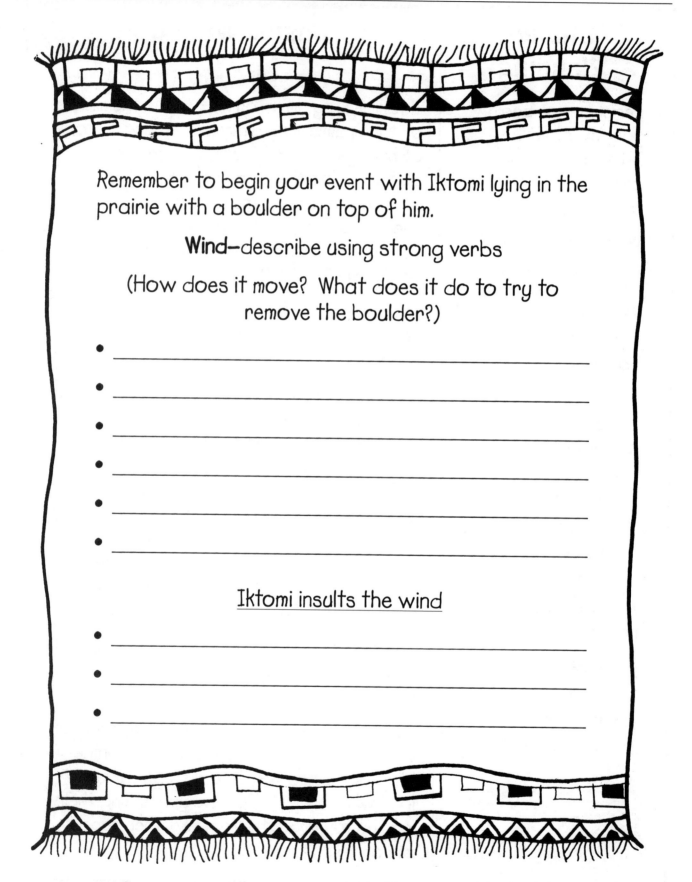

Remember to begin your event with Iktomi lying in the prairie with a boulder on top of him.

Wind—describe using strong verbs

(How does it move? What does it do to try to remove the boulder?)

- _____
- _____
- _____
- _____
- _____
- _____

Iktomi insults the wind

- _____
- _____
- _____

Name(s): _____

_____

_____

_____

_____

_____

_____

_____

_____

_____

_____

_____

_____

_____

Name(s): _____

Rubric for Our Piece

Lesson Focus: Specific Support (developing events)
(Iktomi and the Boulder by Paul Goble)

- We brainstormed our ideas for developing an event with the wind. ___

- We remembered to start and end with Iktomi in the desert with the boulder on top of him. ___

- We described the wind using specific details such as _____

  _____ .

- We used dialogue to make Iktomi speak insults to the wind. ___
  We made Iktomi, say, " _____

  _____." "

- We remembered to check our punctuation, capitalization, and spelling. (Don't forget to put quotation marks around what Iktomi says!)

- We are proud of this piece. ___

- We learned that when writing an event in a story we need to _____

  _____ .

Sample Student Planning

Name(s): ___Aaron　　Kaylee　Marcus Angelique___

Remember to begin your event with Iktomi lying in the prairie with a boulder on top of him.

Wind—describe using strong verbs

(How does it move? What does it do to try to remove the boulder?)

- Tornado
- Rain
- Thunder
- Lightning
- Trees flying
- distroyed objects
  fires

<u>Iktomi insults the wind</u>

- Wind—just a lot of carbon dioxide.
- Wind— weak— can't blow leaves
- Lightning slow — can't even hit a fly

Sample Student Writing

Name(s): Aaron   Kaylee   Marcus   Angelique

Iktomi was still thinking of how to get the boulder off his legs. Suddenly, a storm came into sight. Rain was starting to come down in buckets from the sky. All of a sudden lightning and thunder hit. Iktomi finally had a plan. He said "your wind is so weak it couldn't blow a leaf off a tree." Wind started to pick up speed and it started to become into a tornado. The rock also said, "your lightning is so slow you can't even hit a fly." The tornado started going to it's biggest speed. It was going 185 mph. Trees were flying like jets but the rock didn't budge. Lightning hit the tree and created fires all over the prairie Not long after the tornado stopped the rain continued to pour down on the fires in the prairie, but the rock still did not budge.

Nuttin' Honey

(*two-day lesson if publishing a book*)

Materials

Teacher Materials You Need to Supply:

- read-aloud selection: *Nothing Ever Happens on 90th Street* by Roni Schotter
- overhead projector, transparency markers, pencils for each group of two to three students, cards with the following written on them: office staff—principal, assistant principal, guidance counselor, nurse, secretary, custodial staff, and cafeteria manager; teachers at your school—math teacher, science teacher, reading teacher, writing teacher, social studies teacher, coach, art teacher, music teacher, and speech teacher. *Optional:* If publishing a book, you will need a picture of the school for the book cover, and materials for binding. (ABC ribbon would be perfect for this book. If a digital camera is available, take pictures of the school and your groups of students.)
- overhead transparency of text about the characters (people and advice) (page 125), overhead transparency of text innovation (pages 126 and 127), overhead transparencies of T-chart for planning and stationery for writing (pages 130 and 131)

Teacher Materials Included in the Lesson:

- sample shared planning (page 128) and shared writing (page 129)
- sample student planning and writing (pages 133 and 134)

Student Materials Included in the Lesson:

- For each group of two to three students, you will need to prepare packets containing copies of the T-chart for planning (page 130), stationery for writing (page 131), and rubric for thinking about their writing (page 132).

Read Aloud

1. Build background by eliciting from students some writing assignments that teachers have given them for homework. Ask if anyone has ever had trouble deciding what to write.

2. Explain that the main character in *Nothing Ever Happens on 90th Street* has the exact same problem.

3. Tell students to listen to the story, paying special attention to who Eva meets and what advice about the writing the character gives her.

4. Read *Nothing Ever Happens on 90th Street* by Roni Schotter.

Shared Writing

1. Using the overhead transparency of the text about the characters (people and advice) read and discuss the advice that each character gives Eva. Tell students to notice how the job of the person connects in some way to the advice he or she gives about writing.

2. Explain that you are going to change the setting of the story to take place in your school and that school personnel will become the characters in your story. Point out that the advice they give for wonderful writing will change according to each person's job.

3. Display the overhead transparencies of the text innovation. Read the piece together. Fill in the blanks with the appropriate names for the people who work at your school.

Nuttin' Honey (cont.)

Shared Writing (cont.)

4. Display the T-chart for planning. Tell the students that they are going to plan a piece for Ms._____, the cafeteria manager.

5. Elicit all the things that the cafeteria manager does. (examples: plans menus and orders food, cooks and seasons the food, cleans the kitchen, etc.)

6. Connect the things that she does in the cafeteria to elements of effective writing. For example: orders food—organizes to write; cooks and seasons the food—precise language and sentence fluency to spice-up the writing; cleans the kitchen—conventions of the language.

7. Choose one of the specific things she does and then plan your piece.

8. Using the stationery for writing, together, write your piece. (Save if publishing a class book.)

9. As you write, focus on spelling and grammar issues from your students' last writing sample. Refer to your word wall for those words that are difficult for the students.

Guided Independent Writing

1. To each group of two or three students, distribute the prepared writing packets.

2. Tell students each group may choose a person in your school to write about.

3. Using the T-chart for planning, direct students to list things that person does. Next, direct them to connect those things the person does to the elements of effective writing and decide on one of them to write about.

4. Direct students to write their piece using the stationery for writing. Remind them to begin their piece by placing the main character (a student) at your school sitting on the steps, wondering what to write.

5. When finished writing, direct each group to think about their writing by completing the rubric on their piece. Collect the cards.

Sharing Session

Choose groups to share by selecting a card. Continue drawing cards until all groups have shared.

Follow-up Activity: (teaching points: revision, editing, and publishing a class book)

Using the overhead transparency of the text innovation as the beginning, add the shared writing piece. Model revision to the shared piece. Then edit. Direct each group to read their piece. You will probably have to revise some of the transition between pieces to make them flow gracefully from one event to another. (This transition revision lesson is great authentic experience for the students too!) In groups, direct them to make the necessary revision, and then edit. Together, craft an ending. Then, reread the entire piece. Publish. A great idea for the book cover is to use a digital picture of your school. Add your title and authors' names, and then print. If you add pictures of each group of writers, you further honor their writing. Insert a comment page in the back of the book for readers to share what they enjoyed about the book. (Watch your students race to read what people wrote!) Allow your students to take turns taking your class book home to read to their parents. (A sign-out system works great for getting it returned.) Take a walking tour of the school and share the book with all the school personnel the students wrote about.

Nothing Ever Happens on 90th Street
by Roni Schotter
<u>People</u> and Their <u>Advice</u>

Mr. Morley, who dreamed of a catering business

"Try to find poetry in your pudding," Mr. Morley said softly. "There's always a <u>new way with old words.</u>"

Alexis Leora, dancer

"Stretch," she said sadly. "Use your imagination. If your story doesn't go the way you want it to, you can always <u>stretch the truth</u>. You can ask, 'What if?' and make up a better story."

Mrs. Martinez, a lady who made soup

"Add a little <u>action</u>," Mrs. Martinez said. "Like soup. A little of this. A little of that. And don't forget the <u>spice</u>. Mix it. Stir it. <u>Make something happen</u>. Surprise yourself!"

Nothing Ever Happens on 90th Street
Text Innovation

_____ unwrapped a cinnamon Danish, opened her notebook, and stared helplessly at the wide, white pages. "Write about what you know," her teacher, Mr./Ms. _____ had told her. So _____ sat high on the stoop and looked out over_____ Elementary waiting for something to happen. The intercom beeped. Two kids read. The phone rang. The usual. "Nothing ever happens at _____ Elementary," _____ scribbled in her notebook.

A few doors down, Mr./Ms. _____ was walking down the hallway watching the kids going to class. He/she nodded to Coach and called hello to _____.

Nothing Ever Happens on 90th Street

Text Innovation *(cont.)*

Out the door of _____'s building came _____, our language arts supervisor, carrying her enormous brief case stuffed full of papers. She was dressed in her finest—Brighton shoes with matching handbag and a teacher-jumper that said, "We love writing!"

"Writing?" she asked.

"Trying to," _____ answered, "but nothing ever happens at _____ Elementary!"

"You are mistaken, my dear," _____ said. "The whole world's a stage-even _____ Elementary, and each of us plays a part. Watch the stage, observe the players, and don't neglect the details," she said, smoothing her jumper. "Follow my advice and you will have plenty to write about."

Sample Shared Planning

Nothing Ever Happens on 90th Street
by Roni Schotter

Job Description	Attributes of Strong Writing
Cafeteria Manager—Ms. Eggplant • plans menus, orders food • cooks delicious food • cleans the kitchen	• organizes to write • precise words/sentence fluency • conventions

Sample Shared Writing

Molly sat at the bottom of the steps, tapping her pencil against the paper.

"What to write? What to write?" she repeated over and over again. "I can't think of a thing."

All of a sudden Ms. Eggplant, the cafeteria manager, appeared above her on the steps. Clickety-clack went her heels as she came down the steps.

"Good girl! I see you're thinking. Got any ideas yet? Your page is still blank," said Ms. Eggplant.

"No. I'm fresh out of ideas," Molly sadly replied.

"You got to put black on white, Missy! Start writing. What I always say is you've got to gather your ingredients before you bake the cake. You do the same with your story. Girl, you need some characters! Begin there. Put them in an exciting place and make them do something interesting. Tell us what they think, say, and do, and don't forget to describe, describe, describe! Readers like that!" And with that, Ms. Eggplant wiped her hands on her apron and headed off in the direction of the cafeteria.

Name(s): _____

Nothing Ever Happens on 90th Street
by Roni Schotter

Job Description	Attributes of Strong Writing

Name(s): _____

Name(s): _____

Rubric for Our Piece

<u>Lesson Focus:</u> Specific Support (developing events)
Nothing Ever Happens on 90th Street by Roni Schotter

- We planned our piece by listing things a grownup does in his/her job at our school. ___

- Then we listed some things we know about effective writing. ___

- We remembered to start our piece with the person sitting on the steps. ___

- We selected one thing the grownup does in his/her job and connected it to one thing we know about effective writing. ___

- In our piece, the grownup gave advice about writing well. ___

- Our advice was _____

  _____.

- We remembered to check our punctuation, capitalization, and spelling. ___

- We are proud of our writing. ___

Sample Student Planning

Name(s): __Fred__

Nothing Ever Happens on 90th Street
by Roni Schotter

Nothing   Ever   happens at grahan Elementry

Job Description	Attributes of Strong Writing
writing teacher (Mrs shauf)	• B M E • description • strong lead • verbs • symalics • Good convintions • Organization • ⟨Go slow - pay atention⟩

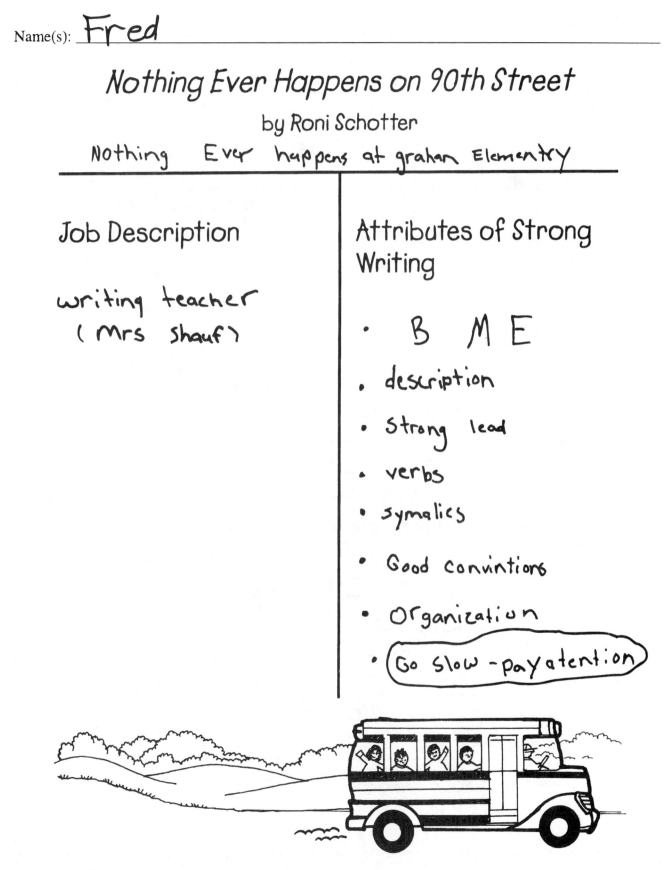

Sample Student Writing

Name(s): Fred

As I sat on the steps wondering what to write along came Mrs. Shauf my writing teacher. As usual she was rushing around with about 15 pounds of books in her hands. Then she stoped at my step and said, "Frederick are ya stuck?" I said, "How did you know? She Answerd with a smile and said, "I could tell be cause you have a frowney face and your pencil isn't moving." I begged, "Pleasss gimme some advice!!" "Fred, writers notice things that other people don't. look around you and pay attention to what's happenig at grahm a elementry school!" With that, she rushed into the faculty lounge. "Hmmm," I thought, "what do I see? Just at that second, I saw three frogs jumping over each other." I could tell a story about three frogs playing leap frog. "Here goes Nothin!"

Creepy Facts

Materials

Teacher Materials You Need to Supply:

- read-aloud selections: *Creepy Creatures* by Sneed B. Collard III, an encyclopedia article on piranhas which is one of the creatures in the book; for modeled writing, an overhead transparency of an encyclopedia article on another animal of your choosing not found in *Creepy Creatures* (alternate read-aloud selection: *Cockroach Cooties* by Laurence Yep, page 37. Begin with: "It's hard to sneak up on cockroaches." End with . . . "like a hand coming down." Page 51. Begin with: "Charlie leaned so close . . ." End with: " . . . but its ancestors migrated here several centuries ago." Page 59. Begin with: "Spiders can be loving mothers . . . ." End with: ". . . . ounce for ounce that face can be stronger than steel.")

- overhead projector, transparency markers, highlighter tape, and pencils for each of your five groups of students. (Optional: If publishing a class book, you might need colored pencils, book binding materials, and two 9" x 12" pieces of white construction paper for each group of students.)

- transparencies of text excerpt on piranhas from *Creepy Creatures* (page 137), trap-door spider facts (page 138), and the stationery for writing (page 145).

Teacher Materials Included in the Lesson:

- sample modeled planning and writing (pages 138 and 139)
- sample student writing (page 147)
- fact sheets for the following animals: alligators, boa constrictors, grizzly bears, horseshoe crabs, and stingrays (pages 140–144)

Student Materials Included in the Lesson:

- For each of your five groups of students, you will need to prepare packets containing copies of a fact sheet on one of five different animals (pages 140–144), stationery for writing (page 145), and the rubric for thinking about their writing (page 146).

Read Aloud

1. Build background by eliciting the effective elements of informational writing. Tell them that the best informational writers include lots of facts and examples in their text so that the reader learns something when they read their pieces.

2. Before reading aloud from *Creepy Creatures* by Sneed B. Collard III, tell the students to listen to the information Collard used. Tell them that the piece is short but filled with intriguing facts about piranhas.

3. Display the transparency of the text of *Creepy Creatures*. Together, read the piece. Elicit some facts in the piece and then point out the interesting way Collard wrote them.

4. Next, tell the students to listen to an encyclopedia article on the same creature. Tell them to listen to the differences in the writing. Read the article.

5. Elicit the differences in the two pieces. (The encyclopedia article is full of facts but not intriguing because its purpose is to provide all known information on a subject. In contrast, Mr. Collard carefully chose interesting tidbits filled with striking information and packed them into just a few words. He left out a lot of the information found in the encyclopedia article, yet his piece holds our attention and invites us to learn more.)

Creepy Facts *(cont.)*

Modeled Writing

1. Display the transparency on the animal you chose to write about. (sample provided: trap-door spiders) Think aloud and underline the information from the piece that you find intriguing. Verbalize why you chose that fact. Make notes on the margins of the fact sheet. (This becomes your plan.) Voice all your thoughts and decisions aloud so that it is clear why you are intrigued by that information.

2. Decide on the order of the information to be used. That will involve selecting an attention-getting lead. Use the most compelling fact as the lead, remembering to say it in your own words. (If you've previously taught different types of leads, try out different ways to begin your piece.) Next, focus on using the information underlined in the piece. Model rephrasing it to make it sound like you (voice). Write your piece referring to your plan to retrieve your ideas. Remember to use your class word wall to help with spelling of high-frequency words. Model convention weaknesses found in your students' writing.

Guided Writing

1. Divide the students into five groups and distribute a packet of writing materials and one roll of highlighter tape. Tell them that each group will write a piece on one of five different creatures.

2. Direct the students to first read all the facts on their creature. Next, decide on the facts that they find interesting. Direct them to place a piece of highlighter tape on the four or five facts they find intriguing. Finally, order the facts by numbering them—choosing the most compelling as the lead.

3. Using the stationery for writing, direct them to write a piece on their creature. Remind them to also include an illustration. Encourage them to use the back of the page for the illustration. Direct them to label their drawing so that it looks like real informational text with graphic support.

4. Have them think about their writing by completing the rubric, and encourage them to make any changes necessary.

Sharing Session

Have each group read their piece. Invite students to talk about the decisions they made in order to write their piece.

Follow-up Activity (teaching point: more specific details, intriguing facts)

Extend the lesson by researching and writing about other creatures. Allow your students to choose their own animal. Research on the Internet or use an encyclopedia. Make a class book. Use one piece of construction paper for the picture, the other for the writing. Possible titles—"Creepy Critters" or "Additional Creepy Creatures."

Excerpt from *Creepy Creatures*

(by Sneed B. Collard III)

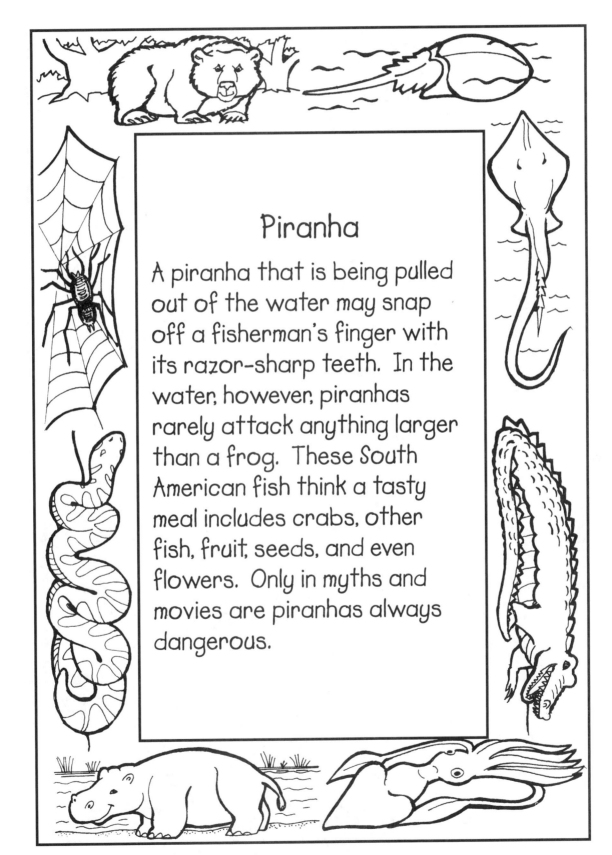

Piranha

A piranha that is being pulled out of the water may snap off a fisherman's finger with its razor-sharp teeth. In the water, however, piranhas rarely attack anything larger than a frog. These South American fish think a tasty meal includes crabs, other fish, fruit, seeds, and even flowers. Only in myths and movies are piranhas always dangerous.

Modeled Planning: Trap-door Spider Facts

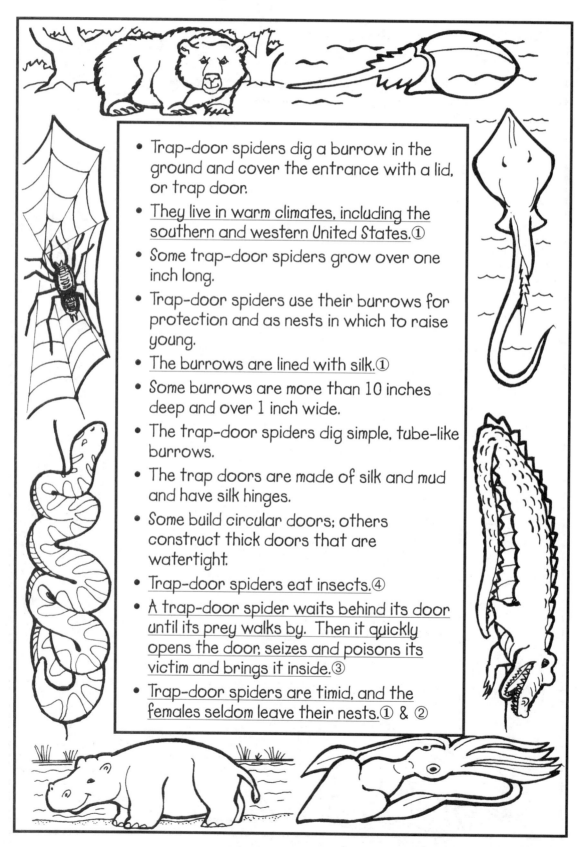

- Trap-door spiders dig a burrow in the ground and cover the entrance with a lid, or trap door.
- <u>They live in warm climates, including the southern and western United States.</u>①
- Some trap-door spiders grow over one inch long.
- Trap-door spiders use their burrows for protection and as nests in which to raise young.
- <u>The burrows are lined with silk.</u>①
- Some burrows are more than 10 inches deep and over 1 inch wide.
- The trap-door spiders dig simple, tube-like burrows.
- The trap doors are made of silk and mud and have silk hinges.
- Some build circular doors; others construct thick doors that are watertight.
- <u>Trap-door spiders eat insects.</u>④
- <u>A trap-door spider waits behind its door until its prey walks by. Then it quickly opens the door, seizes and poisons its victim and brings it inside.</u>③
- <u>Trap-door spiders are timid, and the females seldom leave their nests.</u>① & ②

Sample Modeled Writing:
Trap-door Spiders

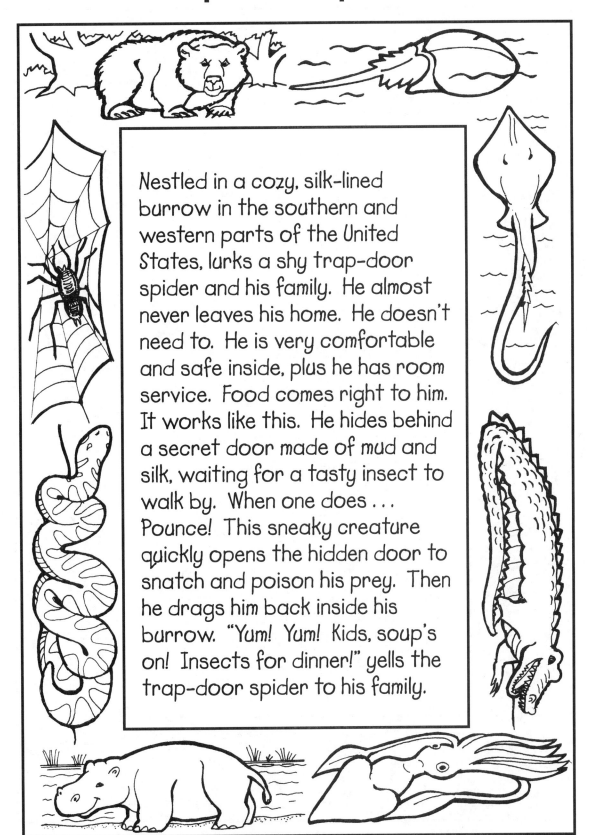

Nestled in a cozy, silk-lined burrow in the southern and western parts of the United States, lurks a shy trap-door spider and his family. He almost never leaves his home. He doesn't need to. He is very comfortable and safe inside, plus he has room service. Food comes right to him. It works like this. He hides behind a secret door made of mud and silk, waiting for a tasty insect to walk by. When one does . . . Pounce! This sneaky creature quickly opens the hidden door to snatch and poison his prey. Then he drags him back inside his burrow. "Yum! Yum! Kids, soup's on! Insects for dinner!" yells the trap-door spider to his family.

Alligators Fact Sheet

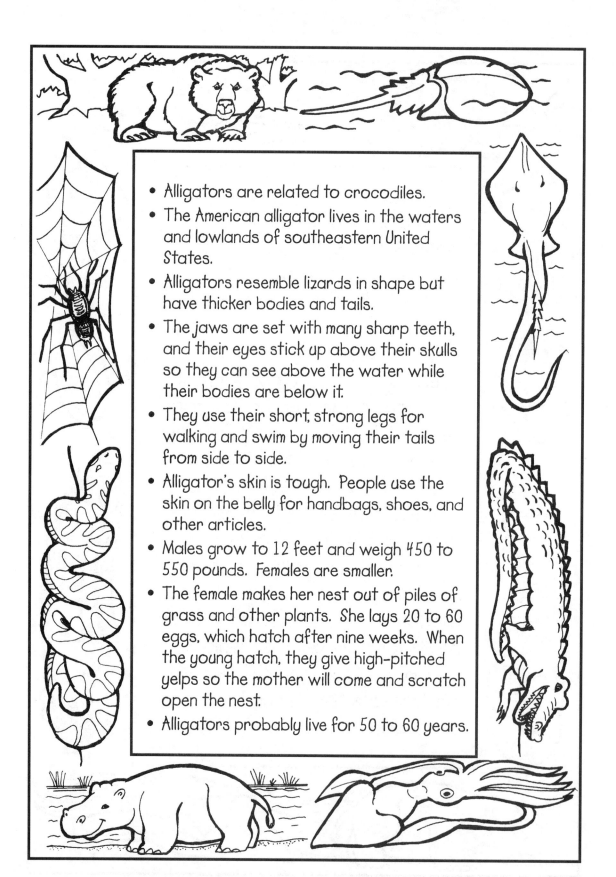

- Alligators are related to crocodiles.
- The American alligator lives in the waters and lowlands of southeastern United States.
- Alligators resemble lizards in shape but have thicker bodies and tails.
- The jaws are set with many sharp teeth, and their eyes stick up above their skulls so they can see above the water while their bodies are below it.
- They use their short, strong legs for walking and swim by moving their tails from side to side.
- Alligator's skin is tough. People use the skin on the belly for handbags, shoes, and other articles.
- Males grow to 12 feet and weigh 450 to 550 pounds. Females are smaller.
- The female makes her nest out of piles of grass and other plants. She lays 20 to 60 eggs, which hatch after nine weeks. When the young hatch, they give high-pitched yelps so the mother will come and scratch open the nest.
- Alligators probably live for 50 to 60 years.

Boa Constrictors Fact Sheet

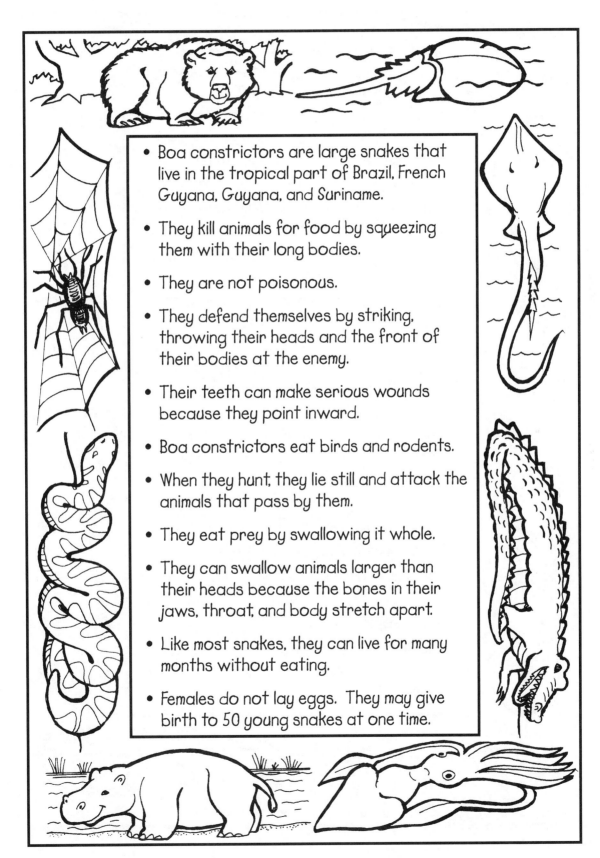

- Boa constrictors are large snakes that live in the tropical part of Brazil, French Guyana, Guyana, and Suriname.

- They kill animals for food by squeezing them with their long bodies.

- They are not poisonous.

- They defend themselves by striking, throwing their heads and the front of their bodies at the enemy.

- Their teeth can make serious wounds because they point inward.

- Boa constrictors eat birds and rodents.

- When they hunt, they lie still and attack the animals that pass by them.

- They eat prey by swallowing it whole.

- They can swallow animals larger than their heads because the bones in their jaws, throat, and body stretch apart.

- Like most snakes, they can live for many months without eating.

- Females do not lay eggs. They may give birth to 50 young snakes at one time.

Grizzly Bears Fact Sheet

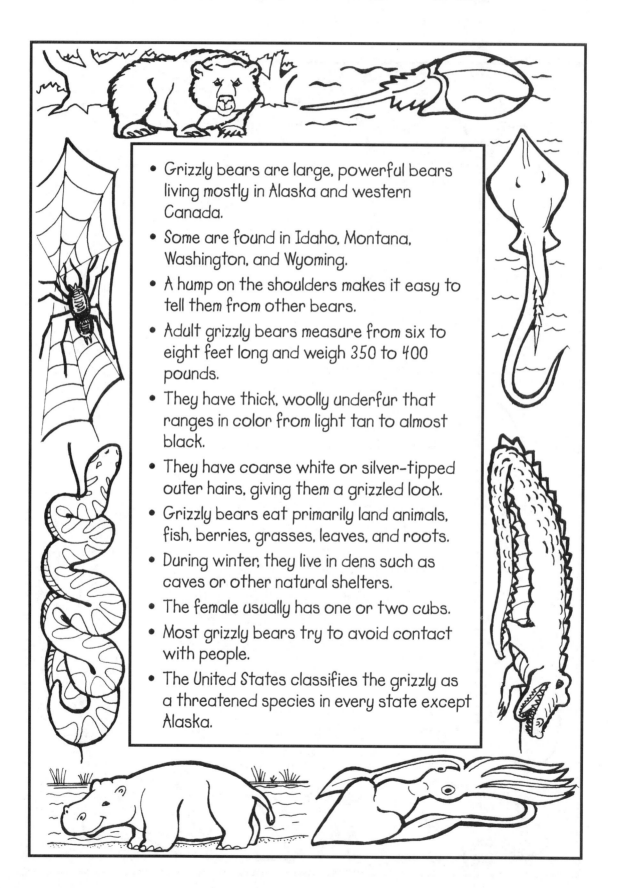

- Grizzly bears are large, powerful bears living mostly in Alaska and western Canada.
- Some are found in Idaho, Montana, Washington, and Wyoming.
- A hump on the shoulders makes it easy to tell them from other bears.
- Adult grizzly bears measure from six to eight feet long and weigh 350 to 400 pounds.
- They have thick, woolly underfur that ranges in color from light tan to almost black.
- They have coarse white or silver-tipped outer hairs, giving them a grizzled look.
- Grizzly bears eat primarily land animals, fish, berries, grasses, leaves, and roots.
- During winter, they live in dens such as caves or other natural shelters.
- The female usually has one or two cubs.
- Most grizzly bears try to avoid contact with people.
- The United States classifies the grizzly as a threatened species in every state except Alaska.

Horseshoe Crabs Fact Sheet

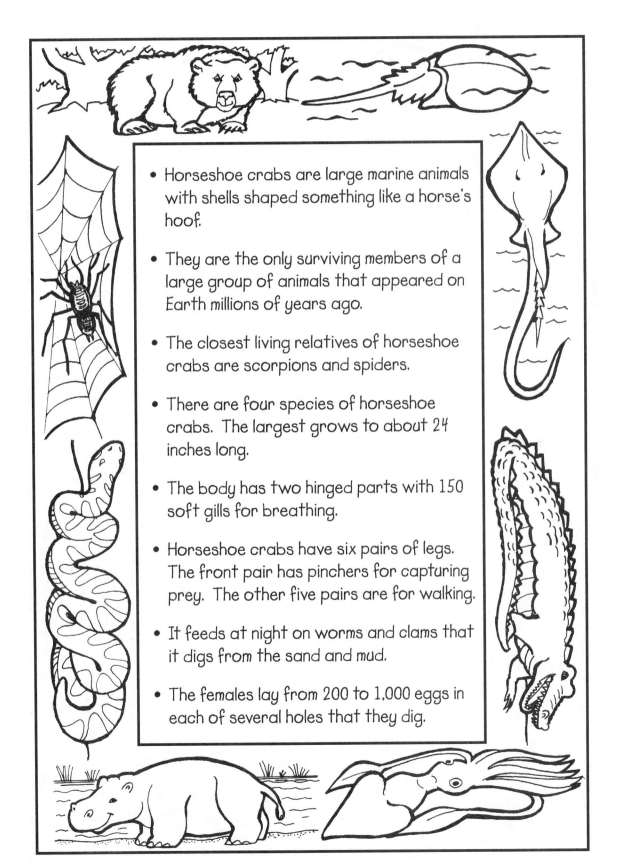

- Horseshoe crabs are large marine animals with shells shaped something like a horse's hoof.

- They are the only surviving members of a large group of animals that appeared on Earth millions of years ago.

- The closest living relatives of horseshoe crabs are scorpions and spiders.

- There are four species of horseshoe crabs. The largest grows to about 24 inches long.

- The body has two hinged parts with 150 soft gills for breathing.

- Horseshoe crabs have six pairs of legs. The front pair has pinchers for capturing prey. The other five pairs are for walking.

- It feeds at night on worms and clams that it digs from the sand and mud.

- The females lay from 200 to 1,000 eggs in each of several holes that they dig.

Stingray Fact Sheet

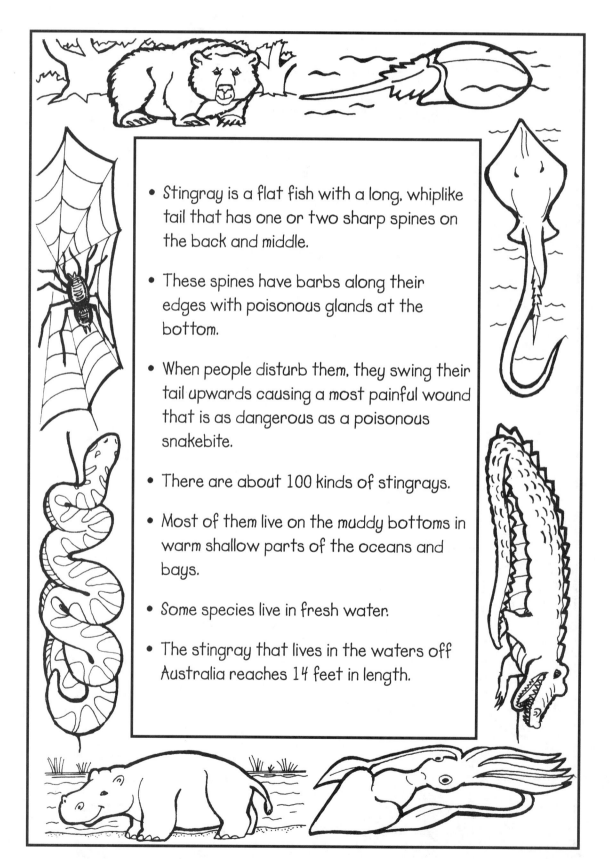

- Stingray is a flat fish with a long, whiplike tail that has one or two sharp spines on the back and middle.

- These spines have barbs along their edges with poisonous glands at the bottom.

- When people disturb them, they swing their tail upwards causing a most painful wound that is as dangerous as a poisonous snakebite.

- There are about 100 kinds of stingrays.

- Most of them live on the muddy bottoms in warm shallow parts of the oceans and bays.

- Some species live in fresh water.

- The stingray that lives in the waters off Australia reaches 14 feet in length.

Name(s): _____

Name(s): _____

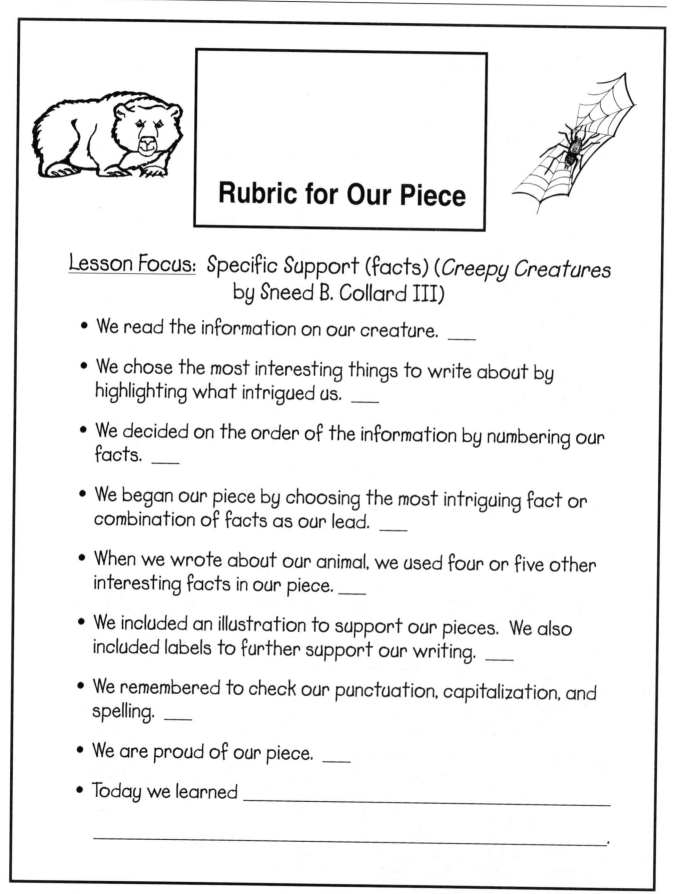

Rubric for Our Piece

<u>Lesson Focus:</u> Specific Support (facts) (*Creepy Creatures* by Sneed B. Collard III)

- We read the information on our creature. ___

- We chose the most interesting things to write about by highlighting what intrigued us. ___

- We decided on the order of the information by numbering our facts. ___

- We began our piece by choosing the most intriguing fact or combination of facts as our lead. ___

- When we wrote about our animal, we used four or five other interesting facts in our piece. ___

- We included an illustration to support our pieces. We also included labels to further support our writing. ___

- We remembered to check our punctuation, capitalization, and spelling. ___

- We are proud of our piece. ___

- Today we learned _____

_____.

Sample Student Writing

Name(s): heonni, Erika, mildred

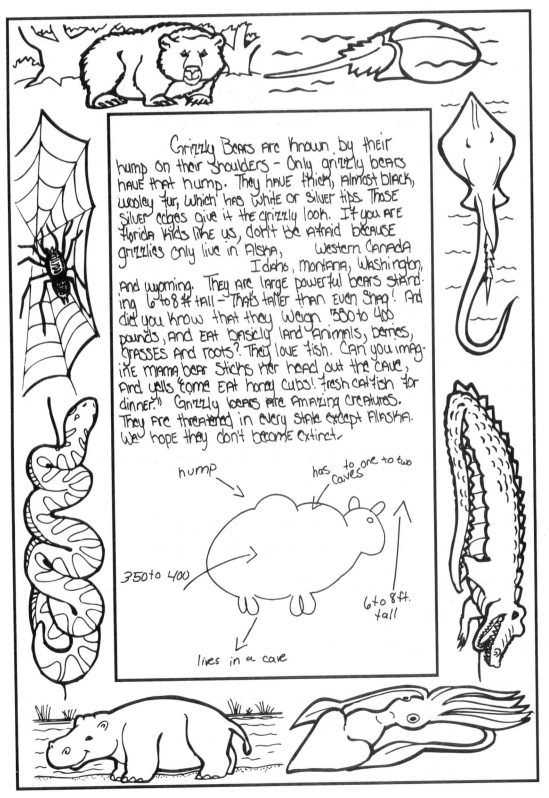

Grizzly Bears are known by their hump on their shoulders - Only grizzly bears have that hump. They have thick, almost black, wooley fur, which has white or silver tips. Those silver edges give it the grizzly look. If you are florida kids like us, don't be afraid because grizzlies only live in Alska, Western Canada Idaho, Montana, Washington, and wyoming. They are large powerful bears standing 6 to 8 ft tall - That's taller than even Shaq! And did you know that they weigh 350 to 400 pounds, and eat basicly land animals, berries, grasses and roots? They love fish. Can you imagine mama bear sticks her head out the cave, and yells "come eat honey cubs! fresh catfish for dinner." Grizzly bears are Amazing creatures. They are threatened in every state except Alaska. We hope they don't become extinct.

hump
has one to two caves
350 to 400
6 to 8 ft. tall
lives in a cave

Facts, Examples, and Something Personal

Materials

Teacher Materials You Need to Supply:

- read-aloud "Nutrition" (page 151), overhead transparency of the cereal text to be revised (page 152), overhead transparency of Cinnamon Toast Crunch Facts (page 153), overhead transparency of the stationery for planning (page 155), overhead transparency of the stationery for writing on Cinnamon Toast Crunch (page 157).

- overhead projector, transparency markers, chalkboard or whiteboard, and a marker

- six signs with cereal names written on them, spinner with sections numbered 1–6, six empty boxes of assorted cereal (this lesson used 1 ⅛ oz. individual serving sizes of Kellogg's Smacks, Frosted Flakes, Cocoa Krispies, Corn Pops, Fruit Loops, and Apple Jacks)

- one large empty box of Cinnamon Toast Crunch used in modeled writing, one sticky-note for each student, and pencils for each of the six groups. *Optional:* highlighter tape for each group of students.

Teacher Materials Included in the Lesson:

- read-aloud selection "Nutrition" (page 151), the cereal text to be revised (page 152), Cinnamon Toast Crunch Facts (page 153), stationery for planning (page 155), stationery for writing on Cinnamon Toast Crunch (page 156).

- sample modeled planning and writing (page 154)

- sample student planning and writing (pages 159 and 160)

Student Materials Included in the Lesson Plan:

- For each of your six groups of students, you will need to prepare packets containing copies of stationery for planning and writing (pages 155 and 157), revision text (page 152), the rubric for thinking about their writing (page 158), and one empty box of cereal.

Read Aloud

1. Build background experience by eliciting the types of cereal the students enjoy eating. Briefly discuss a few of their favorites and why they like them.

2. Tell students that kids know lots about cereal because they read the back of the cereal boxes, eat many boxes of cereal each year, and they watch all the commercials on television. Say that today we are going to explain why certain cereals are good for us.

3. Before reading, elicit and record on the whiteboard the types of support used to develop main ideas in expository writing (*details, facts, examples,* and *personal experiences*).

4. Read the piece "Nutrition." Tell students to listen particularly to the support in each main idea.

5. Elicit the specific details, facts, examples, and personal experiences from the piece.

Facts, Examples, and Something Personal *(cont.)*

Modeled Writing

1. Display and read the overhead transparency of the revision text on cereals.

2. Tell students that the beginning and ending of the piece are strong, and then elicit what is missing from the middle of the piece (support for each main idea—specific details, facts, examples, and personal experiences).

3. Display the overhead transparency of the Cinnamon Toast Crunch piece, the first main idea in the revision text. Then hold up the cereal box. Model how to locate the important information about the cereal found on the box. (Highlighter tape may be used to mark the places.)

4. So that everyone can see the information on the box, display the overhead transparency of the facts and ingredients found in Cinnamon Toast Crunch.

5. Tell the students that you made a list of some things that could be used to provide support in the piece.

6. Display the overhead transparency of the stationery for planning. Model deciding what facts and details you find intriguing about the cereal. Also, explain what facts and details you don't find interesting and why you will not use them in the piece.

7. Display the overhead transparency of the stationery for writing on Cinnamon Toast Crunch. Write your piece including some details, facts, examples, and personal experiences from the plan.

8. Remember to use some high-frequency words from the class word wall. Model rereading the ingredients to locate the spelling of hard words. Focus on punctuation and grammar issues that trouble your students.

Guided Writing

1. Before establishing groups, tell students that in our piece we will be writing about eating. Explain that it will get pretty boring if we keep repeating the word "eat" in our piece. Elicit and record on the whiteboard other words for *eat*. Possibilities are *dine, munch, inhale, scarf down, feast on, gobble, consume*, etc.

2. Hang cereal names in six locations in the room and then distribute one sticky-note to each student. Before having them move, direct their attention to the types of cereals written on the signs. Direct students to write their first and second choices on their sticky-notes. (This will eliminate students choosing a friend's group and also allow you some flexibility if too many choose a particular type of cereal.) Direct the students to move to their first-choice location written on their sticky-note. Adjust the numbers in the groups as needed by having some students move to their second choice. Establish six groups.

Facts, Examples, and Something Personal *(cont.)*

Guided Writing *(cont.)*

3. Distribute the small cereal boxes and the packets of writing materials to each group.

4. Before writing, direct students to locate the sections on the box that contain information about the cereal. Tell them to place highlighter tape there to help them locate some useful information they can use in their piece. (You can have them circle with markers if highlighter tape is not available.)

5. Remind students of the elements of specific support needed in the piece and of the other words for "eat" recorded on the whiteboard.

6. Tell students to copy their main idea sentence from the Revision Text onto the stationery for writing.

7. Direct them to plan their piece. Remind them of the model.

8. Then direct students to write their main idea. Circulate and assist each group as they write their piece.

9. When the paragraph is finished, direct them to complete the rubric for thinking about their writing. Encourage them to make any changes necessary in their paragraph.

Sharing Session

Use a spinner divided into six sections numbered 1–6 for selecting groups to share their piece. Direct each group to stand and read their piece. Invite the audience to give "thumbs up" every time they hear specific support.

Follow-up Activity (teaching points: revision, editing, and publishing)

Direct each group to revise and then edit their piece. Type the fully revised piece, including the beginning, modeled writing, text that each of the six groups wrote, and the ending. Publish the piece. Create an instructional bulletin board with the cereal piece in the center. (If a poster machine is available, enlarge the piece.) On a sentence strip, write your teaching point—specific details, intriguing facts, and examples. Title the bulletin board "Ways Authors Provide Specific Support to Expository Writing" (details, facts, examples, personal experiences). Staple the cereal boxes along the sides. Refer back to the piece and the lesson focus as you continue to write other expository pieces.

Facts, Examples, and Something Personal *(cont.)*

Read-Aloud

> Yum! Yum! Cereal! Cereal for breakfast is good for us!

Nutrition

American children are getting fatter and fatter each year. Did you know that? We eat too many fatty foods at meal times, sit around like couch potatoes, and snack all throughout the day. Doctors have been telling us what we should eat. They even made us a food pyramid to show it. We need to follow it.

Vegetables! Vegetables! Vegetables! That's the answer. The biggest part of our diet needs to be made up of fruits and vegetables. Why, you might ask. They contain vitamins A, B, C, and D. Our body needs those vitamins to keep us healthy. They are also enriched with niacin, copper and zinc. Those minerals help us fight diseases. The last time I saw my pediatrician, Dr. Taylor, she said, "Honey, are you eating large servings of fruits and vegetables?" I was proud to say, "Yes, I am!" My checkup went well because of all those fruits and vegetables I eat.

Dairy products are also important to your diet. One of the main things they have is calcium. Look for labels that say "enriched with calcium." Those foods are better for you. Do you like string cheese, yogurt, or hot chocolate? If you do, then you can eat healthful, tasty foods, and make your dentist and doctor happy too. I just found out that older people need calcium too. My grandmother has to take calcium pills every morning. She says it makes her bones strong so her back won't curve over like an old witch. I heard on TV that four out of five adults don't get enough calcium. If they would start eating dairy products, maybe they would get healthy and have strong teeth and bones like us kids.

Do you like pasta or toast or cereal? If you do, then you can eat lots of those foods. Those foods come from the grain food group. Make sure you eat foods from this group too. After school, I microwave Uncle Ben's Pasta in a Bowl. When I eat that, I get grains and vegetables all at once. This food has the American Heart Association seal of approval. I feel good when I eat something that doctors approve. Grains give you fiber that your body needs. When you eat grains, you have energy too. My coach says, "Attention you kids, I want you to eat a sandwich before practice so you'll have enough energy to play soccer." See, I told you grains were good for you.

It is a fact that Americans need to eat better. Think before you grab those fast foods! Eat healthy! Listen to this kid!

Facts, Examples, and Something Personal *(cont.)*

Revision Text

Yum! Yum! Cereal! Cereal for breakfast is good for us!

Crunch! Munch! Snap! Crackle! Pop! What do kids eat that makes those sounds? Cereal! You've got it! We inhale boxes of it everyday. It tastes so good and it's nutritious too.

Cinnamon Toast Crunch is an all time favorite at my house.

We also gobble down boxes of Frosted Flakes.

If you're craving pop corn, Kellogg's Corn Pops will hit the spot.

Another tasty one is Froot Loops.

There's also Kellogg's Smacks if you need some instant energy!

Since kids love chocolate, Cocoa Krispie is very popular.

Then there's Apple Jacks—sure to please your teacher.

Where you find kids, you're sure to find cereal. We munch on it for after-school snacks, and we beg for it at breakfast. We sure love cereal!

Modeled Writing Facts

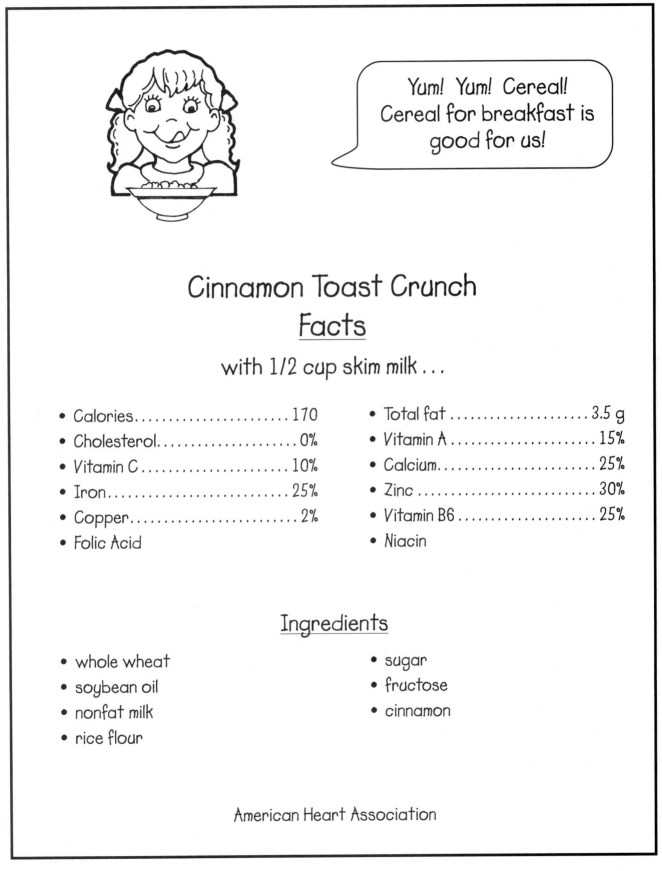

Yum! Yum! Cereal! Cereal for breakfast is good for us!

Cinnamon Toast Crunch
Facts

with 1/2 cup skim milk . . .

- Calories 170
- Cholesterol 0%
- Vitamin C 10%
- Iron 25%
- Copper 2%
- Folic Acid

- Total fat . . . . 3.5 g
- Vitamin A 15%
- Calcium 25%
- Zinc 30%
- Vitamin B6 . . . . 25%
- Niacin

Ingredients

- whole wheat
- soybean oil
- nonfat milk
- rice flour

- sugar
- fructose
- cinnamon

American Heart Association

Modeled Planning

Ideas for My Piece

Specific Details:

- cinnamon/sugar in every bite
- Eat with milk
- For breakfast or snack

Facts and Examples:

- Whole wheat, sugar, & rice flour
- Fructose
- 170 calories
- Recommended by American Heart Association
- Vitamins A, C, and B6
- Zinc, copper, calcium, and niacin
- Get the toy before your brother

Personal Experience:

- All time favorite
- Dad eats it
- Toy inside

Modeled Writing

Yum! Yum! Cereal! Cereal for breakfast is good for us!

Cinnamon Toast Crunch is an all-time favorite at my house. We like it because you get cinnamon and sugar in every bite. It's made with whole wheat, sugar, and rice flour. They even put in fructose to make it taste even better. If you think kids are the only ones who munch it, you'd be wrong. Dads gobble it down too. My dad eats it because there are only 170 calories per serving, and it is recommended by the American Heart Association. Do you have a mom on a health kick? If you do, she'll love Cinnamon Toast Crunch. It contains vitamins A, C, and B6. In every spoonful you'll get zinc, copper, calcium, and niacin too. Let's not forget another perk to this cereal. There's usually a toy inside. It's fun sticking your hand down inside to snatch out the toy before your brother gets it! At our house, we devour it with milk for breakfast, but when we get home from school, we consume it just as it is, right out of the box. Yum! Give me some Crunch!

Name(s): _____

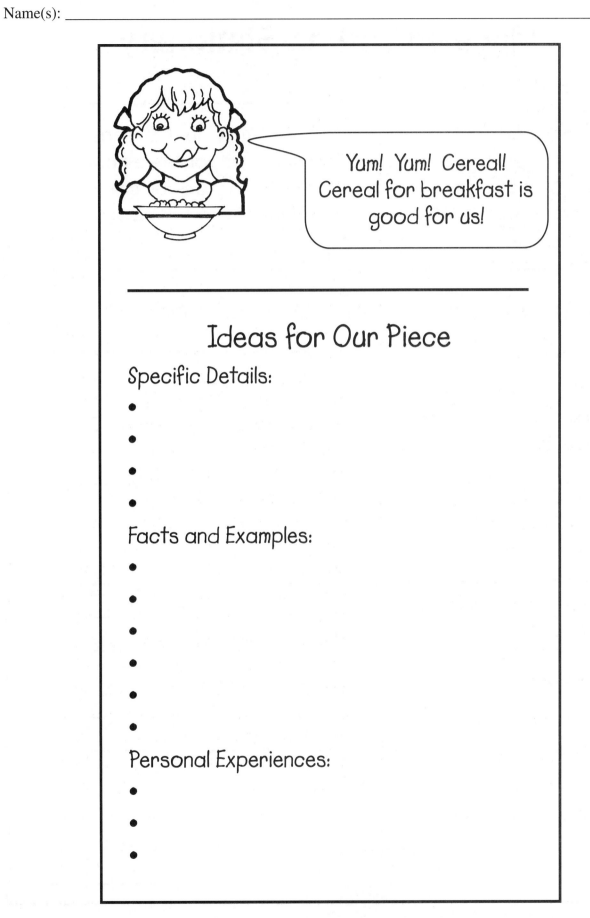

Yum! Yum! Cereal!
Cereal for breakfast is
good for us!

Ideas for Our Piece

Specific Details:

-
-
-
-

Facts and Examples:

-
-
-
-
-
-

Personal Experiences:

-
-
-

Modeled Writing Stationery

Yum! Yum! Cereal! Cereal for breakfast is good for us!

Cinnamon Toast Crunch is an all-time favorite at my house. _____

_____

_____

_____

_____

_____

_____

_____

_____

_____

_____

_____

_____

_____

_____

Name(s): _____

Yum! Yum! Cereal! Cereal for breakfast is good for us!

_____

_____

_____

_____

_____

_____

_____

_____

_____

_____

_____

_____

_____

_____

_____

_____

_____

_____

Name(s): _____

Rubric for Our Piece

Yum! Yum! Cereal! Cereal for breakfast is good for us!

Lesson Focus: Specific Support

"Nutrition"

- We read the information on our cereal. ___

- We chose the most interesting things to write about by highlighting what intrigued us. ___

- We have also included some examples. ___

  We wrote _____.

- We included some facts. ___

  We wrote _____.

- We remembered to check our punctuation, capitalization, and spelling. ___

- We learned that _____

  _____.

- We are proud of this piece. ___

Sample Student Planning

Name(s): **Cesar, Ontario, Nick, and Heather**

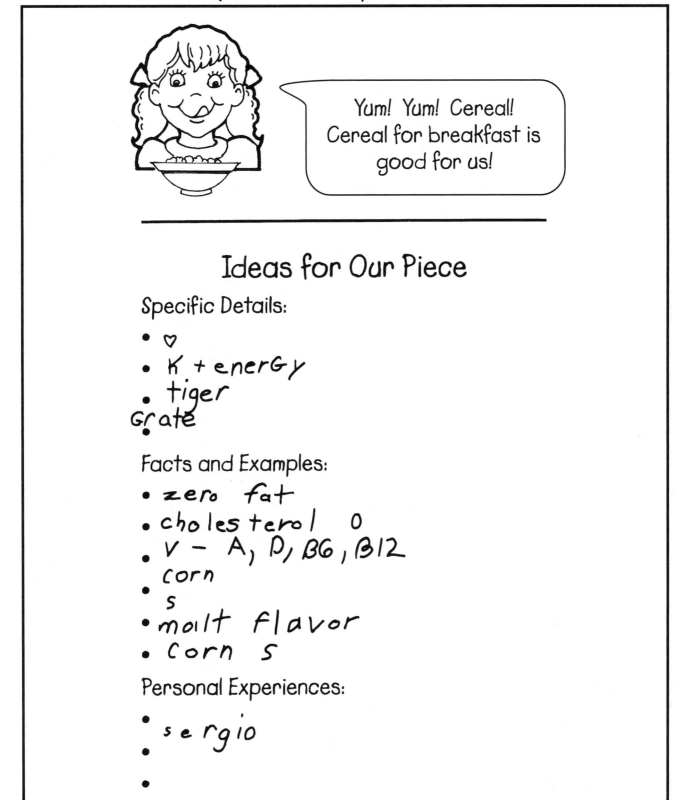

Yum! Yum! Cereal! Cereal for breakfast is good for us!

Ideas for Our Piece

Specific Details:

- ♡
- K + energy
- tiger
- Grate

Facts and Examples:

- zero fat
- cholesterol 0
- V — A, D, B6, B12
- corn
- s
- malt flavor
- corn s

Personal Experiences:

- sergio
-
-

Sample Student Writing

Name(s): Cesar, Ontario, Nick, and Heather

Yum! Yum! Cereal! Cereal for breakfast is good for us!

We also gobble down boxes of Frosted Flakes You Know the box with Tony the tiger on the box. Tony says "THEY'RE GREAT!" We thinck they are great to. They're supper charGeD for energy. Frosted flakes are helthy becduse they have vitamins A, D, B6 and B12. It also has 75% iron wich makes us strong. Are parents like it because it has 0% fat and 0% cholerterol. their Docter has them watching out for that fat! Our friend Sergio scarfs down a box evey week. He likes it because it has corn, suger, fructose and corn syrup in it. He says "with all that grate tasting ingredients it GRRREAT!!!" EVen the American Heart Association likes them. We like them to.

Clumping for Detail

(*Two- to three-day lesson*)

Materials

Teacher Materials You Need to Supply:

- read-aloud selection: *Charlie Anderson* by Barbara Abercrombie
- overhead projector, transparency markers, colored magic markers, and pencils
- one to two overhead transparencies of cat stationery (page 167) for writing
- chart paper cut into the shape of three large cat faces labeled with "Eat," "Do," and "Looks Like"
- *Optional*: Play "The Waltzing Cat" by Leroy Anderson during guided writing, pictures of your cat if you have them, and colored pencils for day two of the lesson; if continuing to day three, make an overhead transparency of the final piece.

Teacher Materials Included in the Lesson:

- sample modeled planning and modeled writing (page 165)
- sample student planning and writing (pages 168 and 169)

Student Materials Included in the Lesson:

- For each group of three to four students, you will need to prepare packets containing copies of cat stationery for planning and for writing (pages 166 and 167) and the rubric for thinking about their writing (page 164).

Read Aloud

1. Before reading, build background by asking questions about pets in general. Elicit animals that make great pets and then elicit the attributes of each pet.

2. Tell them that they know lots of things about cats. Ask the students to raise their hands if they own or have owned a cat themselves. Ask them to raise their hands if they know someone who owns or has owned a cat. Talk briefly about each one. *Optional*: Create interest by displaying pictures of your cat. Then tell students that writers write about the things that they know. Since we know a lot about cats, then we can write about them.

3. Before reading, tell the students to listen carefully to the information on cats found in *Charlie Anderson* by Barbara Abercrombie. Tell them that this book tells a story about a cat and should give us some ideas to use in our writing.

4. Read *Charlie Anderson* by Barbara Abercrombie.

Clumping for Detail *(cont.)*

Shared Writing

1. Tell students that we are going to organize and write a piece about cats. Elicit facts on cats from the story. (They purr, sleep with you, require little care, like to prowl the woods, like to drink warm milk, and have soft fur.) Tell students that when we write, we need to clump our ideas together so that our readers can understand our writing. Writers call these clumps *paragraphs*.

2. Point to the three chart-paper cats with their labels. Elicit the facts found in the book and decide where each would go. Using a marker, record students' ideas on the appropriate cat chart.

3. Elicit some facts that weren't mentioned in the story. Where appropriate, probe for specific details. (Eat: Meow Mix, bluebirds, field mice, etc.) (Do: play with string or small balls, sleep, fight, scratch, etc.) (Looks Like: furry, solid, stripes, spotted, pointed ears, fluffy tail, etc.)

4. Check for understanding by eliciting why you wouldn't write "sleeps under bushes" on the cat labeled "Eat." Continue probing in this manner, checking for understanding.

5. Since the teaching point of the lesson is organization to write with specific details, don't dwell on the lead—write one for them so you can begin the model on organizing and supporting a main idea. (You can always revisit the piece at a later time to work on other teaching points.)

6. Choose one idea for Main Idea # 1. Referring to the appropriate chart-paper cat, direct the students to use the ideas listed there to help them craft sentences for the piece.

7. Together, write your main idea, referring often to the appropriate cat charts. Remind them that since we planned so well, our ideas are already clumped appropriately.

8. After writing, reread sentence by sentence to see if everything you wrote is about your main idea. Direct the students to signal "thumbs up" if they agree the sentence belongs in the paragraph. Tell them that writers always check to make sure all their sentences belong in their main ideas. Continue in this manner until all the sentences in your main idea have been read.

9. Reread your piece to focus on the spelling and grammar issues for your students' last writing sample. Refer to your word wall for those words that are difficult for students. (Save your shared piece if continuing with day two or three.)

Guided Writing

1. Group your class into groups of three to four students.

2. Allow each group to choose one of the other topics not used in your model. (If you allow them to use the topic from shared writing, they will write what you wrote.) Then, direct them to look at the appropriate cat chart for their ideas. Remind them that they can also add other ideas not listed on the chart. Encourage them to come up and add those ideas to the appropriate cat chart.

3. Direct the students to write their main idea. *Optional*: Play "The Waltzing Cat" by Leroy Anderson softly as they write. Tell them the name of the song and that the music will remind them of cats and set the stage for strong writing.

4. After most groups have finished, remind them to reread their piece to make sure all their sentences are about their topic.

5. Direct groups to think about their writing by completing the rubric. Encourage students to make changes where needed.

Clumping for Detail *(cont.)*

Sharing Session

Call on each group of students to read their piece. Collect the pieces and save for the follow-up.

Follow-up Activity (day-two teaching point: writing a piece with a beginning, middle, and ending)

Preparation before the day two lesson: From day one, select two different main ideas your students wrote. Add them to the shared writing transparency from day one. Now you have a beginning and three main ideas. (It is important for students to see that the paragraphs they previously wrote become support to the middle of a full piece of writing.)

Day Two—putting it together for a full piece of expository writing: Review what you did previously in writer's workshop. Display the overhead transparency and reread the lead and the main idea developed during shared writing. Then tell students that you added some of their writing to support the middle of the piece. Read the entire piece. Point out that you indented so that readers can see the separation between each main idea or paragraph. Model checking each sentence to see if what they wrote belongs to the main idea paragraphs. Review the parts of an expository essay. Using your transparency marker, label the parts of the essay: *Beginning, Middle, . . .* Oops, there's no *ending*! Together, craft an ending. Then go back to the shared writing main idea. Using a different colored marker, model revision by making changes to the paragraph. Remind students that these changes make the piece stronger. Establish the same groups as on day one and return the previously written pieces. Direct them to reread what they wrote and make any changes. Encourage them to add more support to make the piece stronger.

Follow-up Activity (day-three teaching point: identifying where specific support belongs)

Preparation before the day-three lesson: Type the entire piece from days one and two and make an overhead transparency and copies for all your students. (Using pieces that students are familiar with makes it easier for them to learn new crafting techniques or review previously taught concepts.)

Day Three—locating where additional specific support should go: Distribute copies of the completed essay to each student. Reread it together. Elicit the parts of an expository essay (beginning, middle, and end). Review the main idea concept. Refer back to the three chart-paper cats. Then, direct students to number each paragraph of the essay (1 through 5). Model this on the overhead transparency.

(Save your shared piece if continuing with day three.)

Clumping for Detail *(cont.)*

Day Three (cont.)—Then, tell the students we are going to play a game called "Where Does It Go?" Tell them that you will read a sentence aloud and they must decide where it should go in the piece. Tell them to hold up the appropriate number of fingers to indicate their answer. Check to see if they understand by saying, "If you think it goes in the paragraph about what cats DO, show me the answer by holding up your fingers." Repeat the process for practice. Vary the response by telling them to whisper to their neighbor; then call on someone to repeat the answer he or she heard. Example sentences that you might ask: Eat—Some people buy Whisker Lickin's cat treats for their cats to gobble up. Do—My neighbor's cat, Snickers, loves to snuggle under the orange tree in my backyard. Looks Like—Whether striped, spotted, or solid, cats usually are as fluffy as feather pillows on my grandmother's bed. Continue in this manner. Form groups of three or four students. Direct each group to write one or two additional sentences for any part of the piece and to label where they think each sentence belongs (paragraphs 2, 3, or 4). Share and have everyone signal thumbs up or down, depending on whether they agree or disagree. Probe to see if a sentence could go in another main idea (sometimes it may). Assess verbal contributions and written sentences to see if the students understand organizing and developing the middle of an expository essay. Most groups will need additional writing focused on small pieces before they understand how to organize and write an entire expository piece from beginning to end.

Name(s): _____

Rubric for Our Piece

Lesson Focus: Specific Support & Organization (*Charlie Anderson* by Barbara Abercrombie)

- Our main idea was _____.

- All our sentences are clumped together in a paragraph. _____

- We wrote about what we know about cats. _____

- Everyone helped with ideas. _____

- Some of our ideas were _____.

- We reread our piece to make sure that all our sentences belong with our main idea and placed a mark after each one to show that it belonged. _____

- We remembered to check our punctuation, capitalization, and spelling. _____

- We are proud of this piece. _____

- Today we learned _____

    _____.

Shared Planning

"What Cats Look Like"

(Our Topic)

- spotted
- fluffy
- ears
- different colors
- four paws–claws
- gray
- striped
- wiggly
- whiskers
- tail

Shared Writing

"Meow!" That's cat talk for, "Hi! Aren't I adorable? Go ahead. Reach out to me. I know you can't resist petting me!" We all like cats, and we know a lot about them.

White cats. Gray cats. Brown cats. Cats can be all different. Some cats are solid colors like black Halloween cats, and others are striped like my brother's basketball socks. We've also seen some that have big blobs of color patches over one eye or down their backs. In fact, color is one way to tell them apart. But, no matter what colors, all cats have long, tickle-whiskers that stick out from the sides of their mouths, and if you look closely at their faces, we bet you'll notice how long their eyebrows are. Whew! Too long if you ask us! Cats also have four feet that are called paws and hiding inside are . . . claws! Cats, we think, look nice.

Name(s): _____

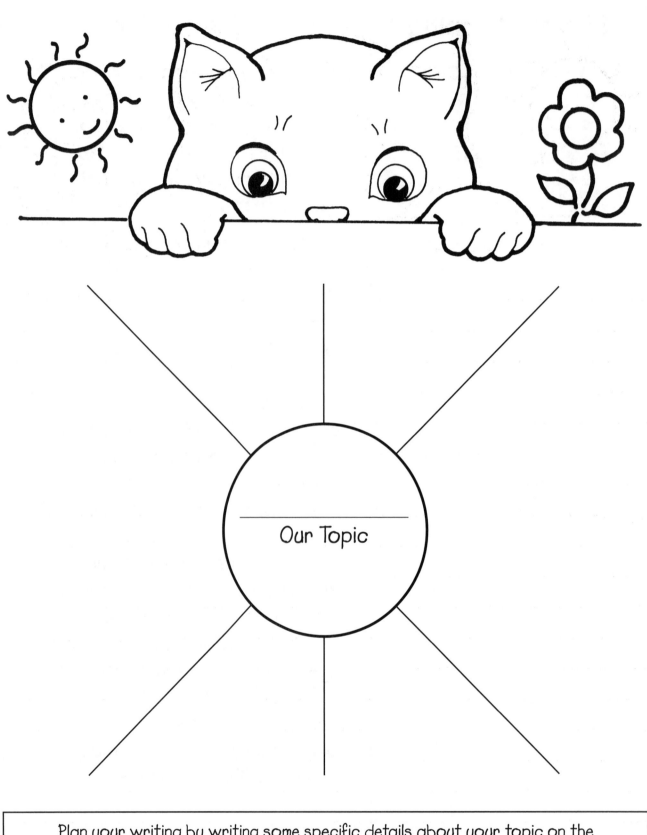

Our Topic

Plan your writing by writing some specific details about your topic on the lines above. Draw more if you need them.

Name(s): _____

_____
_____
_____
_____
_____
_____
_____
_____
_____
_____
_____
_____
_____
_____
_____
_____
_____
_____

Sample Student Planning

Name(s): Stephanie, Busty, Devante, Kellie

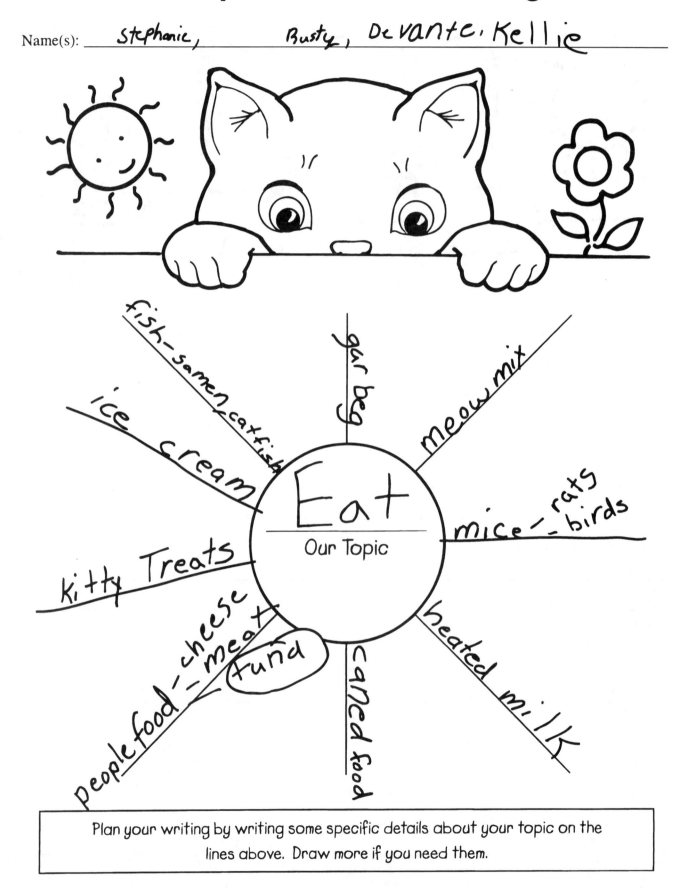

Plan your writing by writing some specific details about your topic on the lines above. Draw more if you need them.

Sample Student Writing

Name(s): _Stephanie,   Busty,   Devante, Kellie_

Cats love to eat all kinds of food!
One of the foods they like is catfish
and salmond. When my cat sees a dish
of that he likes his lipes. People feed
cats Moew mix and heated milk. They rely
like that! If you have a cat that likes
to hunt it mite eat mice or birds. Our
(nabers) cat gets in our garbagh can.
My dad saw him. He said "Scat get out
of there." He didn't get to eat any garbag,
that night. Meow, Meow. Meow, Meow,
Meow Meow.." Thats the sound of
my cat when he is (hungry)!

Some Place Special

Materials

Teacher Materials You Need to Supply:

- read-aloud selection: *If You're Not from the Prairie . . .* by David Bouchard
- overhead projector, transparency marker, pencils for each group of students
- index cards with topics about your state written on them (example: For Florida, these topics might apply: sand, sun, rain, orange juice, palm trees, flowers, ocean, clouds, breeze, tropical storms, bugs, gators, theme parks), cards with the five senses written on them
- (*Optional:* For day two, you will need an overhead transparency of book ending (page 176) and bookbinding materials. Also, each group of students will need a copy of the book ending.)
- overhead transparencies of stationery for planning and for writing (pages 173 and 174)

Teacher Materials Included in the Lesson:

- sample shared planning and writing (page 172)
- sample student planning and writing (pages 177 and 178)

Student Materials Included in the Lesson:

- For each group of three to four students, you will need to prepare packets containing copies of stationery for planning and for writing (pages 173 and 174) and the rubric for thinking about their writing (page 175) and stationery for the ending of the book (page 176).

Read Aloud

1. Before reading, ask the students to hold up their fingers to show the number of years they have lived in your state.

2. Elicit some facts they know about your state.

3. Before reading *If You're Not from the Prairie . . .* by David Bouchard, ask the students if they have ever visited a prairie. (Many will not have had this experience.) Tell them to listen to Mr. Bouchard's description of what a prairie looks like, feels like, smells like, and sounds like. Tell them that we can go there in our heads because of his strong sensory writing.

4. Read *If You're Not from the Prairie . . .* by David Bouchard.

Shared Writing

1. Hold up the five senses cards. Tell the students that we could experience what the prairie is like because of all the sensory detail in the book. Reread or elicit an example from the book for each of the sense cards.

2. Tell the students that we are going to describe our state just as Mr. Bouchard did. In fact, we will structure our piece just as he did. (This is called a book innovation.)

3. Display the overhead transparency of the planning stationery. Hold up the cards with the choices. Select one (e.g., sand). Write your topic in the center of the page; then elicit what your topic looks like, feels like, smells like, tastes like, and sounds like. Tell students that writers don't always use all their senses, but they try to use as many as they can so the reader can picture what they write.

4. Display the overhead transparency of the stationery for writing. Referring to your plan, together write your piece. Point out that you will begin with the same lines that are in the book except you will change the word *prairie* to your state's name and also insert your topic. *Note:* Depending on the fluency of your students' writing, consider focusing on sensory description only, rather than rhyming each line as in the text of the book.

Some Place Special *(cont.)*

Shared Writing *(cont.)*

5. Reread your piece to focus on the spelling and grammar issues from your students' last writing sample. Refer to your word wall to check the spelling and usage of those words that are difficult for students.

Guided Writing

1. Organize students into groups of three or four; then distribute their packets containing the stationery for planning, stationery for writing, and the rubric for thinking about their writing.

2. Direct students to select a topic from the prepared topic cards on your state.

3. Tell students to talk together about their topic and then generate some ideas. Remind them to follow the pattern of the book and to describe their topic using as many of the five senses as possible.

4. Direct students to write their piece using the stationery for writing.

5. Remind them to think about their writing by completing the rubric. Invite them to make any changes necessary in their writing.

Sharing Session

Collect the index cards with the topics written on them. Mix and then draw out one card. Direct that group to share. Continue drawing cards until all the groups have shared. (If making a book, collect student pieces and save for day two.)

Follow-up Activity—(day two teaching points: revising for sensory support; writing an ending to a class book)

Display the overhead transparency from shared writing and reread the piece. Revise the text to further build the sensory support. Encourage students to tell what they liked about the piece and what helped them get a picture. Elicit new ideas and again revise. Then, direct each group to choose a reader to read aloud their previously written piece. Give specific praise and invite comments. Ask, "What did you like best about the piece? What words did the student use that helped you get a picture of the topic? What would you like to know more about?" Encourage revisions to include new ideas brought out in the discussion during sharing. Then, tell students to listen again to the way the author ends the book. Open If You're Not from the Prairie by David Bouchard to page 22 and read to the ending on page 28. Discuss the way you felt at the conclusion of. How does the author create a picture of a prairie for the reader? Tell them that you need an ending to your book. Again, remind them that we can model our writing after the writing in the book. Display the overhead transparency with the frame for the book ending. Together, write your ending. Reassemble the groups of three to four students and direct them to write an ending to their book.

Sharing Session

Invite others—students, teachers, parents, administrators—to comprise an audience. Allow each group of students to perform their piece.

Shared Planning

Sand

Looks like:

  glistening in sun

  salt, grits, sugar

Feels like:

  cat's tongue, concrete,

  grinds in hands

Tastes like:

  (can't do)

Sounds like:

  what we say—makes our day

Smells like:

  sea creatures—catfish, mullet, crabs, sea horses

Shared Writing

If you're not from Florida,

You don't know the sand,

You can't know the sand.

Glistening grits toasted in the sun,

Making sandcastles is so much fun.

Experience the grind of the sand,

In the palm of your hand.

Then take a big whiff and smell

catfish, crab, mullet, and even the horses of the sea,

The memory is there for you and me.

We claim the beach, hear us say,

"Going to the beach makes our day!"

If you're not from Florida,

You don't know the sand.

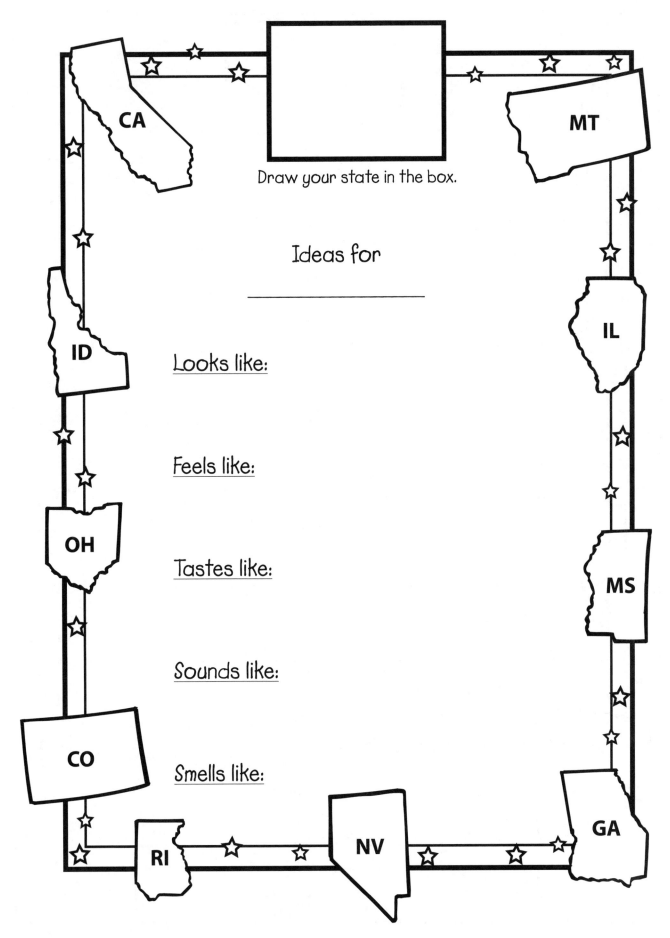

Draw your state in the box.

Ideas for

_____

Looks like:

Feels like:

Tastes like:

Sounds like:

Smells like:

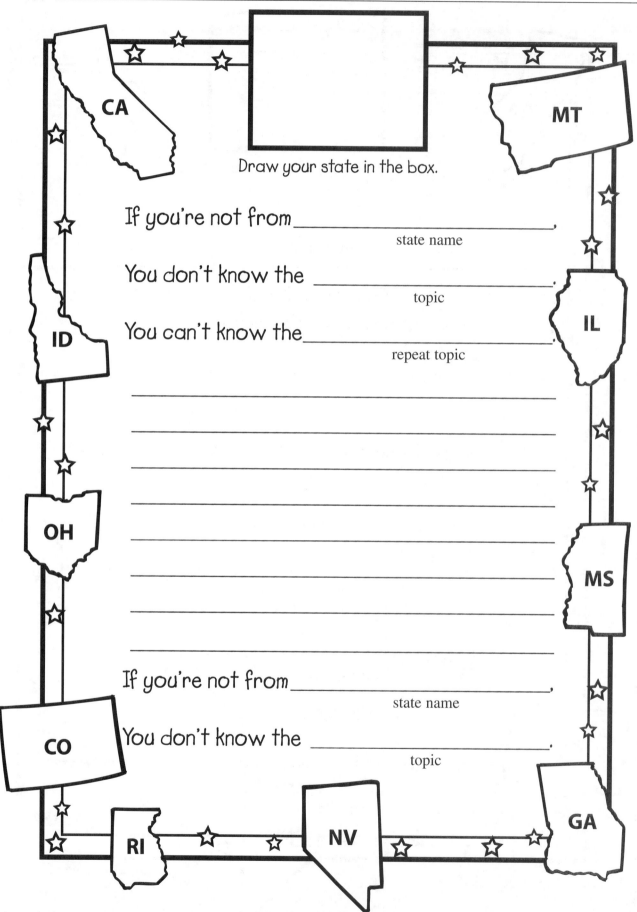

Draw your state in the box.

If you're not from _____,
                              state name

You don't know the _____.
                                    topic

You can't know the_____.
                              repeat topic

_____

_____

_____

_____

_____

_____

_____

_____

If you're not from_____,
                              state name

You don't know the _____.
                                    topic

Name(s): _____

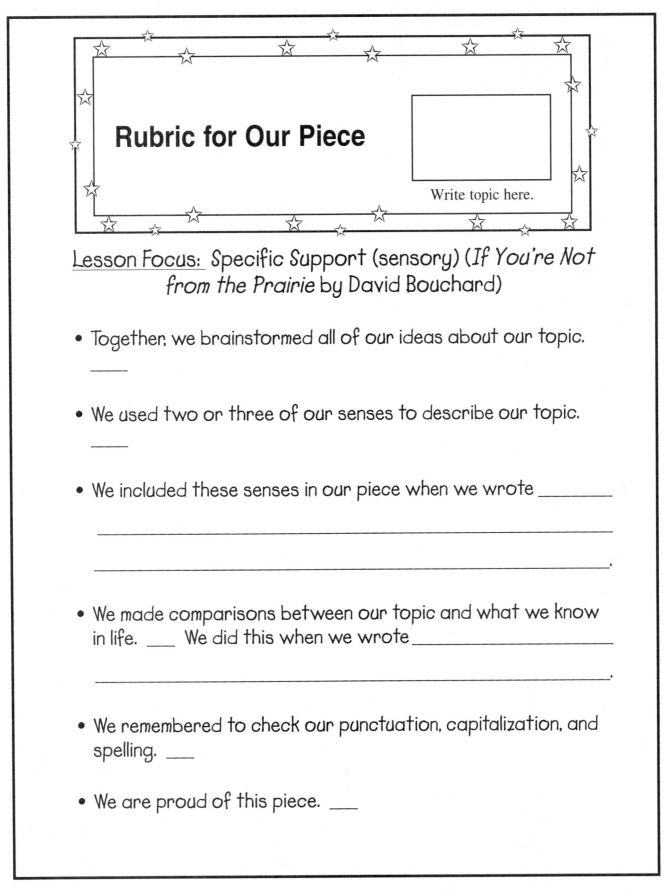

Rubric for Our Piece

Write topic here.

<u>Lesson Focus:</u> Specific Support (sensory) (*If You're Not from the Prairie* by David Bouchard)

- Together, we brainstormed all of our ideas about our topic.
  ____

- We used two or three of our senses to describe our topic.
  ____

- We included these senses in our piece when we wrote _____
  _____
  _____.

- We made comparisons between our topic and what we know in life. ___ We did this when we wrote_____
  _____.

- We remembered to check our punctuation, capitalization, and spelling. ___

- We are proud of this piece. ___

CA

MT

Draw your state in the box.

Ending for Our Book Stationery

If you're not from _____.

If you're not from _____,

You don't know us.

You just can't know us.

You see_____

Our hair _____

Our skin _____

Our lips_____

We've lain _____

_____

We've stared at the_____

_____

We've heard _____

We've tasted _____

We've touched _____

Our home is _____, and we _____

_____

ID

OH

CO

RI

NV

IL

MS

GA

Sample Student Planning

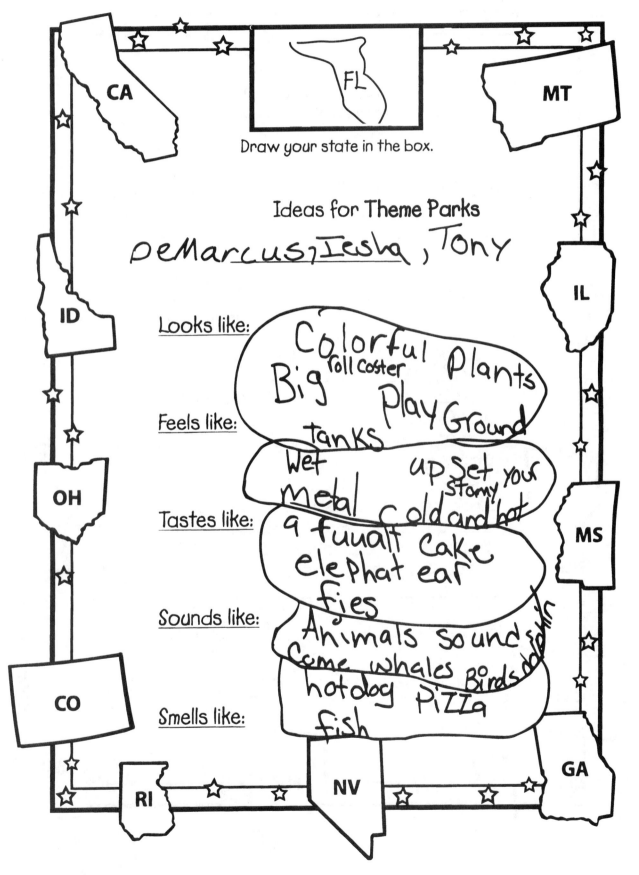

FL

Draw your state in the box.

Ideas for **Theme Parks**

DeMarcus, Iesha, Tony

Looks like:
Colorful Plants
Big roll coster Play Ground

Feels like:
tanks
Wet up set your
metal cold and hot stormy

Tastes like:
a funalt cake
elephat ear
fies

Sounds like:
Animals sound
Come whales Birds
hotdog Pizza

Smells like:
fish

CA   MT   ID   IL   OH   MS   CO   RI   NV   GA

Sample Student Writing

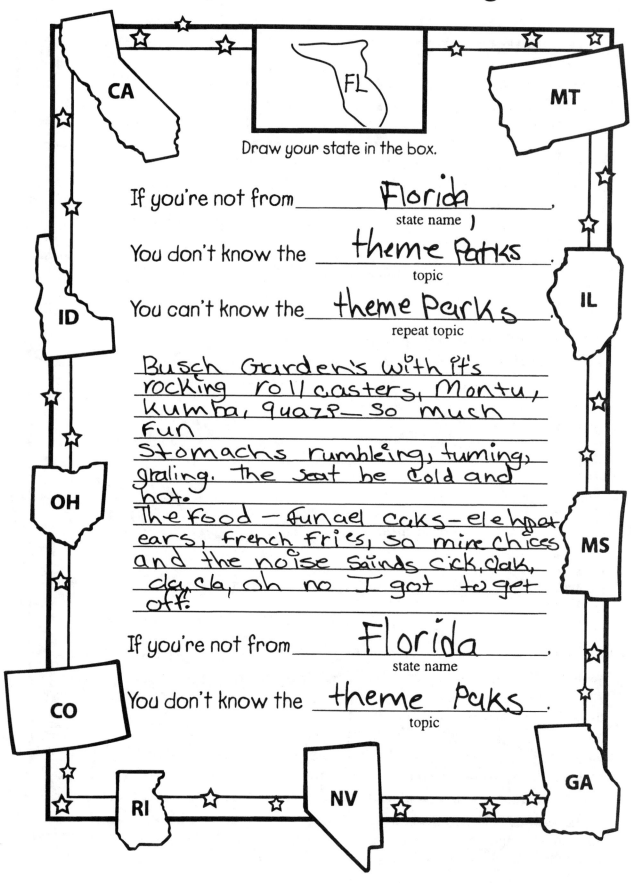

Draw your state in the box.

FL

If you're not from _____Florida_____,
　　　　　　　　　　　state name)

You don't know the ___theme Parks___.
　　　　　　　　　　　topic

You can't know the ___theme Parks___.
　　　　　　　　　　　repeat topic

Busch Garden's with it's
rocking roll casters, Montu,
kumba, quaze— so much
Fun
Stomachs rumbleing, tuming,
graling. the seat be cold and
hot.
The food — funael caks—elehpot
ears, french fries, so mine chices
and the noise sainds cick, clak,
cla, cla, oh no I got to get
off.

If you're not from _____Florida_____,
　　　　　　　　　　　state name

You don't know the ___theme Paks___.
　　　　　　　　　　　topic

Using What You've Got

Materials

Teacher Materials You Need to Supply:

- read-aloud selection: *Bud, Not Buddy* by Christopher Paul Curtis
- alternate read-aloud selections: *But No Candy* by Gloria Houston, page 2. Begin with: "If the weather was nice . . . ." End with: "To Lee, the taste of that chocolate bar was the best thing in the world." *Welcome to the River of Grass* by Jane Yolen.
- For the smells activity, you will need the following materials: seven paper lunch bags numbered 1–7, seven Ziploc plastic bags (smallest size), cotton balls, and seven items for students to smell—e.g., toothpaste, cinnamon, peanut butter, bubble gum, baby powder, shampoo, chocolate. (Suggestions: Use cotton balls to hold liquids inside the containers. Also, to make the activity go faster make two sets of the smell bags.)
- Before the lesson, prepare the smell bags. Put each item to be smelled into a different Ziploc bag or container. Hide each one inside a numbered paper lunch bag. (Remember to create an answer key by listing beside each number, the name of the item included inside each bag.) Hint: For best results, open the containers inside the lunch bags 10 to 15 minutes before the lesson begins. This allows the smell to penetrate the bag.
- overhead projector, overhead transparency markers, and pencils for each student
- Overhead transparencies of the planning stationery and writing stationery (pages 184 and 185) and the smells activity answer sheet (page 182). Using an overhead marker, write the items you place inside the bags.

Teacher Materials Included in the Lesson:

- sample modeled planning and modeled writing (page 183)
- sample student writing (pages 187–189)

Student Materials Included in the Lesson:

- For each student, you will need to prepare packets containing copies of the worksheet for recording smells (page 182), stationery for planning (page 184), stationery for writing (page 185), rubric for thinking about their writing (page 181), and the compliment list for partner sharing (page 186).

Read Aloud

1. Build background by asking students to close their eyes and picture their school lunchroom. Elicit the smells. Continue to elicit smells for other common places and things such as Mom's hair, Grandma's house, their room, the fish section in the grocery store, etc.
2. Tell students that skilled writers often slow down and support their writing by using their senses. Explain that including our senses helps the reader picture what the writing is about and also sharpens the focus for the writer.
3. Tell students to listen to the selection from *Bud, Not Buddy*, focusing on the smells in the library.
4. Read from pages 53–55. Begin with page 53: "The next thing about the air in the library . . ." and end with page 55: ". . . someone's dried up slobber." Elicit the sensory description Curtis used to take the reader to the library.

Using What You've Got *(cont.)*

Smells Activity

1. Introduce the smells activity by explaining that smells generate memories for us. Explain that we are going to do a smelling activity that will help us tap into those memories that each of us has in our lives. Distribute to each child the packet of materials containing the worksheet for recording smells, stationery for planning and for writing, and the rubric for thinking about their writing, and the compliment list.

2. Arrange students into groups of four or five; provide one bag containing an unidentified smell. Ask the students to pass the bag and to smell the item inside it. Then, direct them to record their guess beside the corresponding number on the worksheet. Give each person in the group an opportunity to smell the contents of the bag and record their guess on the worksheet. After a short time, signal students to rotate bags with another table until everyone has had an opportunity to smell each bag. When rotations are complete, display the overhead transparency of the answer key for them to check their guesses.

Modeled Writing

1. Remind students of the library selection found in *Bud, Not Buddy*. Tell them we are going to write like Christopher Paul Curtis by identifying a sense and lingering longer with it so that the reader can be with us wherever we are.

2. Model choosing one item we just smelled to write about. Explain why you chose it and not the others. Tell them about your personal memory that smell triggered. List your ideas on the planning transparency while you talk.

3. Using the overhead transparency of the stationery for writing, write your piece about that memory. Be sure to slow your writing down to capture the sensory description of that smell. Reread often. Revise when needed. Use the writing process to demonstrate what writers do as they make decisions in their writing.

Guided Independent Writing

1. Tell the students that they are also going to write like Christopher Paul Curtis. Direct each student to circle a smell on the worksheet that triggered a special memory for him or her.

2. Using the planning stationery, direct students to jot down ideas for their pieces. Remind them to focus their writing on the memory triggered by that smell.

3. Direct the students to write their pieces on the writing stationery, referring often to their plan.

4. Direct the students to think about their writing by completing the rubric. Encourage them to make any changes necessary.

Sharing Session

Have each student share his or her writing with a partner. Ask the listener to complete the compliment list by jotting down things that the writer did well in the piece. Direct students to exchange their compliment lists with a partner.

Using What You've Got *(cont.)*

Follow-up Activity

Revisit *Bud, Not Buddy* by Christopher Paul Curtis to teach other sensory elements. The following selections focus on these senses:

Sound

- Begin with page 80: "A Man Screamed . . . ." End with page 81: " . . . once we got on the train."
- Begin with page 98: "He stopped and put his fingers to his lips . . . ." End with page 99: "The noise-making critters in that patch of road got quiet."
- Begin with page 200: "I looked up . . . ." End with page 203: " . . . Wow!"

Sight

- Begin with page 113: "I took another drink of the red pop . . . ." End with page 114: " . . . it looks more like red stew."

Taste and Smell

- Begin with page 161: "I closed my eyes and took a big snort of air . . . ." End with page 162: " . . . cause the smell was starting to get me dizzy."

Sight and Feeling

- Begin with page 170: "I didn't see it before . . . ." End with page 171: " . . . that was jumping out of Miss Thomas's chest."

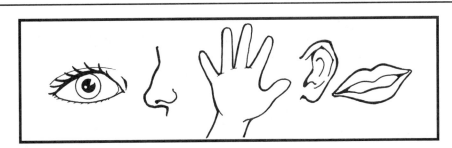

Rubric for My Piece

Lesson Focus: Specific Support—sensory (*Bud, Not Buddy* by Christopher Paul Curtis)

- I described using my sense(s) of _____.
- I chose my words carefully. ____
- Some examples are _____.
- I used comparison between_____ and _____ in my piece.
- I made clear the connection between the sense and my memory. ____
- I stayed with my idea long enough to develop it. ____
- This piece makes the reader FEEL something. ____
- I remembered to check my punctuation, capitalization, and spelling. ____
- I am proud of this piece. ____

Smells Activity Worksheet:

Smells! "What's in the bag?"

My Guess   Memory Evoked

1. _____   _____

2. _____   _____

3. _____   _____

4. _____   _____

5. _____   _____

6. _____   _____

7. _____   _____

Modeled Planning

Ideas for My Memoir

In my writing I will develop the sense of smell.

- focus on love of Papa
- worn-out Tennessee overalls
- me sitting on the bathtub—wiggling, talking, enjoying the attention
- shaving mug—chipped and yellowed
- smell—Slow down writing here!

Describe how the smell gets from the sink to the bathtub where I sit.

Brush—round and round

Mint molecules dance in the air.

Comparison to acrobats

Remember to use strong verbs—dance, fly, wiggle.

Modeled Writing:

Papa Shaves

The smell of menthol shaving lather jerks me back to a wonderful time in my past. My nose starts twitching, and my mouth starts grinning at the thoughts that are conjured up. Papa, dressed in his worn-out Tennessee overalls with his right foot on top of the toilet seat, swirls the brush around and around in his chipped, yellowed shaving mug. Bubbles froth up and stick to the brush. With each trip of the brush around the cup, little minty molecules dance out into the air. Like acrobats, they fly straight up inside my nostrils, teasing little shakes and wiggles out of me. On they sneak, slamming against the hallways of my nose to tickle the goose bumps right out of me. There's nothing like it. One little whiff, and I'm back there again—just my papa and me.

Name: _____

Ideas for My Memoir

In my writing I will develop the sense(s) of

_____

✓ _____

✓ _____

✓ _____

✓ _____

✓ _____

✓ _____

✓ _____

✓ _____

✓ _____

✓ _____

✓ _____

✓ _____

✓ _____

✓ _____

Name: _____

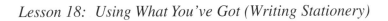

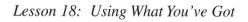

Compliment List

To: _____

From: _____

Great job! Yippee! Hurray! Bravo! Here are the parts I thought were well written.

I was there with you when you wrote _____

_____

_____

You did a wonderful job of using your sense(s) of _____

when you wrote _____

_____

I also noticed _____

_____

Thanks for sharing your writing with me!

Compliment List

To: _____

From: _____

Great job! Yippee! Hurray! Bravo! Here are the parts I thought were well written.

I was there with you when you wrote _____

_____

_____

You did a wonderful job of using your sense(s) of _____

when you wrote _____

_____

I also noticed _____

_____

Thanks for sharing your writing with me!

Sample Student Writing

Name: Bear

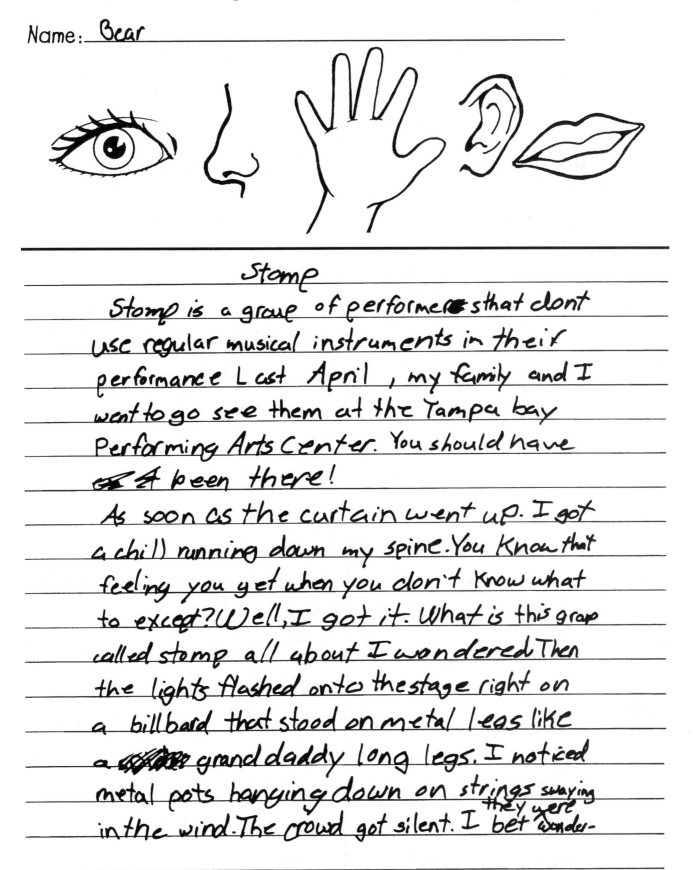

Stomp

Stomp is a group of performers that dont
use regular musical instruments in their
performance Last April , my family and I
went to go see them at the Tampa bay
Performing Arts Center. You should have
been there!

As soon as the curtain went up. I got
a chill running down my spine. You know that
feeling you get when you don't know what
to except? Well, I got it. What is this group
called stomp all about I wondered Then
the lights flashed onto the stage right on
a billbard that stood on metal legs like
a grand daddy long legs. I noticed
metal pots hanging down on strings swaying
in the wind. The crowd got silent. I bet they were wonder-

Sample Student Writing *(cont.)*

Name: Bear

"ing, what will happen next.

Then ~~the~~ about five performers shot out on bongie cords from the stage rafters. They started clanging on those hanging pots with long wooden spoons. I heard a "ting ting ting" when they hit on the edge and "wat wat, boom" when they when they beat on the center. Out from the seacret hatches on the stage floor, exploded more stomp members with brooms in their hands. They started beating on the floor. Along with the "ting, wat wat, boom" came a "whoosh shoosh thud, do, da dwn". The rythem of sound began bourcing off the walls. Do you think you can do that? I sure did. Bring on the squares, lids and trash cans! For the next two hours I sat there stamping my feet and shaking my head to the beat of the music.

Sample Student Writing *(cont.)*

Name: _Bear_

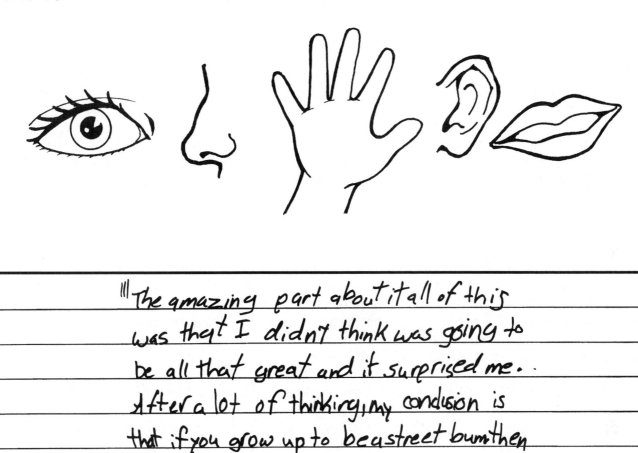

The amazing part about it all of this
was that I didn't think was going to
be all that great and it surprised me.
After a lot of thinking, my conclusion is
that if you grow up to be a street bum then
maybe you can make lots of money banging
on trash cans.

Emphasizing the Middle with Voice

Can you see my personality in my writing? Bet ya can, for I have VOICE!

Voice. What is it? We know it when we hear it. Books by our favorite authors have it. We continually strive to write with it, and we definitely want our children's pieces to have it. But understanding and defining voice is elusive because it comes in so many forms, yet all forms still can have voice. Some of the best writers are serious; some are funny; some are lyrical; some are playful, and some are full of the distinctive dialect of the writer. If you can identify that a particular person wrote it, it has voice.

I think of voice as the writer's DNA in print. Just as our DNA is unique, so are our voices. Written voice is made up of all the things in our lives that make us who we are. Our culture influences the way we combine words and also the way we punctuate them. Also, things that we value make our voices unique. Word choice and the particular way we turn a phrase help create our voices too. In addition, sentence structure and even punctuation play a big part in making our writing have the sound and the rhythm to depict who we are. See what I mean? Voice is complex, and it can be evident in any genre.

Are you guilty of taking your students' writing home and carefully selecting certain students' pieces to read first or if you prefer . . . last? I admit it, and I'm not ashamed either! Every time I assess my kids' writing, there are those kids that I search out. I burrow down through the pile to seek them out. I want to savor their pieces—those little nuggets that keep me going. Those kids in our classes become our oasis in the desert. We search their writing out because they sustain and bolster us as we struggle to free the voices within all of our students.

As teachers, we just want someone to tell us how to teach it. Here's what I do. Read to them—books that have strong voices, and when you get them, kids' pieces too. If shown, we can learn to write in other people's and objects' voices. I've found that it's easier for students who are just learning to find their own voice to write in a voice other than their own. I think the reason it's easier is because the essence of one's own self is not on the line. The object talks, not the kid. If the reader doesn't respond to the voice of the object, it's not personal. Also, teach students to consider their audience when they write. Boy, does audience influence the voice in our writing! And try to pin down the voices of some of the authors they read and then compare their voices to others. Write letters and write pieces where the opinions of your students are strong. When our emotions are involved, it's easier for our voices to emerge. And don't forget to model writing in your own voice. They need to see you struggle to get your writing to sound just the way you want it. To find their own voices, they need examples of others reverberating in their heads.

Voice. It makes all the difference. Kids can learn to write with their own voices if we set the stage. We guide them so that they can unleash the voices inside each of them that clamor to get out. It is what we do. We do it today. We do it tomorrow and soon . . . they do it all by themselves.

. . . defining voice is elusive. . . .

. . . think of voice as the writer's DNA in print.

. . . things we value make our voices unique.

Miss Nelson Said What?

Materials

Teacher Materials You Need to Supply:

- read-aloud selection: *Miss Nelson Is Missing* by Harry Allard and James Marshall
- overhead projector, transparency markers, dice (for sharing session), envelopes, and pencils for each of the five groups (*optional*: clothes for the teacher to dress as Viola Swamp)
- overhead transparency of the activity card for shared writing (page 194), overhead transparency of planning stationery (page 197), one to two transparencies of stationery for writing (page 198), and an overhead transparency of a sample envelope

Teacher Materials Included in the Lesson:

- activity card for shared writing, five voice activity cards (pages 199–201)
- sample shared planning (page 195)
- sample shared writing (page 196)
- sample student planning and writing (pages 202 and 203)

Student Materials Included in the Lesson:

- For each group of four to five students, (size can vary depending on the number of students in your class) you will need to prepare packets containing copies of stationery for planning and for writing (pages 197 and 198), the rubric for thinking about the writing (page 201), and one envelope for each group.

Read Aloud

1. (*Optional*) Set the stage for the lesson by rushing into the classroom dressed in the character of Viola Swamp. Walk around the classroom saying things such as, "Go to the chalkboard and write 50 times, 'I will listen and obey my teacher.'" To any who appear skeptical or amused, say, "You think this is funny? Just wait until homework time tonight."

2. Hold up *Miss Nelson Is Missing* by Harry Allard and James Marshall. Tell them that this book is about a teacher with a class of very naughty students.

3. Before reading, tell the students to pay attention to the character Viola Swamp.

4. Read *Miss Nelson Is Missing.*

Shared Writing

1. Explain that the author developed the character of Miss Swamp by showing how she looks, what she does, and what she thinks and says. When a character's personality emerges in a piece of writing, we say that the piece has *voice*.

Miss Nelson Said What? *(cont.)*

Shared Writing *(cont.)*

2. Tell the students that we are going to write a letter to Miss Swamp in the voice of Miss Nelson. In order to do this, we must consider our audience. Explain that if the audience changes, so does the voice of the writer. An example of this might be a letter written to an adult and another one to a child. Naturally, the voice of the two pieces would sound quite different because the audience changed.

3. Display the overhead transparency of the activity card for shared writing. Explain that the purpose of this letter is to explain to Miss Swamp (the substitute) details about this difficult class. Miss Nelson needs to tell Miss Swamp about the troublemakers and what she has tried to do in order to establish an orderly classroom where students can learn.

4. Explain that this letter will be teacher to teacher. Remind students of the times they have overheard teachers talking, and the times they've actually played "school." Explain that when we write, we need to sound like a teacher. If we do this, our writing will have a very important quality called "voice."

5. Display the overhead transparency for planning. Elicit the naughty things from the book and list them. (Examples from the book: *Spitballs stuck to the ceiling. Paper planes whizzed through the air. Children whispered and giggled while Miss Swamp taught. They squirmed and made faces. They were rude during story time. They refused to do their work.*) Also include some naughty things from your students but assign fictitious names to the deeds.

6. Using the stationery for writing, compose a letter to Miss Swamp, telling about her class. Model referring back to the plan for your ideas. Reread and then write, focusing on getting the voice just right.

7. Model using high frequency words from your class word wall. Model correcting those punctuation and grammar weaknesses found in your students' writing.

8. Display the overhead transparency of the envelope. Model making up an address for Miss Swamp. Add your school's information in the return address. Point out the location of the stamp in the top right-hand corner.

Guided Writing

1. Group students into five groups and assign a number (1–5) to each group. Allow each group to select a card. Then distribute the packets for writing to each group. (Students have the same situation, but their audience changes. They will write in the voice of Miss Swamp to one the following people: (1) *her previous fourth grade teacher*, (2) *her best friend*, (3) *one of her school board members*, (4) *her brother or sister*, or (5) *her principal*.

Miss Nelson Said What? *(cont.)*

Guided Writing *(cont.)*

2. Read one of the activity cards to the class and explain that everyone has the same situation; for each group, however, the person they are writing to will be different. That means the voice will change to match the audience, the person they are writing to.

3. Remind students that since they are writing a letter, they should address their letter to the person to whom they are writing.

4. Using the stationery for planning, direct students to plan their piece. Remind them to continually ask, "How would Miss Nelson say this?"

5. Using the stationery for writing, direct students to write their letter and then to address their envelope. Tell them to draw a stamp in the upper right-hand corner.

6. As students finish their letter and envelope, direct each group to think about their writing by completing the rubric. Remind them to make any necessary changes in their letter.

Sharing Session

Before sharing, tell the students when they read their letters, the class will try to guess their audience. So that they don't accidentally read the person's name, direct them to fold down the Dear line on the top of their paper. Roll the die to determine the order for each group to share their piece. If the die lands on #6, they get to choose. Allow each group to read their letter. To increase their fun, tell them that when they read their letter they should make their voice sound like Miss Swamp's.

Follow-up Activity (teaching point: revising for voice)

The day following this lesson, teach a revision lesson focusing on voice in a piece previously written. During modeled or shared writing, demonstrate how you can make changes in the piece so that it will reflect the writer's personality. Your read-aloud selection for this lesson extension could be one or several of the group letters from this lesson. (Consider dressing up as the character you are writing about. It makes writing fun for the kids and frees up the voices inside them!)

Shared Writing Activity Card

The class had been horrid all day. They've called out, hit you and other students with paper balls, and disobeyed you all day long. At one point, fighting even erupted in your classroom! You, Miss Nelson, the teacher, need a vacation from this class, so you decide to write a letter. <u>Your audience is the substitute teacher, Miss Viola Swamp.</u> Your letter details what she can expect when she takes over your class. <u>Your purpose is to paint a picture of this difficult class.</u> Choose words and phrases that sound like Miss Nelson.

Write a letter to <u>Miss Viola Swamp, your substitute teacher.</u>

Shared Planning

Ideas for Our Piece

- lock up purse

- jacket up the flagpole

- kids treating glitter like confetti

- glue and tacks in chairs

- spitballs

- paper airplanes

- gummy bears stuck everywhere

- clumps of towels on the ceiling

- kids' good arms—ducking/dodging

- snake in the teacher's desk

Shared Writing

Allard Elementary Room 207,
1567 Marshall Drive
Tampa, FL 33629
March 12, 2003

Good luck! You're going to need it with this class. Make sure you lock up your purse and anything else that is not nailed down. I'm warning you right now—it'll be gone if you don't. I hope you're good at ducking and dodging because these little suckers all have good right arms. And another thing to watch out for is your chair. I recommend standing all day, but if you must sit, do a hand-swipe of the chair bottom before you sit down, for these kids all have pockets filled with tacks! I've laid out the pens and pencils because opening my desk drawer could be hazardous to your health. FYI Johnny's dad owns Pete's Snake Shack. Leave your jacket in the teacher's lounge. If you don't, it might be sent up the flag pole out in front of the school. Also, ignore all those clumps of paper towels on the ceiling. They'll only fall if there's an earthquake.

I'm sorry to do this to you, but I need a day off. After today, you'll understand why.

My prayers are with you,
Miss Nelson

P.S. Hide the glitter and glue!

Name(s): _____

Ideas for Our Piece

_____

_____

_____

_____

_____

_____

_____

_____

_____

_____

_____

_____

_____

_____

Dear _____,

Voice Activity Card One

The class had been horrid all day. They've called out, hit you and other students with paper balls, and disobeyed you all day long. At one point, fighting even erupted in your classroom! You, Miss Nelson, the teacher, need a vacation from this class so you decide to write a letter. <u>Your audience is your previous 4th grade teacher.</u> Your letter details the problems you are having with your class. <u>Your purpose is to paint a picture of this difficult class.</u> Your purpose is to get advice on how to handle this difficult class.

<u>Write a letter to your previous 4th grade teacher.</u>

Voice Activity Card Two

The class had been horrid all day. They've called out, hit you and other students with paper balls, and disobeyed you all day long. At one point, fighting even erupted in your classroom! You, Miss Nelson, the teacher, need a vacation from this class so you decide to write a letter. <u>Your audience is your best friend.</u> Your letter finds the humor in all the things your students do in your class. <u>Your purpose is to entertain her with the events from your day.</u>

Choose words and phrases that sound like Miss Nelson.

<u>Write a letter to your best friend.</u>

Voice Activity Card Three

The class had been horrid all day. They've called out, hit you and other students with paper balls, and disobeyed you all day long. At one point, fighting even erupted in your classroom! You, Miss Nelson, the teacher, need a vacation from this class so you decide to write a letter. <u>Your audience is the chairman of your school board of education.</u> Your letter details the experiences you have had with unruly children while teaching in their district. <u>Your purpose is to get the board to make policy changes regarding school discipline.</u> Choose words and phrases that sound like Miss Nelson.

<u>Write a letter to the Chairman of your school board of education.</u>

Voice Activity Card Four

The class had been horrid all day. They've called out, hit you and other students with paper balls, and disobeyed you all day long. At one point, fighting even erupted in your classroom! You, Miss Nelson, the teacher, need a vacation from this class so you decide to write a letter. <u>Your audience is your brother or sister.</u> Your letter details all the naughty things your students do. <u>Your purpose is to get sympathy for your rough day trying to earn enough money to put bread on the table.</u> Choose words and phrases that sound like Miss Nelson.

<u>Write a letter to your brother or sister.</u>

Voice Activity Card Five

The class had been horrid all day. They've called out, hit you and other students with paper balls, and disobeyed you all day long. At one point, fighting even erupted in your classroom! You, Miss Nelson, the teacher, need a vacation from this class so you decide to write a letter. <u>Your audience is the principal.</u> Your letter details the total disrespect of some students in your classroom. <u>Your purpose is to inform him/her of your experiences while in his/her school and to secure office support for discipline problems.</u> Choose words and phrases that sound like Miss Nelson.

<u>Write a letter to the principal.</u>

Name(s): _____

Rubric for Our Piece

Lesson Focus: Voice (*Miss Nelson Is Missing* by Harry Allard and James Marshall)

- Our audience is_____, and we have written for the purpose of _____.

- When the reader reads what we wrote, Miss Nelson's personality shines through. ___

- We chose words and phrases that sound like Miss Nelson. ___ We said_____

  _____

  _____.

- We used our experiences listening to teachers talk to help us with the voice for this piece. ___

- This piece makes the reader feel something and get a sense of who Miss Nelson is. ___

- Voice makes our writing_____.

- We remembered to check our punctuation, capitalization, and spelling. ___

- We are proud of this piece. ___

Sample Student Planning

Ideas for Our Piece

- roon 207
- Graham
- Pound Math – x $\frac{243\cancel{7}}{\cancel{684}8}$
- Kick out of Control – Airplanes – spit balls –
- Johney and Frank Fight – Paper swords
- Noise Level ∧ful blast (Radio)
- Teacher shouting top of her lungs

Sample Student Writing

2915 Mass. Ave.
Tampa, FL 33602
25 April 2002

Dear ___Mrs. Taylor___,

    I don't know what you were thinking when you hired that substitute teacher. First of all she gave us a pound of math homwork. The easiest problem was 2437×8848. I don't feel like writing the hardest one. The were compleTly out of control. Airplanes are flying to the left and spit balls flying to the right. I had to get under my desk to avoid getting hit. Then there was the noise problem. It sounded like a boom box tuned in on 98.0 - The heavy metal rock station. Next came the paper sword fight between Johney and Frank. Those swords here moving so fast I didn't see there hands. If you had walked down our hallway, you could have heard her shouting from top of her lungs. So take some advice for a kid Fire Herrrrr!!!

                Love,
                Frederick.

All in the Name

Materials

Teacher Materials You Need to Supply:

- read-aloud selection: *The House on Mango Street* by Sandra Cisneros (Alternate selection: *Williwaw!* by Tom Bodett, pages 28–29. Begin with: "Brilliant and unpredictable . . . ." End with: "To me: she'd say, gathering them up close in her arms.")
- overhead projector, overhead transparency markers, pencils and crayons for each student (*optional*: refrigerator letter magnets for sharing session)
- overhead transparencies of stationery for planning and for writing (pages 209 and 210)

Teacher Materials Included in the Lesson:

- letter to parents (page 206), stationery for planning (page 209), and stationery for writing (page 210)
- sample modeled planning (page 207) and sample modeled writing (page 208)
- sample student planning and writing (pages 211–213)

Student Materials Included in the Lesson:

- For each student, you will need to prepare packets containing copies of the planning stationery (page 209), stationery for writing (page 210), and the rubric for thinking about their writing (page 205).

(One or two days prior to this lesson, send home a copy of the letter to the parents (page 206), asking them to participate in an interview with their child about the child's name.)

Read Aloud

1. Build background by eliciting information about your students' names. Find out who they were named after and what they wish they had been named. Tell them that when writers feel strongly about a topic, it is easier to write with voice.

2. Before reading pages 11–13 from *The House on Mango Street* by Sandra Cisneros, tell the students to listen carefully to Ms. Cisneros's ideas and the way she says them. She writes with a distinctive voice. Tell them we want to discover how she does it. Tell them to listen to her ideas, her word choice, and her arrangement of words and sentences.

Modeled Writing

1. Tell the students that you are going to write about your name, focusing on voice—writing so that it sounds like you.

2. Display the overhead transparency for planning (page 209). Jot down your ideas on both sides of the line as you talk.

3. Plan your piece, paying special attention to your word choice and the phrasing of your ideas. Tell students that in the vignette "My Name" you noticed that Ms. Cisneros used a dash to slow down her writing and to give a little bit more information about her idea. Also, point out that she boldly wrote what she thought, stating her opinions freely and confidently. Note, too, that she gave us information about who she was named for and what she thought about that. Tell them that readers want to know what writers think, and they want us to say it in our own words so that it sounds like us speaking our thoughts from the page. Readers want to see our personality; and when they can, we have voice.

All in the Name *(cont.)*

Modeled Writing *(cont.)*

4. Display the overhead stationery for writing (page 210). Referring back to the plan, continue to voice aloud your ideas as you translate them into sentences. Model using the dash to slow down or to alert the reader that you are adding to an idea. Be selective of your word choice. Reread and change your words until it sounds as if you were talking from the page. Include some information on how you got your name and be sure to state your opinion about your name choice.

5. Model pulling words from your class word wall and remember to stress conventions that are weaknesses in your students' writing.

Guided Writing

1. To each student, distribute the prepared packets for writing. Direct them to take out the interview completed with their family. Remind them to include some of the information obtained from interviewing their family members as they plan their piece. Encourage them to write down some words that sound just like their personality. Tell them you can't wait to read what they think about their name. Challenge them to use the dash to slow down their writing or to stress a point.

Sharing Session

Using the refrigerator letter magnets, randomly draw one letter at a time and allow those students whose name begins with that letter to share their piece. Invite the students to tell the writer what parts sound most like the self.

Rubric for My Piece

Name: _____

(Write your first name on the line above)

Lesson Focus: Voice (*The House on Mango Street* by Sandra Cisneros)

- I prepared to write by remembering what my parents have told me about how they chose my name. ___
- I reread the information from my interview with my family. One interesting thing I learned was _____.
- I planned my piece by listing my ideas along the name line. ___
- I chose words that sound like me. ___ One of those words or phrases was_____ _____.
- I included what I thought about my name. ___
- The place where my voice sounds best is when I wrote _____.
- I remembered to check my punctuation, capitalization, and spelling. ___
- I am proud of this piece. ___
- I learned _____.

Dear Parents,

Part of each child's writing homework tonight is to interview members of the family about his or her name. We are interested in learning a bit of the history about how students got their names so that they can write about it. Children are always interested in hearing stories about how they got named and the day of their birth. Please allow your child to ask you some questions about his or her name.

Thanks for your support in helping your child learn to write.

Questions for Your Family

1. Who named me? _____

2. Why did they choose that name for me? _____

   _____

3. Am I named for a relative? If yes, who? _____

4. Am I named for a famous person or place? _____ If yes, who or where?

   _____

   _____

5. What did Mom want to name me? _____

6. What did Dad want to name me? _____

7. If I had been born the opposite sex, what would have been my
   name? _____

8. If my brother/sister could have named me, what would be my
   name? _____

9. What does my name mean? _____

Questions for You, the Writer

1. What do you like about your name? _____

2. What do you not like about your name? _____

3. Do you have a nickname? ____ If yes, what is it? _____

   _____

4. If you could choose another name, what would you choose? _____

   Why? _____

Modeled Planning

All about My Name
RuthAnn
Name Line of Ideas

Beginning	Middle
first gift	parents worry
saddled with the name	double name
	sister–Tina
Mom–beautiful	
	angry–red face, bite my tongue
Travis–Bible–his shenanigans	
	Ending
Makaila–three syllables like molasses	ONE good name

Modeled Writing

RuthAnn

Your name is your parents' first gift to you. Some parents worry about naming their new baby for months and months before it's born and even buy books on names. It's a good thing that parents worry, for their poor little baby will be saddled with that name for the rest of his or her life. Take me for example. My name is RuthAnn. Not plain Ruth or just Ann, but RuthAnn—all together. They decided to name me Ann after both of my grandmas. Now that makes sense to me. Ann is a nice sturdy name—an old name that's been around for years, so it can't be all that bad if people are still naming their babies that name. When I asked my mother where they got that awful Ruth part of my name, my mom said, "I just thought Ruth was a beautiful name." I wished she had thought more about that. I think she rushed it. I don't think they even thought about what I'd have to put up with. When I meet new people the first thing they say is, "Oh! You're from the South. People from the South are so partial to double names." Every time I hear this comment, I get so irritated. My face gets red. I have to force-plaster a fake smile on my face, and I have to BITE my tongue. I think my parents should have thought longer about all the possibilities before naming me that hateful old double name. Even my own sister wanted to name me another name. Tina. She said that she thought that would look good on a cheerleader sweatshirt. But, they just ignored her. Travis, my older brother, said that they probably named me a Bible name so I could grow up and be godly. I say, "Mind your own business—you who are always up to some shenanigan or another." Now, if I could choose, I would name myself Makaila. Say it. Makaila. Now that's what I call a name! Three syllables that roll off your tongue like molasses. And best of all, it is one name. Doesn't each person deserve ONE good name?

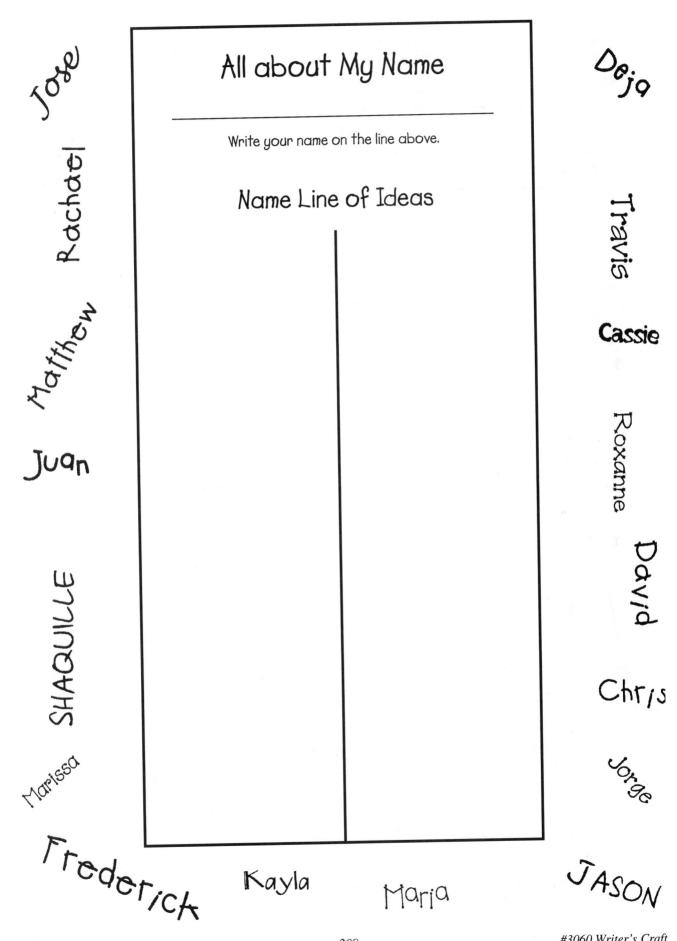

All about My Name

_____

Write your name on the line above.

Name Line of Ideas

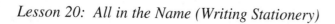

Write your name on the line above.

Sample Student Planning

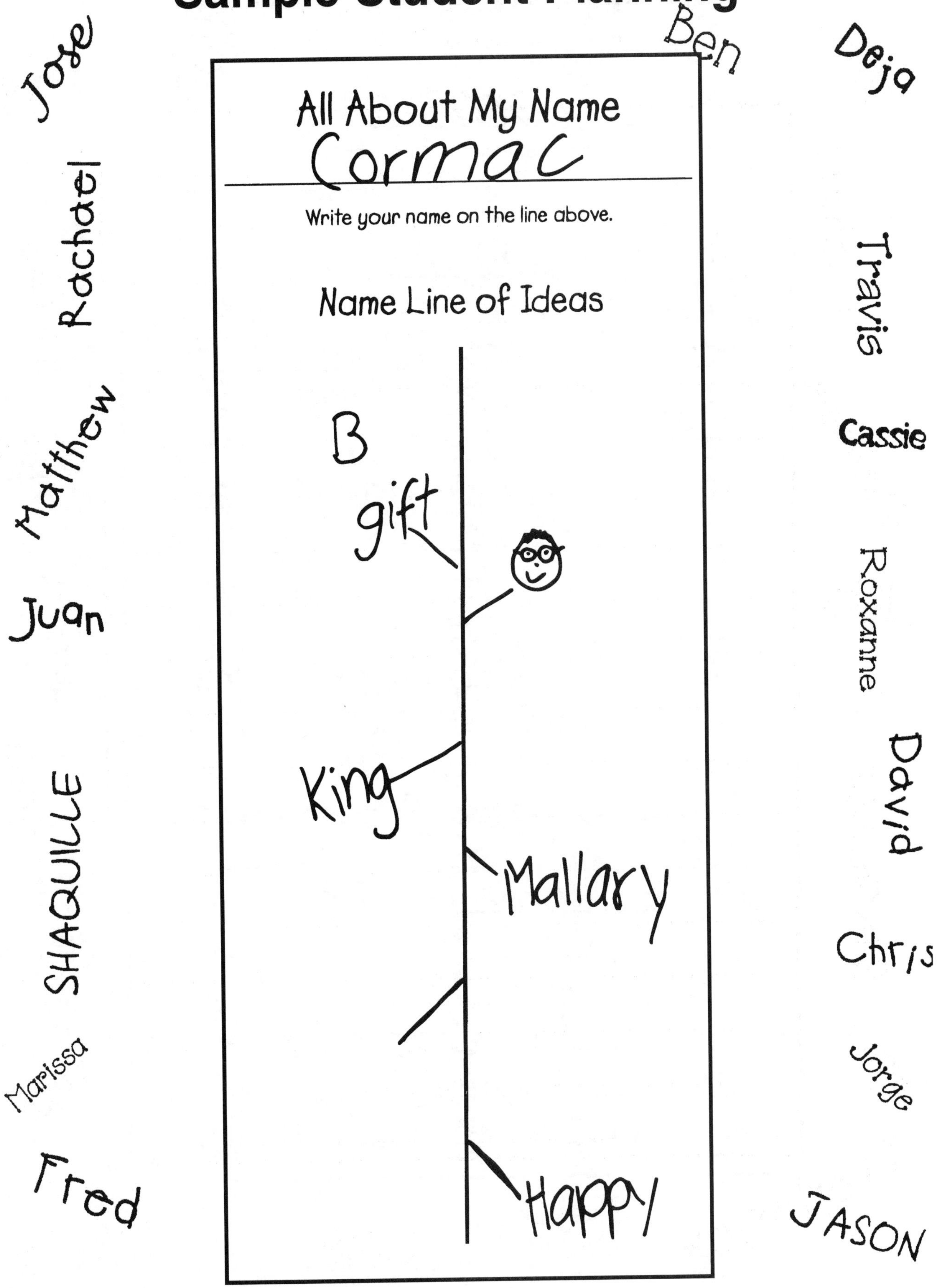

Jose

Ben

Deja

Rachael

Travis

Matthew

Cassie

Juan

Roxanne

David

SHAQUILLE

Chris

Marissa

Jorge

Fred

JASON

All About My Name
Cormac

Write your name on the line above.

Name Line of Ideas

B

gift

King

Mallary

Happy

Sample Student Writing

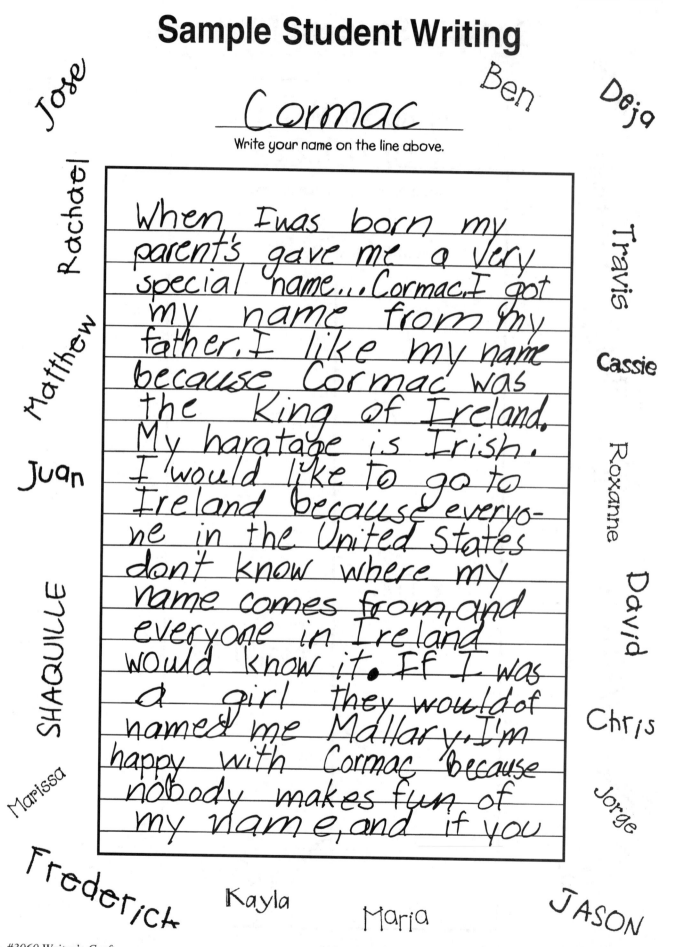

Cormac

Write your name on the line above.

When I was born my parent's gave me a very special name...Cormac. I got my name from my father. I like my name because Cormac was the King of Ireland. My haratage is Irish. I would like to go to Ireland because everyone in the United States don't know where my name comes from, and everyone in Ireland would know it. If I was a girl they would of named me Mallary. I'm happy with Cormac because nobody makes fun of my name, and if you

Sample Student Writing *(cont.)*

Jose   Ben   Deja

Cormac

Write your name on the line above.

Rachael

Travis

Matthew

Cassie

Juan

Roxanne

SHAQUILLE

David

Marissa

Chris

Jorge

Frederick   Kayla   Maria   JASON

You think about it kings are wise and strong people and I think I'm wise and strong. I got my middle name from my great grandpa that served in a war. He must of been brave. So I get my courage from him. Strong names make people strong and beleve in them selves.

Characters Come Alive

(*two- to three-day lesson if it includes revision*)

Materials

Teacher Materials You Need to Supply:
- read-aloud selection: *Missing May* by Cynthia Rylant
- overhead projector, overhead transparency markers, pencils for each group of students, unusual pictures from magazines or calendars (You will need enough pictures for each group of two to three students to have four or five choices. Ideas for unusual pictures are cake on a woman's head, lotion—alligator standing over a woman, cookie—leprechaun tied to a tree, etc.)
- overhead transparency of stationery for planning (page 218), overhead transparency of stationery for writing (page 219), and a picture for modeled writing. (If possible, make an overhead transparency of the picture.)

Teacher Materials Included in the Lesson:
- stationery for planning and for writing (pages 218 and 219), a picture for modeled writing (If possible, make an overhead transparency of it.)
- sample modeled planning and modeled writing (pages 216 and 217)
- sample student writing (page 221)

Student Materials Included in the Lesson:
- For each group of two to three students, you will need to prepare packets containing copies of stationery for planning (page 218), stationery for writing (page 219), and the rubric for thinking about their writing (page 220).

Read Aloud

1. Build background, by asking the students if they have ever seen a billboard or flipped through a magazine and seen pictures that started them thinking or caught their attention. Explain that ads are purposefully designed that way. They grab our attention if they are effective. Hold up one or two of the magazine pictures. Model making up a brief story about two or three of the pictures. Assume the voice of the object or person as you talk.

2. Before reading, explain that while reading *Missing May*, you got an idea for a writing lesson. Tell them to listen to how Cletus, one of the main characters in the book, collects magazine pictures and then makes up stories about them. The pictures come to life because of voice. He makes them tell their stories using his imagination.

3. Before reading, tell students to pay special attention to the story Cletus makes up about a picture in his magazine collection. Remind students that one way authors build characters in their stories is by writing what the characters say and do and think. When authors do this, they think about the personality of the character and what that character thinks and says. Read from pages 17–21 in *Missing May* by Cynthia Rylant. Begin reading with: "If Cletus gets wind . . . ." End reading with, "But all the rest, I figure is right on the money."

Characters Come Alive *(cont.)*

Modeled Writing

1. Tell students that, like Cletus, you also collected some pictures from magazines. Model choosing a picture from two or three pictures. Tell students your ideas for each of them and then choose one to use with your model. Explain why you chose it.

2. Display the picture. Using the transparency for planning stationery, jot down your ideas. Focus on writing in the voice of the object in the picture. Tell the students what you think the object is thinking and describe what intrigues you about the object.

3. Using the overhead transparency stationery for writing, write your piece. Use your imagination about the object to write in the voice of the object. In fact, upon completion, ask your students if what you wrote sounds like the personality of the object. Remind them that writers call this "voice." (*Note:* When gaining fluency, it may sometimes be easier for young writers to write in the voice of a character or an object other than their own. They are still discovering their voice and may lack self-confidence in using it. Writing in other person's voices helps students to gain that confidence and fluency.)

4. Remember to model using your class word wall to help with the spelling of high frequency words. (Save your modeled writing if planning to teach the follow-up revision lesson.)

Guided Writing

1. Distribute four or five pictures to each group of two to three students. Tell them to choose a picture that triggers their imagination.

2. Distribute to each group the previously prepared packets containing stationery for planning, stationery for writing, and the rubric for thinking about their writing. Then direct the students to record their ideas on the planning sheet. Remind them to think about the object and use their imagination to make that object tell his/her story.

3. Using the stationery for writing, direct students to write their pieces.

4. Remind students to answer the questions on their rubric. Invite them to make any changes necessary to show the personality of the object in the picture.

Sharing Session

Group the students for sharing by labeling designated areas by picture categories. For example, group all those students who wrote about animals in one area. Other categories might include food, people, toys, places, etc. Direct each group to share their piece with another group. Collect the writing if you plan to teach the follow-up revision lesson.

Follow-up Activity (teaching point: revising for stronger voice)

During the following day's writer's workshop, read aloud a few of the pieces your students wrote. Choose pieces that have strong voice. Using your shared writing or a previous piece, model how to revise it to make the voice stronger. Ask the students, "Does this sound as if the object would say this?" (Use a different-colored overhead transparency marker for your revisions.) For guided writing, direct them to revise their piece from yesterday or select a previously written piece from their writing folder. Have them read the piece to their partners. Tell them to assess it for voice. Tell them to decide where and what the piece needs so that it sounds more like the writer's personality. *Note:* Depending on the fluency of the class, this revision lesson might be extended for two days—one to talk and record ideas, another day to actually revise. Share the revised pieces.

This writing sounds like my voice!

This writing sounds like my voice!

This writing sounds like my voice!

Modeled Planning

<u>Whose Voice?</u>—Dalmatian puppy tells the story (personification).

<u>Focus:</u> Buy me and take me home.

<u>What and Where:</u> Locked in a cage at Pet's Mart—for sale.

<u>Specific Details about the Puppy to Convince the Reader to Buy Him:</u>

- black ear—Uncle Rex – Milk Bone record
- right leg—two spots – sign of good breeding – royal line in England
- chin—spot from mama's side – Grandma Tippy – intelligence

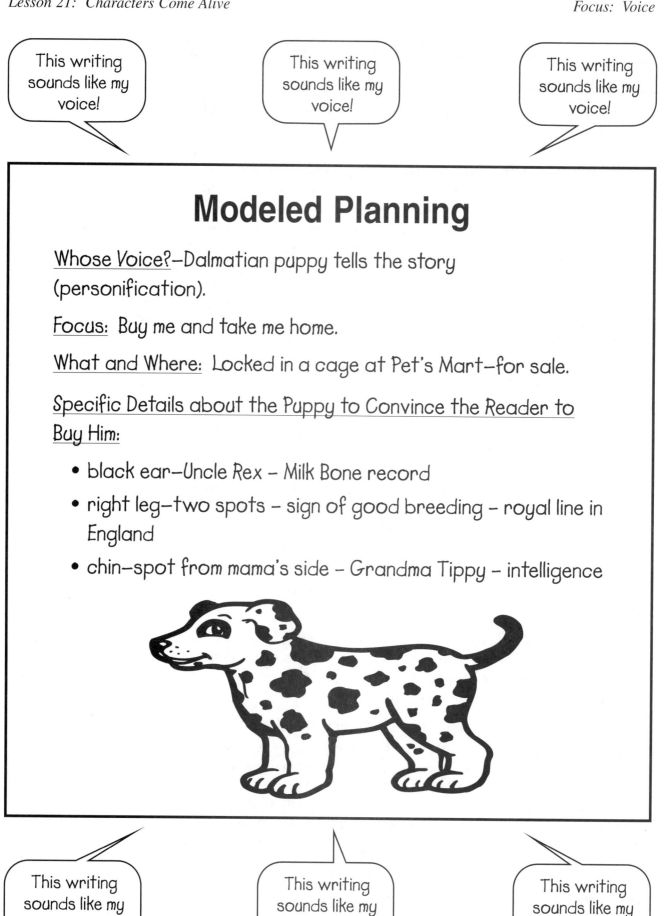

This writing sounds like my voice!

This writing sounds like my voice!

This writing sounds like my voice!

Modeled Writing

Just look at me! My mommy says I'm just too cute! I got my right black ear from Uncle Rex. He holds the world's record for eating Milk Bones. He once ate 87 and didn't even burp! If you look closely at my right leg, you will see three spots clustered together. My pop says those spots are a sign of good breeding. All my ancestors from the royal line in England have them. Of course, you've noticed the big spot nestled underneath my distinguished chin. I inherited that from my mama's side of the family. Her relatives have several black spots chunked like mine. Grandma Tippy says that's a mark of extreme intelligence and that I should walk tall and be proud because of it. As you can plainly see, I'm a dog to die for! I don't look like those other Dalmatian puppies—I'm unique. I'm tired of being locked in Pet's Mart. With all these qualities, how could you leave me here? I need a home and you've got one! Buy me! P-L-E-A-S-E!

This writing sounds like my voice!

This writing sounds like my voice!

This writing sounds like my voice!

Name(s): _____

Ideas for Our Writing

Whose Voice? _____

Focus: _____

What and Where: _____

Specific Details about the Object to Show the Object's Personality:

- _____
- _____
- _____
- _____
- _____
- _____
- _____
- _____

This writing sounds like my voice!

This writing sounds like my voice!

This writing sounds like my voice!

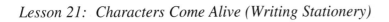

This writing sounds like my voice!

This writing sounds like my voice!

This writing sounds like my voice!

Name(s): _____

_____

_____

_____

_____

_____

_____

_____

_____

_____

_____

_____

_____

_____

_____

_____

_____

_____

_____

_____

_____

This writing sounds like my voice!

This writing sounds like my voice!

This writing sounds like my voice!

Name(s): _____

Rubric for Our Piece

> This writing sounds like our voice!

Lesson Focus: Voice (*Missing May* by Cynthia Rylant)

- We selected a picture that we could make a connection with. ___

- We chose words that sound like the object in our picture would use. ___

- We did this when we wrote_____
_____.

- The reader will get a sense of the object and what intrigues us. ___

- We used specific description when we wrote in the object's voice. _____ We described _____ when we wrote _____.

- We remembered to check our punctuation, capitalization, and spelling. ___

- We are proud of this piece. ___

Sample Student Writing

This writing sounds like my voice!

This writing sounds like my voice!

This writing sounds like my voice!

Name: Bear

"Oh yah! look at these muscles! 1! 2! 3! I work out every day. And I can lift anything! I can pump ~~have~~ twice my body wait." "I ~~growled~~ wich is about 250 lbs." I growled

I'm a panda bear. I eat bamboo, and I'm bad to the bone. I can lift anything from my wife to all my five kids I'm always on the move to show off my HUGE muscles. I enjoy bamboo, sushi and Hawianpunch.

I'm the best bowler in my league. And I hold the world's record for most pins by a panda bear. What's you highest score? I'm pretty sure it's less than mine, for I am the man-the Bear Man

Panda Bear
alias
Barrett (Bear) McCoy Townsend
↑
this is my real name

This writing sounds like my voice!

This writing sounds like my voice!

This writing sounds like my voice!

Pledging with Our Voices

Materials

Teacher Materials You Need to Supply:

- read-aloud selection: *I Pledge Allegiance* by Bill Martin Jr. and Michael Sampson (alternate read-aloud selection: *America Is . . . .* by Louise Borden)
- overhead projector, overhead transparency markers, pencils for each group of two to three students, whiteboard, markers, and crayons (*optional*: patriotic music to play as students write)
- overhead transparencies of stationery for planning and for writing (pages 226 and 227) and of the rubric for thinking about their writing (page 228)

Teacher Materials Included in the Lesson:

- stationery for planning and writing (pages 226 and 227)
- sample modeled planning and sample modeled writing (pages 224 and 225)
- sample student planning and writing (pages 229 and 230)

Student Materials Included in the Lesson:

- For each group of two to three students, you will need to prepare packets containing copies of stationery for planning (page 226), stationery for writing (page 227), and the rubric for thinking about their writing (page 228).

Read Aloud

1. Build background by asking the students to share their thoughts on patriotism. List their ideas on the whiteboard and then categorize them. Possible categories are "Patriotic Things That We See" and "Patriotic Songs That We Sing." Elicit their feelings when they say the pledge or see a flag flying or visit a national monument such as the Statue of Liberty. Now add a feeling category, "Patriotic Feelings That We Have," to the whiteboard and list their ideas below it.

2. Before reading *I Pledge Allegiance*, tell students that you want them to listen for the authors' voices as they explain the words in the pledge and the colors in our flag. Tell them when you finish reading that we will make a list of the facts we learned from the text of the book. Invite them to look closely at the pictures because they also contribute to the meaning.

3. Read *I Pledge Allegiance* by Bill Martin Jr. and Michael Sampson.

4. Record facts learned from the text on the whiteboard under a new category, "What We Learned About Being Patriotic."

Modeled Writing

1. Explain that we are going to write about patriotism, telling what we already know and also including what we've learned. Tell them that these rich experiences evoke strong feelings in us, and we can write about them using our voice. When writers write with strong feelings and concentrate on writing about what's in their hearts, the writing has the voice or personality of the writer.

2. Tell them that you are going to record some of your personal thoughts about what being an American patriot means to you.

Pledging with Our Voices (cont.)

Modeled Writing (cont.)

3. Display the overhead transparency of the stationery for planning. Tell the students that you are going to draw yourself dressed patriotically. Tell them that your face is painted red, white, and blue like our flag and that you have on a patriotic hat. In your hands, you hold and wave the American flag. As you talk, draw yourself in the box labeled, "A Patriotic Me." Then list your ideas about patriotism.

4. Begin your piece with a song lyric lead. Tell students that a lyric lead will help the readers feel your emotion. So that they understand how much of the song to write, remind them of the "ABC song." Tell them that readers only need to hear, "A, B, C . . . ." (the first few letters of the song) before their brains take over to supply the rest of the lyrics in the song. Using the overhead transparency of the stationery for writing, model selecting one of the patriotic songs from the whiteboard. Model writing enough of the song's lyrics so that everyone recognizes it. Add ellipses to demonstrate how writers tell readers that their brains need to supply the rest.

5. Model writing your piece, referring back to the plan. Your piece should reflect your true feelings, and personality. Concentrate on choosing words that sound like you, your voice. Reread as you write to see if your ideas are communicated to the reader. Make sure you've shown how you feel and what you think. In fact, upon completion, ask your students if what you wrote sounds like you. Remind them that writers call that voice, and it's easier to write in your own voice when you feel strongly about something.

6. Remember to use your class word wall for help with spelling high frequency words and to model convention weaknesses from in your students' writing.

7. Reread your piece and make changes. Then display the overhead transparency of the rubric. Read the questions aloud and answer them. Refer back to your text as needed to make changes. (If we want our students to revise, we need to model it in our own writing.)

Guided Writing

1. Establish groups of two to three students and then distribute their prepared packets containing the planning stationery, stationery for writing, and the rubric for thinking about their writing.

2. Direct students to draw themselves dressed patriotically. Remind them of the book and the information they learned from the text. Have them list their ideas on their planning sheet. Remind them of the ideas listed on the whiteboard. Invite them to use some of them and to come up with others of their own.

3. Direct students to write their piece on the stationery for writing.

4. After writing, remind students to think about their writing by answering the questions on their rubric. Invite them to make any changes necessary to improve the voice in their piece.

Sharing Session

Share students' writing in small groups or, if time permits, with the entire class. Invite the students to tell the writers what they liked about their piece and what more they would like to know. Also, tell the audience to write down any good ideas they heard.

Modeled Planning

I pledge allegiance to the flag of the United States of America and to the republic for which it stands, one nation under God, indivisible, with liberty and justice for all.

To me, being patriotic means:

- lead–song lyrics
- means more today
- lucky
- chest–swells with pride
- squeeze eyes
- picture soldiers–Show!
- pride
- freedoms
- privileges/responsibility
- kids
- Can they do it?
- ending–song/feeling

Modeled Writing

"Oh beautiful for spacious skies, for amber waves of grain . . . ."

The lyrics of the song mean more to me today than ever before. I've sung it a thousand times and always felt proud while I was singing it too. But, today when I sing it or say the pledge of allegiance, I think about how lucky I am. My chest swells with the pride. I squeeze my eyes closed and picture soldiers dressed in full uniform standing at attention—one by one, row after row, column after column, my own husband and brother among them. My heart pounds out a message to my brain—we are Americans—proud people, truly living in the land of the free. We can vote. We can go where we want and say what we think. Millions of Americans have died to give us those privileges, including those who were killed on September 11, 2001. But with that freedom, comes responsibility. Our future depends on the wisdom of the old passed down to the young—those little people that we've nurtured and treasured. So much responsibility. Too much responsibility. I wonder, will their little shoulders break with it?

When I hear the words of "America the Beautiful" or "The Star-Spangled Banner" or see our flag unfurled in all its glory, I feel both pride and concern.

Name(s): _____

A Patriotic Me

I pledge allegiance to the flag of the United States of America and to the republic for which it stands, one nation under God, indivisible, with liberty and justice for all.

To me, being patriotic means:

- _____
- _____
- _____
- _____
- _____
- _____
- _____
- _____
- _____
- _____
- _____
- _____

Name(s): _____

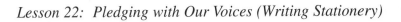

Name(s): _____

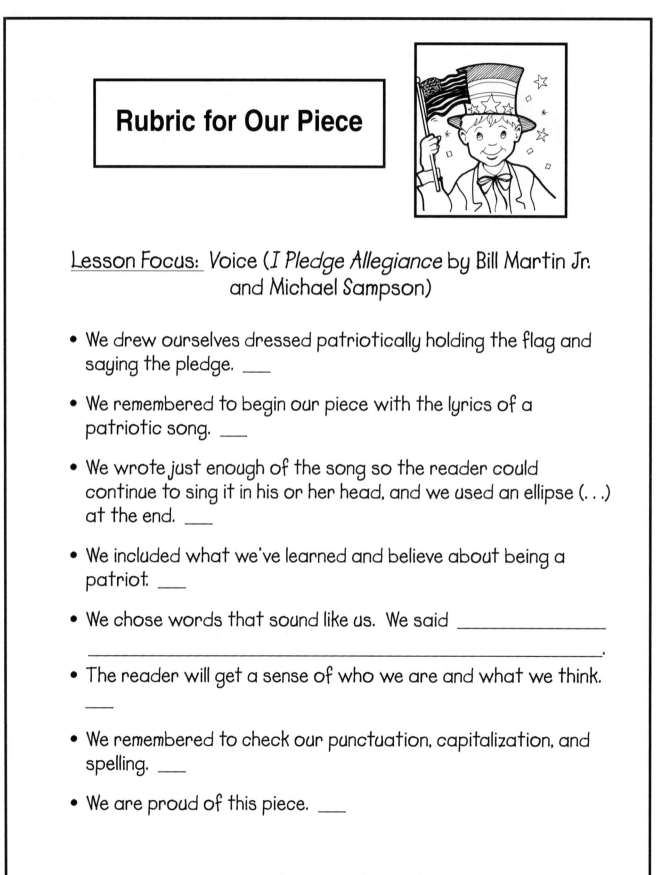

Rubric for Our Piece

<u>Lesson Focus:</u> Voice (*I Pledge Allegiance* by Bill Martin Jr. and Michael Sampson)

- We drew ourselves dressed patriotically holding the flag and saying the pledge. ___

- We remembered to begin our piece with the lyrics of a patriotic song. ___

- We wrote just enough of the song so the reader could continue to sing it in his or her head, and we used an ellipse (. . .) at the end. ___

- We included what we've learned and believe about being a patriot. ___

- We chose words that sound like us. We said _____
_____.

- The reader will get a sense of who we are and what we think. ___

- We remembered to check our punctuation, capitalization, and spelling. ___

- We are proud of this piece. ___

Sample Student Planning

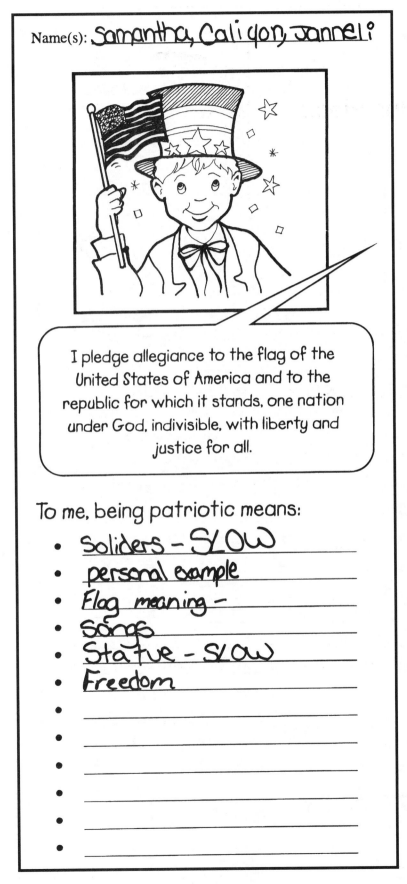

Name(s): Samantha, Cali yon, Janneli

I pledge allegiance to the flag of the United States of America and to the republic for which it stands, one nation under God, indivisible, with liberty and justice for all.

To me, being patriotic means:

- Soliders - SLOW
- personal example
- Flag meaning -
- Songs
- Statue - SLOW
- Freedom
-
-
-
-
-
-

A Patriotic Me

Sample Student Writing

Name(s): Jarrelli, 5th grade Calixon 5th grade Samantha, 4th

"Oh beautiful for spacious skies, for Amber wayves of grain..." This song means alot to us. we sing it all the time in our minds. we sing it all the time because its a patriotic song also because it's our favorite song. When we sing the song we picture soliders standing at attenchen in rows waving the red, white, and blue flag. Did you ever wonder what the colors of the flag mean? Well guess what you won't have to wonder any more. Red stands for courage, Blue stands for loyaly and fairness. White stands for purity and innocence. Also, the Statue of Liberty stands for America. There she is for all to see. In her right hand she holds a torche prodly saying, "welcome to America. land of the free home of the brave." We are a nation full of brave heros. Policeman. Fire fighters. They proved their bravery on September 11, 2001. A tragidy that we will remember always. The flag swoves slowlie, smothly out front Shaw Elementry. When we see it we think — "I pledge allegiance to the flag of the United States of America"...."

Personality Plus

(Day One)

Note to teacher: Lessons 23 and 24 are connected. They both make use of the same read-aloud selection, but the lesson focus shifts from *voice* to *sentence variety*. It will be helpful to read through both lessons before starting.

Materials

Teacher Materials You Need to Supply:

- read-aloud selection: *Woman Hollering Creek and Other Stories* by Sandra Cisneros

- overhead projector, overhead transparency markers, pencils for each group of three to four students, and sticky-notes for each child (used during sharing session)

- overhead transparencies of the stationery for planning and for writing (pages 236 and 237) and the rubric for thinking about their writing (page 238) (*optional*: the hard copy of "Does this writing sound like us talking?" Duplicate page 235 on construction paper and laminate. Fold along dotted line to make a three-D stand-alone.)

Teacher Materials Included in the Lesson:

- stationery for planning and writing (page 236 and 237)

- sample shared planning and shared writing (pages 233 and 234)

- sample student writing (See lesson 24—page 244.)

Student Materials Included in the Lesson:

- For each group of three to four students, you will need to prepare packets containing copies of stationery for planning (page 236), stationery for writing (page 237), and the voice rubric for thinking about their writing (page 238).

Read Aloud

1. Build background by eliciting the students' ages. Tell them that they know a lot about being eight or nine or ten . . . because they ARE that age and have had many experiences. Tell them that writers write about things that they know. They know more about being their age than anyone else. Ask, "What is it like to be You and Your Age?" Call on several students to contribute.

2. Before reading "Eleven," the vignette from *Woman Hollering Creek* by Sandra Cisneros, tell the students to listen for the personality of the writer as she writes about what it is like to be 11. Explain that the personality of the writer is called "voice." It is created primarily through sentence structure and word choice. Tell them that the best writers have identifiable voices when they write. Read "Eleven." Begin with: "What they don't understand about birthdays . . . ." End with: "And you don't feel smart at eleven, not until you're almost twelve. That's the way it is."

3. Elicit specific examples that show Cisneros's personality.

Personality Plus (cont.)

(Day One)

Shared Writing

1. Tell the students that we are going to write with our strong voices just like Sandra Cisneros. Display the overhead transparency of the planning stationery. Tell them that we are going to write a piece about being age five, since we've all been that age. Make decisions on how to begin. (You may want to reread the lead from "Eleven" and craft one similar or choose a lead strategy previously taught.) Elicit ideas for age five and record them on the lines of the arrow. Encourage students to consider the unique attributes of that age—things that happen only at age five. Decide how to end the piece. If you have previously taught strategies for endings, use one of them.

2. Display the overhead transparency of the stationery for writing. As you write, reinforce over and over by saying, "How would we say this so that it sounds like us?" Together, write your piece. Use your class word wall to focus on the high-frequency words that your students find troublesome. Model the conventions that are weaknesses in your students' writing. Reread each sentence before you craft the next one. (This models what we want them to do when they write.)

3. Reread your entire piece. Invite your students to change words or phrases so that it has their voice. Display the sign "Does this writing sound like us talking?" Evaluate your piece to see if it has voice. (Save your transparency if continuing with the Day Two—sentence variety.)

4. Edit your writing focusing on the spelling and grammar issues from your students' last writing sample. Refer to your word wall for those words that are difficult for the students. Display the overhead transparency of the rubric. Model how to reflect on your writing to answer the questions. Revise as needed. (Save your transparency if continuing with Day 2—sentence variety.)

Guided Independent Writing

1. Group students in groups of the same age. Put three to four in a group. Distribute packets of writing materials. (*Optional:* Distribute the sign "Does this writing sound like us talking?")

2. Direct students to talk about their age. Remind them to think of some unique things that happen at their age and record them on their plan. Circulate and assist. When their ideas have been recorded, direct them to write their piece. (Save your overhead transparency if continuing withthe Day 2 portion of the lesson-sentence variety.)

Sharing Session

Distribute two to three sticky-notes to each student. Call on groups to share their piece. Direct them to write down any ideas on the sticky-notes that they hear and want to remember. Tell them to jot only one or two words and put the kids' names by it. At the conclusion, direct the students to stick the notes to their piece. Collect and save for the day-two portion of the lesson.

Follow-up Activity (day-two teaching point: revising for sentence variety)

- Save the shared writing overhead transparency and student pieces for Lesson 24: Age Matters; So Does Sentence fluency.

Shared Planning

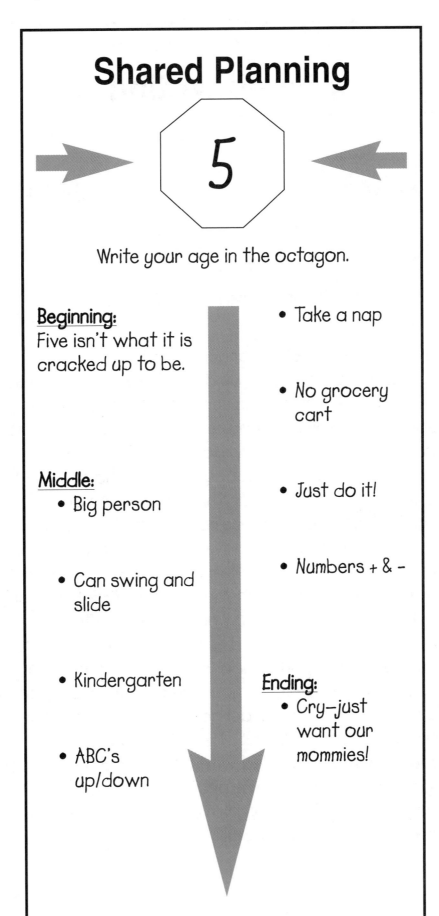

5

Write your age in the octagon.

Beginning:
Five isn't what it is cracked up to be.

Middle:
- Big person

- Can swing and slide

- Kindergarten

- ABC's up/down

- Take a nap

- No grocery cart

- Just do it!

- Numbers + & –

Ending:
- Cry–just want our mommies!

Shared Writing

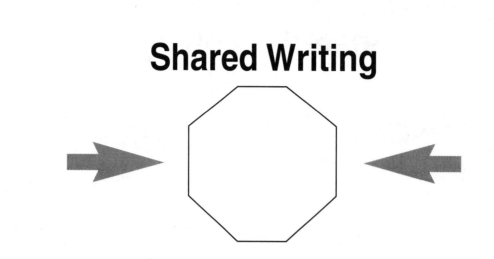

Write your age in the octagon.

Being five years old is not all it's cracked up to be. Sure, you're old enough to go on the swings or slide down the slide by yourself, and you don't have to ride in the baby seat of the grocery cart any more. But when you're five years old, you're expected to act like a big person. You have to suck it up and go off to kindergarten whether you want to or not. People expect you to know how to do things. It's not like when you were four or three or two or one. They have less patience with you because you're older and you should know more. Also, when you're five, you have a lot to learn. There's left from right and up from down. Little letters. Big letters. Put them together so you can make the sounds when the teachers point to them with their stick. Then there's numbers. Whew! You need to count them and read them, and if that wasn't hard enough, they want you to add them together and when you get done with that, they want you to take them away. We say make up your mind! Teachers try to cram so much inside your head in that kindergarten classroom. There's never a minute to rest until you get to nap time! Then you're expected to lie down on your mat in a room filled with 20 kids and promptly fall asleep. And when you can't, they start to look at you like you're a big, fat troublemaker. It's a heavy burden being five. Some days you just want to scream, "I Want My Mommy!"

"Does this writing sound like us talking?"

Name(s): _____

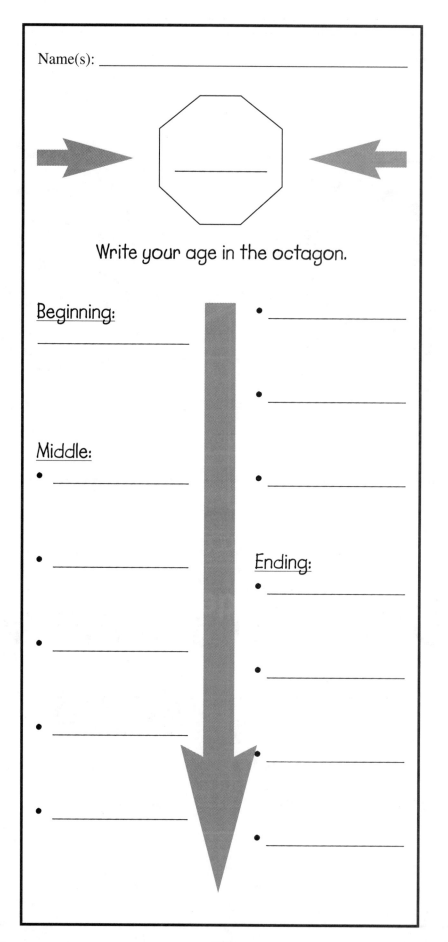

Write your age in the octagon.

Beginning:
_____

Middle:
• _____

• _____

• _____

• _____

• _____

• _____

• _____

Ending:
• _____

• _____

• _____

• _____

Name(s): _____

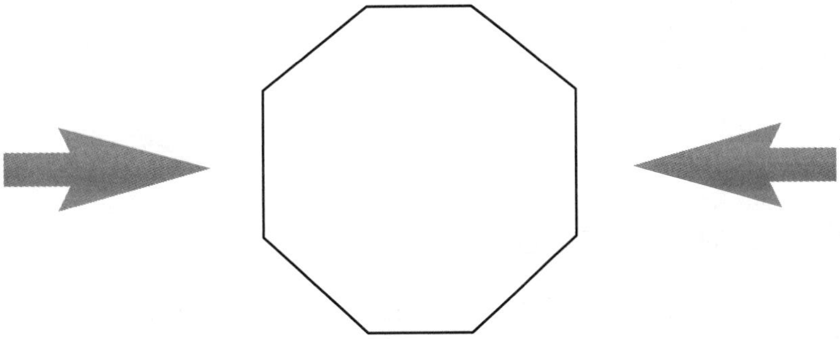

Write your age in the octagon.

_____

_____

_____

_____

_____

_____

_____

_____

_____

_____

_____

_____

_____

_____

Name(s): _____

Rubric for Our Piece

8 or **9** or **10** or _____

> This writing sounds like our voice.

<u>Lesson Focus:</u> Voice (*Woman Hollering Creek and Other Stories*, "Eleven," by Sandra Cisneros)

- We chose words that sound like us. ___ Some of those words are_____.

- The reader will get a sense of who we are and what intrigues us about our age. ___

- We made comparisons about our age to other things to help the reader understand what we think it's like to be a kid our age. ___

- We reread our writing to ask ourselves if it sounded like us. ___

- We remembered to check our punctuation, capitalization, and spelling. ___

- We are proud of this piece. ___

- Today we learned _____

  _____.

Emphasizing the Middle with Sentence Variety

Our youngest writers write pieces very much like this: "I like pizza. It tastes good. It has cheese. It has sauce. It has meat. I love pizza." Oh, and let's not forget . . . "The End!"

While we applaud their ideas and effort, we struggle to teach them to fill their writing with specific details and to use sentence variety while doing it. Often you might say, "You could beat a drum to that piece." That's because all of the sentences are basically the same length with a subject followed by a verb—and if we are very lucky, another word.

At its best, sentence variety becomes the *rhythm* of the piece, and it's much more than the basic four types of sentences—exclamatory, declarative, interrogative, and imperative. Sentence variety is also the *word order* within the sentence. It is also the *length* of each sentence. It is also the *punctuation* within the sentence. The best writers orchestrate their sentences so that they literally sing to us from the page, and the melody of the piece emerges and stays with us long after the words are read. Writers do this by making conscious decisions about how to present their ideas so that the reader is spellbound. They know when to slow us down so that we can feel and think and have time to react, and in some cases have time for our brains to catch up with the flow of ideas presented. Sometimes writers stop us cold with a purposeful fragment or a short three- or four-word sentence. At other times they string ideas together using phrases to build and build and build on an idea. That mixture of sentence structure makes the rhythm that Bill Martin, Jr., speaks about so often and models for us so expertly in his books. Sometimes it is the part of the piece that we respond to first—that rhythm. The ebb and flow of the words marching toward us. Gathering us up and taking us along for the experience. Have you ever been reading silently and something sounds so wonderful that you have to stop and read it aloud? I'd bet money that you've noticed the fluency of the piece and it's reached out and yanked you in! That's it—sentence variety. Sometimes it is the repetition of a word or a phrase or a sentence pattern written to create a mood or point. Other times it's words or phrases combined and punctuated in such a way that you are forced to respond. And how you respond depends entirely on the writer's purpose. What power we have when we hold the pen!

If you want your students to write pieces that have this rhythm, you should read pieces to them that have it. Pieces like Sneed B. Collard's nonfiction book *Forest in the Clouds*. Read and point out how he invites you into the forest. You notice right away the description and learn some information, yet you also notice how he says it. Long sentences mixed with medium ones. Occasionally a short one. He also punctuates to further create our pacing as we read. When he writes, you can't discern a pattern, and that motivates you to keep on going. You have to continue reading, partly because you want to know what is coming next in the piece and partly because the rhythm draws you in very much like the old spider-and-the-fly scenario.

After we get our students to notice sentence variety and value it, we have to figure out how to teach it. Why not spend a class period crafting one sentence just like an author we've read? If we examine how it is constructed, we can teach our kids to write one just like it, using their own ideas. It's like money in the bank. When they learn to write like the authors they read, there is a payoff—and guess what? We teachers have the combination to the vault! I wish it were as easy as right—36, left—25, right—42, but I've found that it really isn't so very hard. But be selective! Teach only those structures that will dramatically influence what you and your students are writing about. Then stand back to watch and wait. They'll do it once. They'll do it again in another piece, and they'll save it in their memory banks to retrieve any time they want. It will become a strategy they can bring out of the vault to use when they decide it is needed.

Teach! It is an active verb.

Age Matters; So Does Sentence Fluency

(Day Two: Continuation of Lesson 23)

Materials

Teacher Materials You Need to Supply:

- read-aloud selection: *Woman Hollering Creek and Other Stories* by Sandra Cisneros
- overhead projector, overhead transparency markers, shared plan and writing from day one (Lesson 23: Personality Plus), student pieces from guided writing from day one, chart paper, markers and colored pencils for each group of three to four students.
- overhead transparencies of non-example of "Eleven" and rubric on sentence variety (pages 242 and 243)

Teacher Materials Included in the Lesson:

- non-example of "Eleven" (page 242)
- rubric on sentence variety (page 243)
- sample student writing (page 244)

Student Materials Included in the Lesson:

- For each group of three to four students, you will need to prepare copies of the rubric on sentence variety for thinking about their writing (page 243). (Students will also need their writing from day one—Lesson 23: Personality Plus).

Read Aloud

1. Reread "Eleven" from *Woman Hollering Creek and Other Stories* by Sandra Cisneros, directing the students to listen this time for the sentence structure.

2. Tell students that previously we worked on voice, but today we will be working on sentence fluency in our lesson.

3. Direct students to listen to the different ways Cisneros organizes her sentences. Tell them that the sentences change so the reader won't get bored. Call attention to the sentence lengths and word order in the piece.

4. Elicit the specifics from the piece and record them on chart paper.

   Examples might include something like the following:

   - variety of length—short, medium, and long
   - variety of structure—word order, phrases
   - variety of punctuation—commas, dashes, and end punctuation

Age Matters; So Does Sentence Fluency

(Day Two: Continuation of Lesson 23)

Shared Writing

1. Display the non-example paraphrasing "Eleven."

2. Read it to the class and then point out that the piece says essentially what Cisneros wrote, only this piece is boring. The sentences are all between eight and nine words, and all of them are constructed the same: namely, with a subject followed by a verb. Tell students that writers have to pay attention to sentence structure so that their writing is interesting to the reader.

3. Choose a notable sentence from Cisneros's "Eleven" and revise your piece by crafting one similar to hers. (Use a different color of overhead transparency marker so that your revision stands out.) Together, write an entirely new sentence, or rearrange a previous one you have written, or combine two sentences. Your purpose is not only to model the writing process but also to demonstrate how writers give careful consideration to the structure of each sentence.

   (When students see us revise our writing, it sets the stage for them to revise theirs.)

Guided Writing

1. Establish the same groups from day one. Direct the students to reread their piece and revise it for sentence variety, using their colored pencils. Remind them of the sticky notes on their writing that contain some good ideas they gathered yesterday when the groups shared their writing. Encourage them to consider including some of those ideas in their writing. (This may help them achieve sentence variety.)

2. Direct students to think about their writing by completing the rubric on sentence variety. Encourage them to revisit their piece to make additional changes if warranted.

Sharing Session

Pair two groups and direct them to share their writing. Direct them to share both the before and after efforts. Elicit the specific changes they made as to length or structure of their sentences and the reasons why.

Celebrate their efforts.

Day Two: Shared Writing

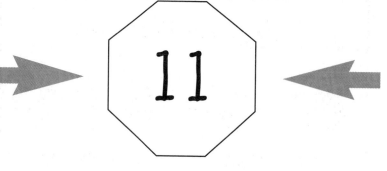

Write your age in the octagon.

<u>Day Two</u> Non-example of "Eleven"

You don't feel eleven when it's your eleventh birthday. (9 words) You really don't feel any different at all. (8 words) Your birthday is just like the day before. (8 words) You expect it to feel differently, but it doesn't. (9 words) You have to keep reminding yourself that you're eleven. (9 words)

Name(s): _____

Rubric for Our Piece

8 or **9** or **10** or _____

<u>Lesson Focus:</u> Sentence Variety (*Woman Hollering Creek and Other Stories*, "Eleven," by Sandra Cisneros)

- We reread our piece and looked at our sentence length. ___

- The reader won't get bored because we made some sentences short, medium, and long. ___

- We made some changes to the sentence structure. We changed some to begin with a phrase. (Example: When you're eight, ...) ___

- We wrote _____.

- We looked at our sentence type. We changed some to questions (?) or exclamation marks (!). ___

- We added some good ideas from our classmates. (sticky notes) ___

- We remembered to check our punctuation, capitalization, and spelling. ___

- We are proud of this piece. ___

- Today we learned _____.

Sample Student Writing

Name(s): Racheal Jasmine Denise Jesse

8

Write your age in the octagon.

Being eight years old is like a roller coaster around the world. Roller coasters go up and down and around in a loopty-loop. An eight year olds ups are fun things like playing spider man in the family room and playing hopscotch and ^ Jumprope in the yard on ^the sidewalk.

An eight year olds downs are always having to be smart. Moms and Dads always tell you to do better at math and science and writing and tests.

An eight year olds loopty-loops are having to do things over and over again like cleaning your bedroom and taking out the garabage and washing disheshes. Now you know what an eight year olds ride is in life.

A Show Sentence

Materials

Teacher Materials You Need to Supply:

- read-aloud selection: *The Seashore Book* by Charlotte Zolotow
- overhead projector, overhead transparency markers, pencils for each group of three to four students, chalkboard and chalk.
- (*optional*: transparent tape and additional paper if doing the revision lesson follow-up)
- overhead transparency of the sentence "The Sky" from *The Seashore Book* by Charlotte Zolotow (page 248), overhead transparencies of the T-chart stationery for planning and the stationery for writing (pages 251 and 252)

Teacher Materials Included in the Lesson:

- sample modeled planning (page 249)
- sample modeled writing (page 250)
- sample copy of "The Sky" sentence (page 248)
- sample student planning and writing (pages 254 and 255)
- stationery for planning and writing (pages 251 and 252)

Student Materials Included in the Lesson:

- For each group of three to four students, you will need to prepare packets containing copies of the T-chart stationery for planning and stationery for writing (pages 251 and 252) and the rubric for thinking about their writing (page 253).

Read Aloud

1. Before reading aloud *The Seashore Book* by Charlotte Zolotow, ask the class to raise their hands if they have ever been to the beach. Build background by eliciting talk about the beach. Probe for description.

2. Now tell students to listen carefully to the description found in *The Seashore Book* by Charlotte Zolotow. Tell them that after reading part of the book, you will ask them to notice a beautiful sentence filled with specific description. Tell them that Ms. Zolotow created a special sentence structure in order to slow the writing down so that readers can see what the sky looks like at the beach. Read from the beginning of the book up to the sentence about the sky, "They are the same smoky . . . ."

A Show Sentence *(cont.)*

Modeled Writing

1. Tell students that you are going to write a sentence like Charlotte Zolotow. Display the overhead transparency of the sentence about the sky. "They are the same smoky gray until the mist shifts from gray to dark white, from dark white to pale purple, from pale purple to hazy blue and then, suddenly, the sun breaks through!" Tell them that Ms. Zolotow used specific detail and also varied her sentence structure when she described the clouds. Point out the pattern of the writing—"from" and "to" with the repetition of a color word.

2. Tell students that you just went to Wal-Mart to buy school supplies, and you think you can use this crafting technique to describe what you saw there.

3. List four things you saw at Wal-Mart on the overhead transparency of the T-chart for planning. Items could include spiral notebooks, Tweety Bird book bags, binders, and pencils—for example, yellow ones, bright colored ones, some with animals, and neon glow-in-the-dark ones. (When we model several ideas and then choose one among all of them, we are modeling what we want our students to do.) Remember that you will need a pattern of four in order to use the crafting technique found in *The Seashore Book*.

4. Tell students that of all the things you saw there, you think you can use Ms. Zolotow's crafting technique best with the pencils. Remind them that you will need four different kinds of pencils in order to write like Charlotte Zolotow.

5. List the four different kinds of pencils that you saw. Stress the sentence pattern—a type of "piggyback repetition," using the words "from" and "to."

6. Using the overhead transparency of stationery for writing, write your piece focusing on crafting a sentence like the author. Often refer to the "sky" sentence from *The Seashore Book*. Voice the decisions you make as you write your piece. Refer to the plan to retrieve your ideas. Remind students that Zolotow repeats the previous color ("piggybacks") each time she introduces a new one.

7. Model pulling words from the class word wall as you write. Also, model punctuation and grammar issues in your students' writing.

8. Before moving to guided writing, generate a list of places students can write about. List the places on the chalkboard. Tell them they are possible ideas for their writing.

9. Display again the overhead transparency of "The Sky" from *The Seashore Book* by Charlotte Zolotow. Leave it up on the overhead so that they can refer to the sentence as they write.

A Show Sentence *(cont.)*

Guided Writing

1. To each group of three to four students, distribute the prepared writing packets. Direct them to find a place that every member in their group has been to, and then have them list some things they saw there. Remind them to find four attributes for their topic. An example might be topic: grocery store and attributes: Campbell's Chicken Noodle Soup, Froot Loops Cereal, Ben and Jerry's Fudge Ripple Ice Cream, and Cheese Doodles.

2. Direct students to once again reread the sentence from *The Seashore Book* by Charlotte Zolotow, examining the pattern of her sentence.

3. Tell each group to write their piece, crafting like Ms. Zolotow. Remind them that they will need a beginning sentence that tells the reader where they are. (Supporting them with a lead structure allows them to concentrate on the sentence structure we are learning.) Allow them to write their middle. When they are almost finished, stop them and direct them to write a concluding sentence that finishes the paragraph off. (Remind them of any ending strategies previously taught.)

4. After students complete their pieces, direct them to think about their writing by completing the rubric. If any changes need to be made in their piece, direct them to revise.

Sharing Session

Call on each group to read aloud their pieces. When moving from group to group, model the crafting technique by stating, "From students who wrote about _____ to those children who wrote about _____. (Repeat the last group's topic and add the next group.) Continue in this manner until all groups have shared.

Follow-up Activity (teaching point: revision to include sentence variety)

Model revision by going back to a previous piece of class writing. Together, reread the piece to find a place where you can slow the writing down to include Charlotte Zolotow's crafting technique. Model the technique again by generating four ideas or attributes, "piggyback" each, and connect them with the words "from" and "to." Revise your piece, using "Cut and Paste Elaboration"— a technique of cutting the paper (or overhead transparency) at the point where a revision is needed, inserting a new piece of paper by taping it to the original text, writing your revision, and then reattaching it to the original text. Direct the students to choose a piece from their writing folders and revise it by using this crafting technique.

The Seashore Book

by Charlotte Zolotow

The sky . . .

"They are the same smoky gray until the mist shifts <u>from</u> gray <u>to</u> dark white, <u>from</u> dark white <u>to</u> pale purple, <u>from</u> pale purple <u>to</u> hazy blue, and then suddenly the sun breaks through."

Modeled Planning

"They are the same smoky gray until the mist shifts from gray to dark white, from dark white to pale purple, from pale purple to hazy blue, and then suddenly the sun breaks through."

The Seashore Book by Charlotte Zolotow

Ideas for Writing	Specific Details about My Idea
Wal-Mart	who ☑ Kids ☑ parents ☑ some teachers ☑ plain yellow ☑ dinosaurs ☑ neon orange ☑ smiley faces
school supplies	
notebooks	
lunchboxes	
pencils	

We can craft like Charlotte Zolotow!

Modeled Writing

School Supplies

In August, I went shopping for school supplies at Wal-Mart. I saw kids and parents and even some teachers hunting through all the goodies on the shelves. But what I noticed most of all was the variety of pencils! <u>From plain yellow ones to some with dinosaurs on them, from ones with dinosaurs on them to neon orange ones that glowed in the dark, from neon orange that glowed in the dark to pencils with smiley faces on them.</u> Boy! So many pencils to choose. How will a writer like me ever decide?

We can craft like Charlotte Zolotow!

Name(s): _____

Plan for Writing

"They are the same smoky gray until the mist shifts from gray to dark white, from dark white to pale purple, from pale purple to hazy blue, and then suddenly the sun breaks through."

The Seashore Book by Charlotte Zolotow

Ideas for Writing	Specific Details about Our Idea

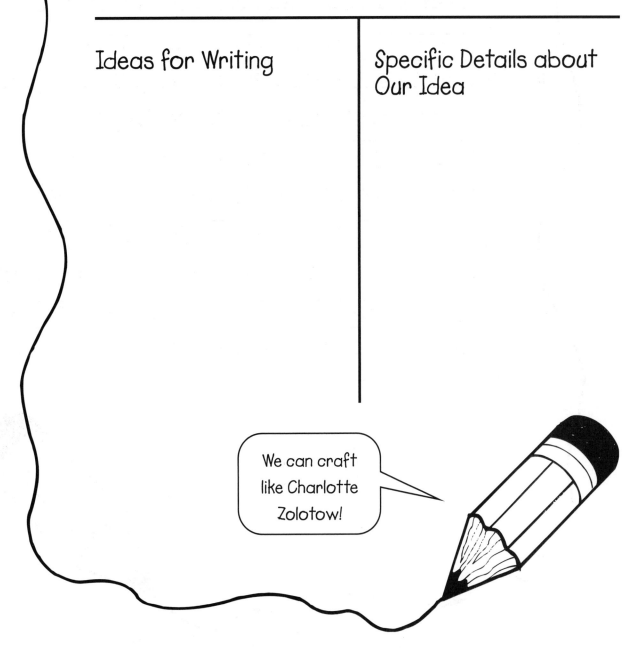

We can craft like Charlotte Zolotow!

Name(s): _____

We can craft like Charlotte Zolotow!

Name(s): _____

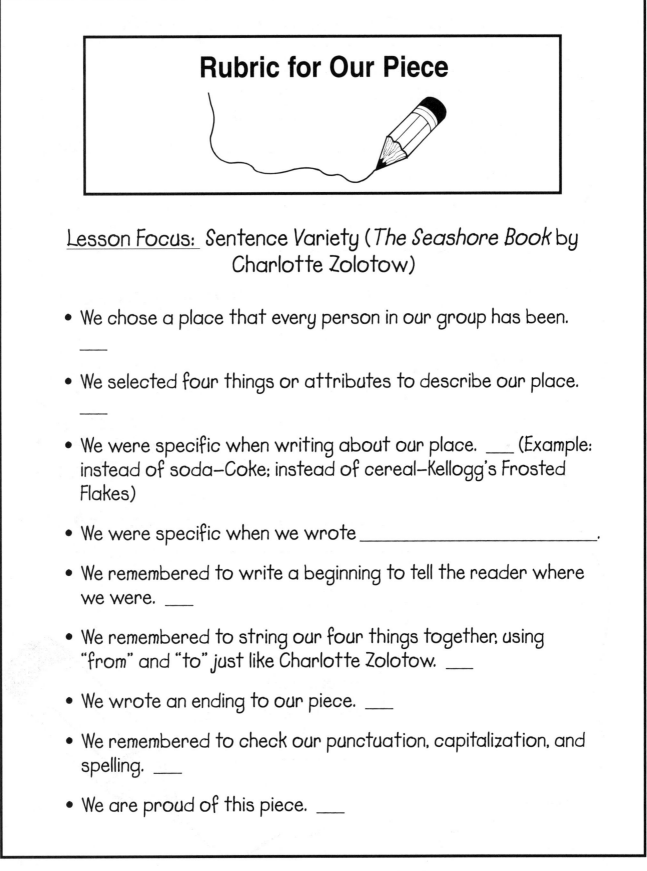

Rubric for Our Piece

Lesson Focus: Sentence Variety (*The Seashore Book* by Charlotte Zolotow)

- We chose a place that every person in our group has been. ___

- We selected four things or attributes to describe our place. ___

- We were specific when writing about our place. ___ (Example: instead of soda–Coke; instead of cereal–Kellogg's Frosted Flakes)

- We were specific when we wrote _____.

- We remembered to write a beginning to tell the reader where we were. ___

- We remembered to string our four things together, using "from" and "to" just like Charlotte Zolotow. ___

- We wrote an ending to our piece. ___

- We remembered to check our punctuation, capitalization, and spelling. ___

- We are proud of this piece. ___

Sample Student Planning

Name(s): __Tyree, Derick, Tituneshia, Reginald, Alexia__

"They are the same smoky gray until the mist shifts from gray to dark white, from dark white to pale purple, from pale purple to hazy blue, and then suddenly the sun breaks through."

The Seashore Book by Charlotte Zolotow

Ideas for Writing	Specific Details about Our Idea
Skating Rink	People skating
	People falling
	Kids gobblin food at the food shack
	(Arcade) games

We can craft like Charlotte Zolotow!

Sample Student Writing

Name(s): Tyree, Derick, Tituneshia, Reginald, Alexia

Most people have been to the Skating Rink. We have. What about you? From People Skating to people falling. from people fallingg to kids gobbling food from the food Shack. from kids gobbling food from the food shack, to kids crowding at the Arcade games. There are many games to chose. At the Skating Rink we can do anything!.

We can craft like Charlotte Zolotow!

Yo! It's All in the Beat

Materials

Teacher Materials You Need to Supply:

- read-aloud selection: *Knots in My Yo-Yo String (The Autobiography of a Kid)* by Jerry Spinelli
- alternate read-aloud selection: *Library Card* by Jerry Spinelli (Begin on page 29 with: "Rain fell . . ." End with: "Gotta go somewhere."
- overhead projector, overhead transparency markers, and pencils for each group of four to five students
- overhead transparency of "Johnson's Highway" text from *Knots in My Yo-Yo String* (page 259), overhead transparency of Examine with Your Writers' Eyeballs (page 260), overhead transparency of Revision Text: Fun After School (page 261), overhead transparency of the stationery for planning (page 265), and an overhead transparency of Shared Revision: Main Idea #1 (page 262)
- (*Optional:* For the follow-up activity, you will need to type up and make overhead transparencies of the revised text from today's lesson and duplicate it for each student.)

Teacher Materials Included in the Lesson:

- "Johnson's Highway" text (page 259)
- Examine with Your Writers' Eyeballs (page 260)
- sample shared planning (page 263)
- sample shared writing (page 264)
- planning stationery (page 265)
- writing stationery: Main Ideas #2, #3, #4 (pages 266–268)
- sample student planning and writing (pages 270–275)

Student Materials Included in the Lesson:

- For each group of four to five students (size can vary depending on the number of students in your class), you will need to prepare packets containing copies of "Johnson's Highway" text from *Knots in My Yo-Yo String, The Autobiography of a Kid* (page 259), Examine with Your Writers' Eyeballs, one of the non-example main ideas for revision (page 260) (The lesson contains main ideas #2, #3, and #4. Each group will work on only one of the main ideas, so you will need to customize each packet.), stationery for planning (page 265), stationery for writing (pages 266–268), and the rubric for thinking about their writing (page 269).

Read Aloud

1. Before reading page one of *Knots in My Yo-Yo String, The Autobiography of a Kid* by Jerry Spinelli, tell the students to listen for the variety of sentence structure the author uses in this one passage of the book. Tell them to notice the mixture of short, medium, and long sentences in the passage and also to listen to the way the words in the sentences are arranged.

2. Read page one of the *Knots in My Yo-Yo String.*

Yo! It's All in the Beat *(cont.)*

Shared Writing

1. Establish groups of four to five students and then distribute the packets to them. (There are three different main ideas in the revision piece. Depending on your class size, two different groups could be revising the same main idea.)

2. Display the overhead transparency of "Johnson's Highway" text from *Knots in My Yo-Yo String*. Tell the students that we are going to examine the sentence structure of the writing with our "writers' eyeballs." Point out the numbers in front of each sentence. Tell them that we will refer to the sentences by using the numbers beside them.

3. Display the overhead transparency of Examine with Your Writers' Eyeballs. Explain that we are going to count the number of words in each sentence of the text from *Knots in My Yo-Yo String*.

4. Model counting the number of words for sentences one and two. Record the information on Examine with Your Writers' Eyeballs. Direct students to record the number on the same sheet in their packets. Elicit the number of words for the remaining sentences, and then explain that the best writers vary the length of their sentences so that the reader doesn't get bored with the writing. Invite them to listen to the rhythm of the passage as you read it together.

5. Continue responding to the other elements of sentence variety found on Examine with Your Writer's Eyeballs. Explain that when you examine writing for sentence variety, you look at the structure of each sentence. List the number of each sentence which you identify as belonging beside each item listed under Sentence Structure and also Sentence Type.

6. Display the overhead transparency Revision Text: Fun After School. Tell students to listen to the rhythm of this piece. Point out that this writing sounds different from Spinelli's because of the sameness of these sentences.

7. Using the overhead transparency of the stationery for planning, together plan your revision for the first main idea paragraph of the piece. (The introduction needs no revision. Reminders from Examine with Your Writers' Eyeballs are included on your plan.)

8. Display the overhead transparency Shared Revision: Main Idea #1. Use as many elements of sentence variety as possible when revising main idea #1. Elicit ideas for revising the piece.

9. Referring back to your plan, reread your piece and place check marks beside each of the items on the plan that you used in your piece. Revise to include other sentence structures in the piece. The goal is to try to use as many as possible. Remind them that they are learning to write like the Newbery Award winner, Jerry Spinelli.

Yo! It's All in the Beat *(cont.)*

Guided Independent Writing

1. Direct the students to read their main idea that needs to be revised. (Remember that there are three different main ideas. Depending on your class size, two different groups could be revising the same main idea.) Using the stationery for planning, direct them to record their ideas for revising their piece. Then, direct them to write their piece on the stationery for writing. Remind them to check off each item on their plan as they write. Tell them this will help them remember to include it in their piece.

2. To help students think about their writing, direct them to complete the rubric provided in the lesson packet. Encourage them to make any changes needed in their writing.

Sharing Session

Again display the overhead transparency of Shared Revision: Main Idea #1. Reread the introduction and the main idea revised during shared writing. Then call on each group to read their pieces in order—main ideas two, three, and four. Conclude by rereading the original ending found in Revision Text: Fun After School.

Follow-up Activity (teaching point: revision and publishing)

So that students understand how their main ideas combine to make a well–written final piece, publish the revised text using the original lead, the main idea #one from shared writing, along with each group's revised main ideas #two, #three, and #four. Include the ending from the original text. Duplicate for the students so that you can refer back to this piece when writing other pieces. Using their writing as examples of excellence makes juggling all elements of effective writing easier for your students. Each time they reread familiar text which they helped to write, it becomes easier for them to see possibilities.

Note: Revisit the piece for homework. The revision possibilities are endless. Revise for a new lead or conclusion; include some facts or examples, dialogue, appeals to senses; rewrite a main idea sentence, polish transitions, or learn to write wrap-up sentences. In the weeks to come, continue revising the piece for homework in order to practice the lessons taught during writer's workshop.

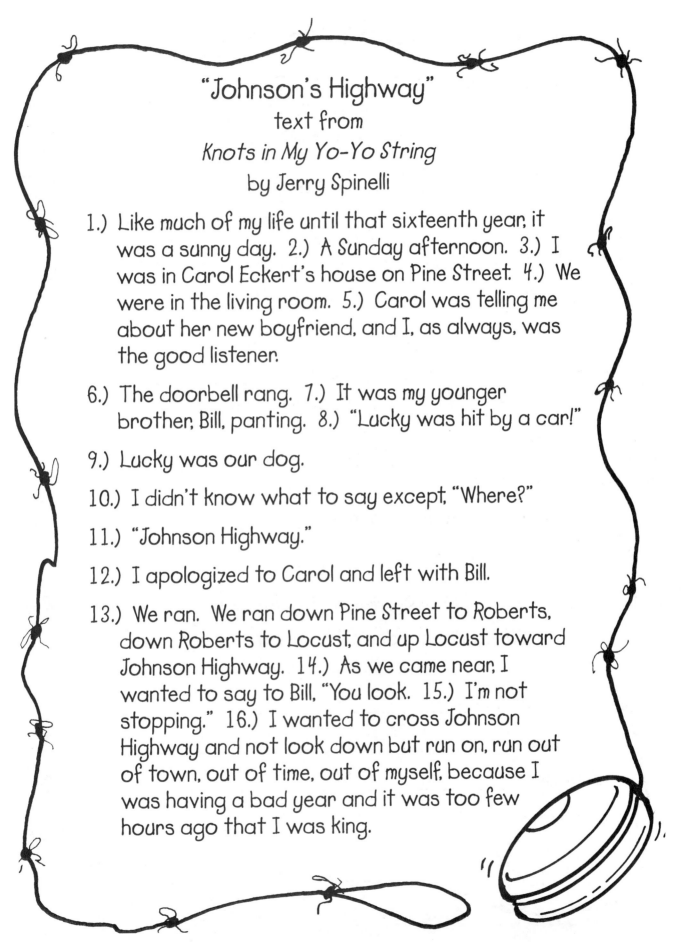

"Johnson's Highway"
text from
Knots in My Yo-Yo String
by Jerry Spinelli

1.) Like much of my life until that sixteenth year, it was a sunny day. 2.) A Sunday afternoon. 3.) I was in Carol Eckert's house on Pine Street. 4.) We were in the living room. 5.) Carol was telling me about her new boyfriend, and I, as always, was the good listener.

6.) The doorbell rang. 7.) It was my younger brother, Bill, panting. 8.) "Lucky was hit by a car!"

9.) Lucky was our dog.

10.) I didn't know what to say except, "Where?"

11.) "Johnson Highway."

12.) I apologized to Carol and left with Bill.

13.) We ran. We ran down Pine Street to Roberts, down Roberts to Locust, and up Locust toward Johnson Highway. 14.) As we came near, I wanted to say to Bill, "You look. 15.) I'm not stopping." 16.) I wanted to cross Johnson Highway and not look down but run on, run out of town, out of time, out of myself, because I was having a bad year and it was too few hours ago that I was king.

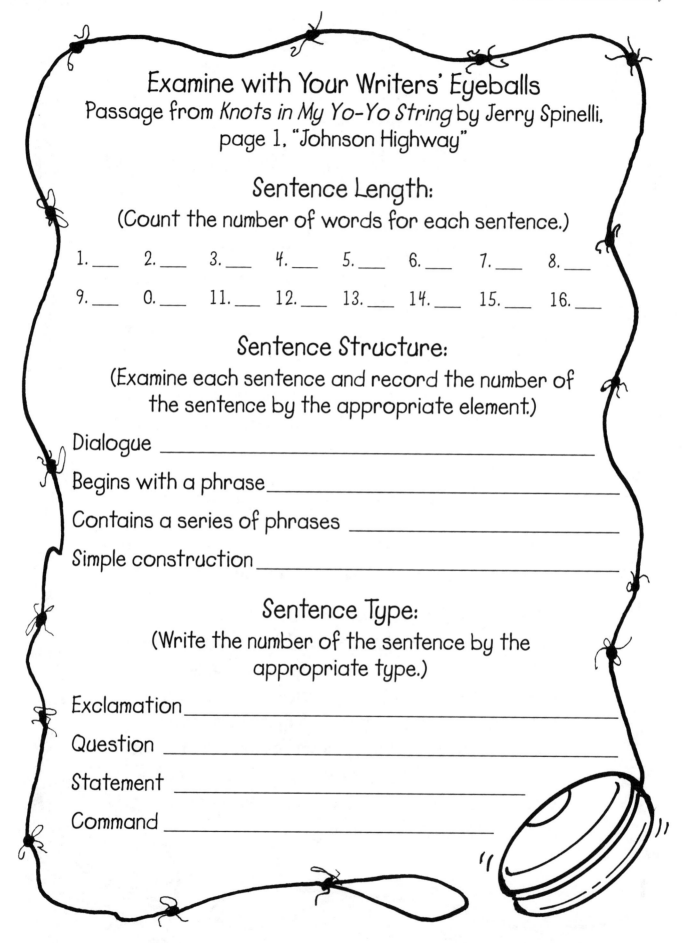

Examine with Your Writers' Eyeballs
Passage from *Knots in My Yo-Yo String* by Jerry Spinelli, page 1, "Johnson Highway"

Sentence Length:
(Count the number of words for each sentence.)

1. ___   2. ___   3. ___   4. ___   5. ___   6. ___   7. ___   8. ___

9. ___   0. ___   11. ___   12. ___   13. ___   14. ___   15. ___   16. ___

Sentence Structure:
(Examine each sentence and record the number of the sentence by the appropriate element.)

Dialogue _____

Begins with a phrase_____

Contains a series of phrases _____

Simple construction_____

Sentence Type:
(Write the number of the sentence by the appropriate type.)

Exclamation_____

Question _____

Statement _____

Command _____

Revision Text

Fun After School

Yippee! It's 2:30 and school is over. Kids everywhere love this time of the day. The possibilities are limited only by your imagination . . . or your mom.

It's fun to get snacks. I'm hungry after school. I like chips and coke. I go outside under a tree. I sit down and eat them. Messes are okay outside. Mom doesn't care at all.

I also like to watch TV. I usually watch cartoons. Scooby Doo is my favorite. That dog is funny. He gets into trouble. I think that is funny.

Sometimes I ride my bike. I go up and down my street. I take off fast. I can do tricks too. We have a ramp. I like to ride up on it. I like to do jumps. I usually don't fall. I like my bike.

I also go to Mark's house. He is my friend. We play Nintendo 64. We play "Blitz Football" on it. I like to be the quarterback. Mark likes to be the kicker. We score points for our teams.

Often I play with my dog. She likes to play ball. Her favorite is a tennis ball. I throw it far away. She runs fast and gets it. She always brings it back. We play most afternoons.

I look forward to my playtime after school. There are so many choices of things to do. Tag. Board games. Friends. Food. When my school work is done, I call my friend, Mark and say, "Let's play!"

Shared Revision: Main Idea #1

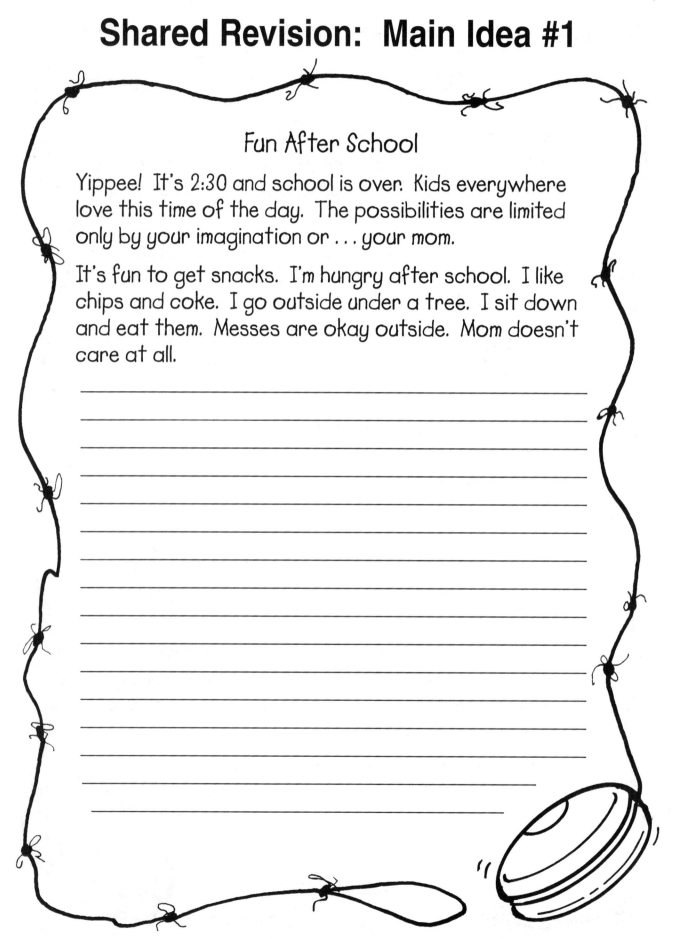

Fun After School

Yippee! It's 2:30 and school is over. Kids everywhere love this time of the day. The possibilities are limited only by your imagination or . . . your mom.

It's fun to get snacks. I'm hungry after school. I like chips and coke. I go outside under a tree. I sit down and eat them. Messes are okay outside. Mom doesn't care at all.

_____

_____

_____

_____

_____

_____

_____

_____

_____

_____

_____

_____

_____

_____

_____

Shared Planning

<u>Reminders:</u>
Sentence Length:
- short
- medium
- long

<u>Sentence Structure:</u>
- dialogue
- begins with a phrase
- contains a series of phrases
- simple construction

<u>Sentence Type:</u>
- exclamation
- question
- statement
- command

✓ Begin with a phrase.

✓ Make Mom talk.

✓ Chips—list kinds.

✓ Outside—tree – Use three phrases: under a tree, next to the big rock, and lean back against the tree trunk.

✓ Mmmmm!

✓ Short sentences—salty, crispy, crunchy, mess

✓ Who cares about messes?

✓ Ants love me.

✓ Kitchen clean.

✓ Ending – Good until gone.

Shared Writing

Fun After School

Yippee! It's 2:30 and school is over. Kids everywhere love this time of the day. The possibilities are limited only by your imagination . . . or your mom.

After a hard day at Sulphur Springs Elementary, it's fun to rush home and gobble snacks. Since I work so hard, I'm hungry after school. Junk food. It calls me. I love it all! As soon as Mom says, "B-e-n-n-n-n, what do you want to eat?" My mouth starts watering for chips and Coke! Whether it's Fritos, Doritos, or Cheetos, I want them. I head outside under a fifty-year-old water oak next to the big rock and lean back against the tree trunk. Then I rip open the bag and start popping them in. Mmmmm! So salty. And crispy! And crunchy! And messy! But I don't worry about a thing. Who cares about messes? Not me! Hey, I'm outside! The ants love both my messes and me. Mom loves me too because the kitchen stays clean. Snacks give kids energy. We love them . . . until they're all gone.

Name(s): _____

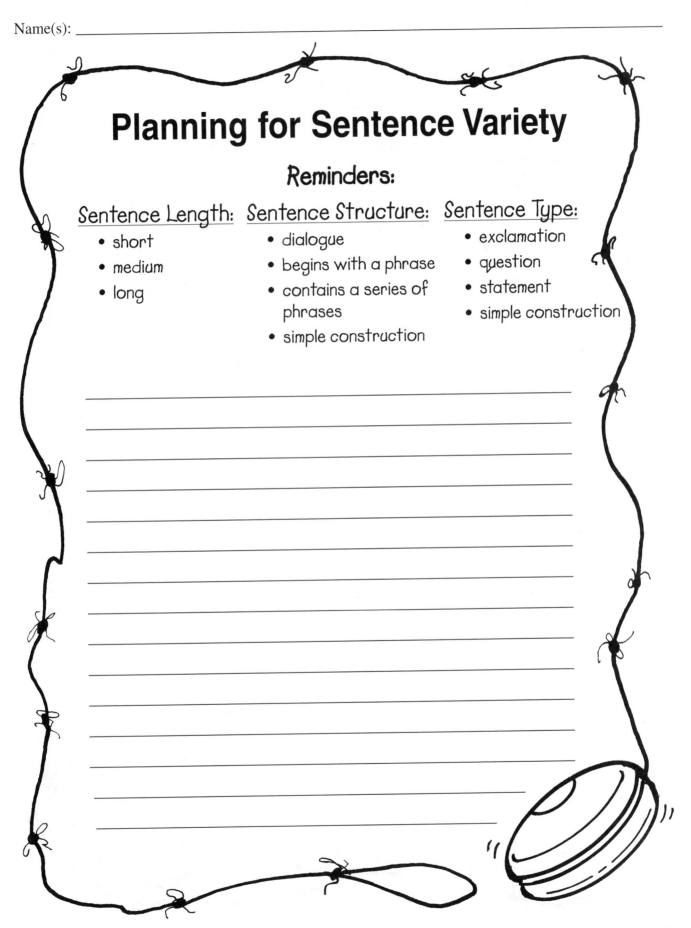

Planning for Sentence Variety

Reminders:

Sentence Length:	Sentence Structure:	Sentence Type:
• short	• dialogue	• exclamation
• medium	• begins with a phrase	• question
• long	• contains a series of phrases	• statement
	• simple construction	• simple construction

Name(s): _____

Main Idea #2

I also like to watch TV. I usually watch cartoons.
Scooby Doo is my favorite. That dog is funny. He gets
into trouble. I think that is funny.

_____

_____

_____

_____

_____

_____

_____

_____

_____

_____

_____

_____

_____

_____

_____

_____

_____

_____

_____

Name(s): _____

Main Idea #3

Sometimes I ride my bike. I go up and down my street. I take off fast. I can do tricks too. We have a ramp. I like to ride up on it. I like to do jumps. I usually don't fall. I like my bike.

_____
_____
_____
_____
_____
_____
_____
_____
_____
_____
_____
_____
_____
_____
_____
_____
_____

Name(s): _____

Main Idea #4

Often I play with my dog. She likes to play ball. Her favorite is a tennis ball. I throw it far away. She runs fast and gets it. She always brings it back. We play most afternoons.

_____

_____

_____

_____

_____

_____

_____

_____

_____

_____

_____

_____

_____

_____

_____

_____

_____

_____

Name(s): _____

Rubric for Our Piece

<u>Lesson Focus:</u> Sentence Variety (*Knots in My Yo-Yo String* by Jerry Spinelli)

- We have some short, _____ medium, _____ and long _____ sentences.
  _(number)   _(number)   _(number)

- We have sentences that begin with phrases. ___

- We have a sentence with two or more phrases. ___
  A sentence we wrote that has two or more phrases is _____.

  _____

  _____

- We have some simple sentences. ___

- We have all types of sentences in our piece. ___
  (Examples: . ! ?)

- We remembered to check our punctuation, capitalization, and spelling. ___

- We are so proud of this piece. ___

- We learned _____

  _____.

Sample Student Planning

Name(s): **Ricole**

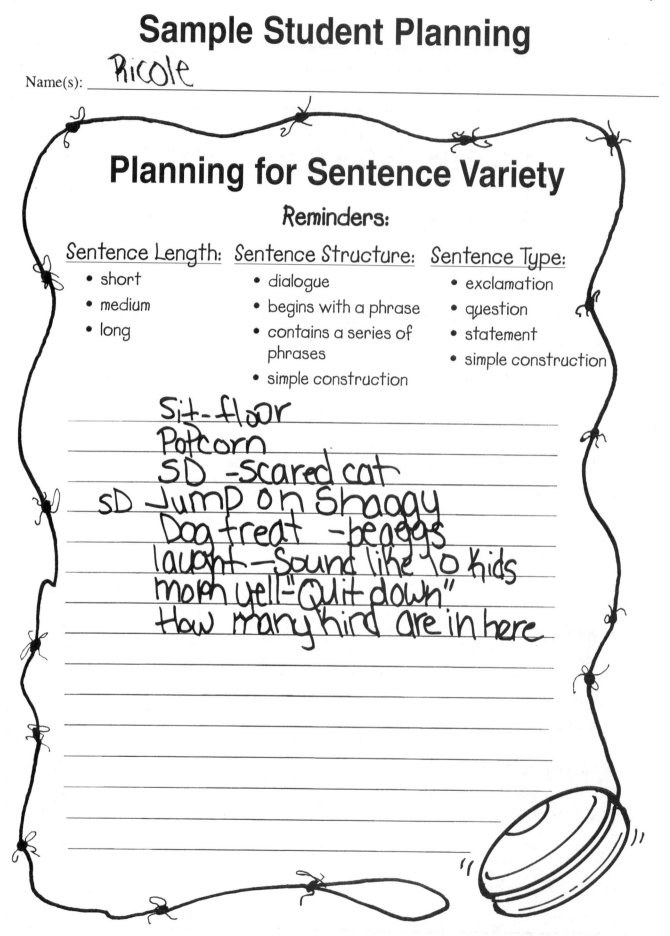

Planning for Sentence Variety

Reminders:

Sentence Length:
- short
- medium
- long

Sentence Structure:
- dialogue
- begins with a phrase
- contains a series of phrases
- simple construction

Sentence Type:
- exclamation
- question
- statement
- simple construction

Sit-floor
Potcorn
SD -scared cat
SD Jump on Shaggy
Dog treat -begas
laught-Sound like 10 kids
mom yell-"Quit down"
How many bird are in here

Sample Student Writing

Name(s): __Ricole__

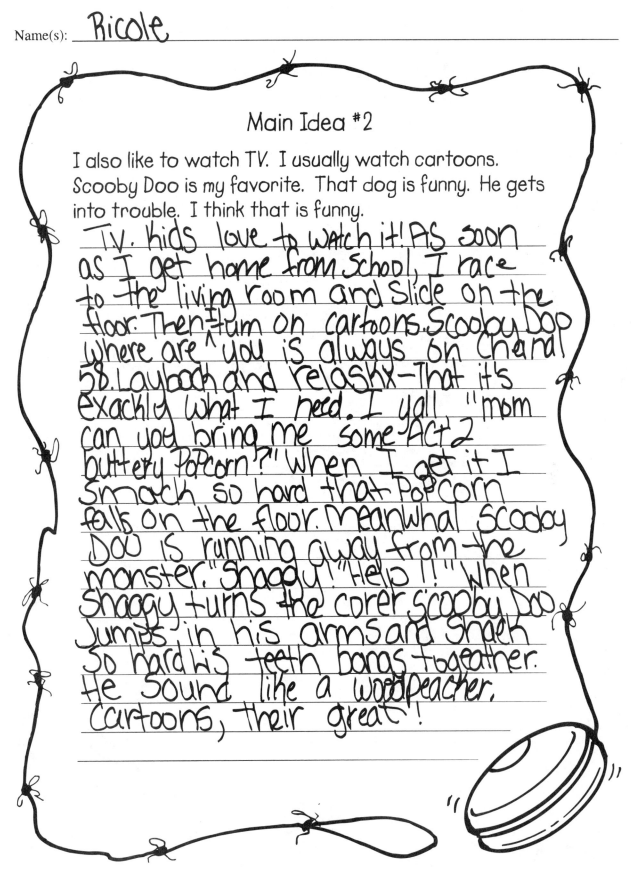

Main Idea #2

I also like to watch TV. I usually watch cartoons.
Scooby Doo is my favorite. That dog is funny. He gets
into trouble. I think that is funny.

TV. kids love to watch it! As soon
as I get home from school, I race
to the living room and slide on the
floor. Then I turn on cartoons. Scooby Doo
where are ^you is always on chanal
58. Lay back and relasky—That it's
exachly what I need. I yall "mom
can you bring me some Act 2
buttery Popcorn?" When I get it I
smach so hard that Popcorn
falls on the floor. Meanwhal Scooby
Doo is running away from the
monster. "Shaggy! Help!!" When
Shaggy turns the corer scooby Doo
Jumps in his arms and shack
so hard his teeth bangs togeather.
He sound like a woodpeacher.
Cartoons, their great!

Sample Student Planning

Planning for Sentence Variety

Reminders:

Sentence Length:
- short
- medium
- long

Sentence Structure:
- dialogue
- begins with a phrase
- contains a series of phrases
- simple construction

Sentence Type:
- exclamation
- question
- statement
- simple construction

Phillips   Street on 52ᵗʰ ✓
Rodrunner - purple 15speed ✓
Cat walk ✓
Sat. Sun. ✓
Ricole Victor ✓
cuts - bruses ✓

Sample Student Writing

Name(s): Jayna

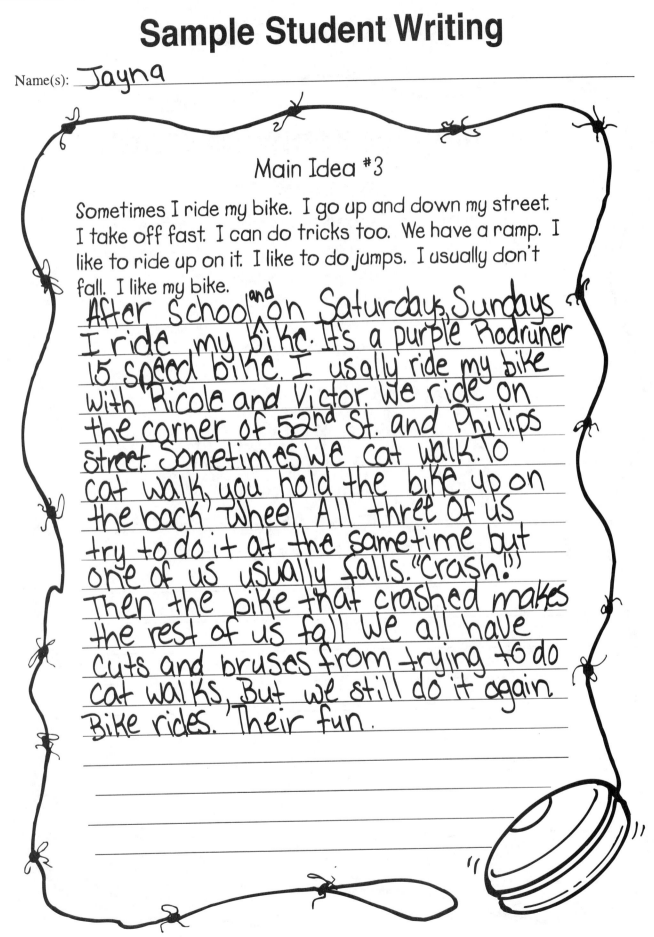

Main Idea #3

Sometimes I ride my bike. I go up and down my street. I take off fast. I can do tricks too. We have a ramp. I like to ride up on it. I like to do jumps. I usually don't fall. I like my bike.

After School and on Saturdays, Sundays I ride my bike. It's a purple Rodruner 15 speed bike. I usally ride my bike with Ricole and Victor. We ride on the corner of 52nd St. and Phillips street. Sometimes we cat walk. To cat walk, you hold the bike up on the back wheel. All three of us try to do it at the same time but one of us usually falls. "Crash!" Then the bike that crashed makes the rest of us fall. We all have cuts and bruses from trying to do cat walks, But we still do it again. Bike rides. Their fun.

Sample Student Planning

Planning for Sentence Variety

Reminders:

Sentence Length:	Sentence Structure:	Sentence Type:
• short	• dialogue	• exclamation
• medium	• begins with a phrase	• question
• long	• contains a series of phrases	• statement
	• simple construction	• simple construction

Tennis ball ✓
middle of the yard   ✓
Catch, then bring it back
friendly Golden Retriever ✓
throw ✓ far away as a street block ✓
runs so fast his ✓ feathers on his
back legs swish ✓

Sample Student Writing

Name(s): __Victor__ _____

Main Idea #4

Often I play with my dog. She likes to play ball. Her
favorite is a tennis ball. I throw it far away. She runs
fast and gets it. She always brings it back. We play
most afternoons.

Most days I come home and
play with my dog, Rex. He's a Golden Retriever.
We always play ball in the middle of my yard. His
favorite kind of ball is a tennis ball. I throw it a
short distance to get him warmed up. I throw it as
far as my Slip in Slide. He runs so fast his feathers
on his back legs swish. He always catches it. Then
brings it back and drops it at my feet. "Good boy,"
I say. Then I pick it up and throw it farther into
the neighboors' yard "Oops! I didn't mean to do that."
Rex never gets tired. I do. When I sit down in the
grass he jumps in my lap and drops that slobbery ball
on me. "Eew. gross." I like Rex but not his slobber
balls.

Rhythm That Paints Pictures

Materials

Teacher Materials You Need to Supply:

- read-aloud selection: *Homer Price* by Robert McCloskey
- alternate read-aloud selection: *Haunting at Home Plate* by David Patneaude (Begin on page 26 with: "There are things about baseball . . . ." End with: " . . . . the smells of leather and grass and dirt.")
- overhead projector, overhead transparency markers and pencils for each pair of students (*optional:* 3" by 5" sticky-notes if revising a previously written piece)
- overhead transparencies of sentence from the book (page 278), directions for writing (page 280), and stationery for writing (page 281)

Teacher Materials Included in the Lesson:

- quoted sentence from *Homer Price* (page 278)
- sample directions for writing (page 280)
- sample modeled planning (page 279)
- writing stationery (page 281)
- rubric for thinking about the writing (page 282)
- sample student directions for writing and writing (pages 283–287)

Student Materials Included in the Lesson:

- For each student, you will need to prepare packets containing copies of the sentence from *Homer Price* by Robert McCloskey (page 278), directions for writing (page 280), stationery for writing (page 281), and the rubric for thinking about their writing (page 282). (Students will also need their writing folders in order to select a piece of writing to revise for this technique.)

Read Aloud

1. Tell the students that today's lesson is on sentence variety. Tell them that writing with sentence variety can give our piece an inviting rhythm and make it interesting to the reader.

2. Tell students that we are going to write one sentence in the same pattern as the fine author, Robert McCloskey.

3. Display the overhead transparency of the sentence from the book. Read it together.

4. Tell students that the repetition of the word *mice* helps the reader see the mice. Point out the phrases and how McCloskey connected them together. Tell students that constructing our sentences like this will help us s-l-o-w down our writing so the reader can see what we are writing about and give the piece a rhythm that is intriguing. Reread the sentence again so the students can hear the rhythm of the sentence. Elicit the details that show the mice.

Rhythm That Paints Pictures *(cont.)*

Modeled Writing

1. Display the overhead transparency of the directions for writing the sentence. Tell the students that we are going to examine the sentence structure of the writing with our "writers' eyeballs." Tell them that you are going to break the sentence down into parts and then write each part using your own ideas. Point out that the sentence from *Homer Price* is written right there on the plan.

2. Model coming up with an idea to show. (Think of something you've previously written about; then choose a noun from that piece that you could show.) For example, one class had just written about doing a good deed, and many students wrote about picking up trash. This sample modeled plan (page 279) uses Corn Pops as an example of how a sentence constructed like McCloskey's would help show the spilled Corn Pops that one person cleaned up.

3. Follow the directions, writing each part of the sentence. Don't be afraid to play with the words until it sounds just the way you want it. You want them to see you labor over each word so that they won't give up when they try to do it.

Guided Independent Writing

1. Establish pairs of students. (When learning something new, it sometimes helps to group a strong writer with a weaker writer.) Distribute a writing packet to each student. (Each student may want his or her own stationery if choosing to rewrite a previous piece. Also, we want them to refer back to this sentence structure to use again and again.)

2. Direct students to decide on something (a noun) to write about. Again, remind them of previous pieces they've written where this technique might fit.

3. Using their directions for writing, direct them to write their sentence.

Sharing Session

- Direct each pair to share their sentence with any other pair in the class.

Follow-up Activity (teaching point: revision)

- Direct each student to take out a previously written piece from his or her writing folders. Have them reread to locate a place where this sentence pattern will help them achieve rhythm and show their idea.
- Using the sticky-notes, direct students to revise by writing a sentence in the same pattern as Robert McCloskey's.
- If your students have Writer's Notebooks, direct them to record their sentence in their books.

"Fat, doughnut fed mice from Uncle Ulysses' lunchroom,

"Fat, doughnut fed mice from Uncle Ulysses lunchroom, thin mice from the churches, ordinary mice from houses and homes, mice from the stores, and mice from the town hall."

—— *Homer Price by Robert McCloskey*

Modeled Planning

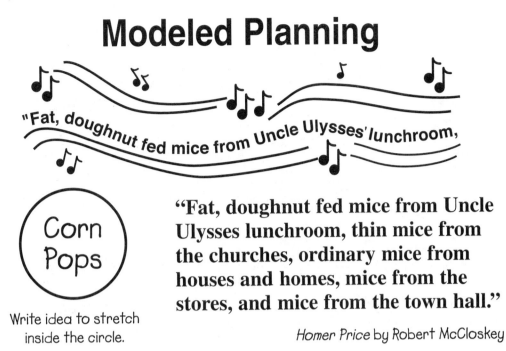

"Fat, doughnut fed mice from Uncle Ulysses' lunchroom,

Corn
Pops

Write idea to stretch
inside the circle.

"**Fat, doughnut fed mice from Uncle Ulysses lunchroom, thin mice from the churches, ordinary mice from houses and homes, mice from the stores, and mice from the town hall.**"

Homer Price by Robert McCloskey

Think of <u>a word to describe</u> your idea, write it, and then add a comma. Write your <u>idea word</u> and then add some more words to describe <u>where</u>. Add a comma.

<u>Round, sugarcoated Corn Pops rolled around my kitchen floor,</u>

Think of <u>another word to describe</u> another <u>type</u> of your idea, write it, and then write your <u>idea word</u>. Add some more words to tell <u>where</u> and then add another comma.

<u>Squished Corn Pops mashed flat from Daddy's big boot,</u>

Think of another word to describe another <u>type</u> of your <u>idea</u>, write it, and then write your idea word. Add some more words to tell <u>where</u> and then add another comma.

<u>Pale yellow piles of Corn Pops peeked from under the cabinets and appliances,</u>

Write your <u>idea</u>, add some more words to tell <u>where</u>, and then add another comma.

<u>Corn Pops scattered and then flew out the door,</u>

Write <u>and</u> repeat your <u>idea</u>, add some more words to tell <u>where</u>, and then end with a period.

<u>and Corn Pops now dirty and broken decorate my floor.</u>

Name(s): _____

Directions for Writing

"Fat, doughnut fed mice from Uncle Ulysses' lunchroom,

"Fat, doughnut fed mice from Uncle Ulysses lunchroom, thin mice from the churches, ordinary mice from houses and homes, mice from the stores, and mice from the town hall."

Homer Price by Robert McCloskey

Write idea to stretch inside the circle.

Think of <u>a word to describe</u> your idea, write it, and then add a comma. Write your *idea word* and then add some more words to describe <u>where</u>. Add a comma.

_____

Think of <u>another word to describe</u> another <u>type</u> of your idea, write it, and then write your <u>idea word</u>. Add some more words to tell <u>where</u> and then add another comma.

_____

Think of <u>another word to describe</u> another type of your <u>idea</u>, write it, and then write your <u>idea word</u>. Add some more words to tell <u>where</u> and then add another comma.

_____

Write your <u>idea</u>, add some more words to tell <u>where</u>, and then add another comma.

_____

Write <u>and</u> repeat your <u>idea</u>, add some more words to tell <u>where</u>, and then end with a period.

_____

Name(s): _____

"Fat, doughnut fed mice from Uncle Ulysses' lunchroom,

Name(s): _____

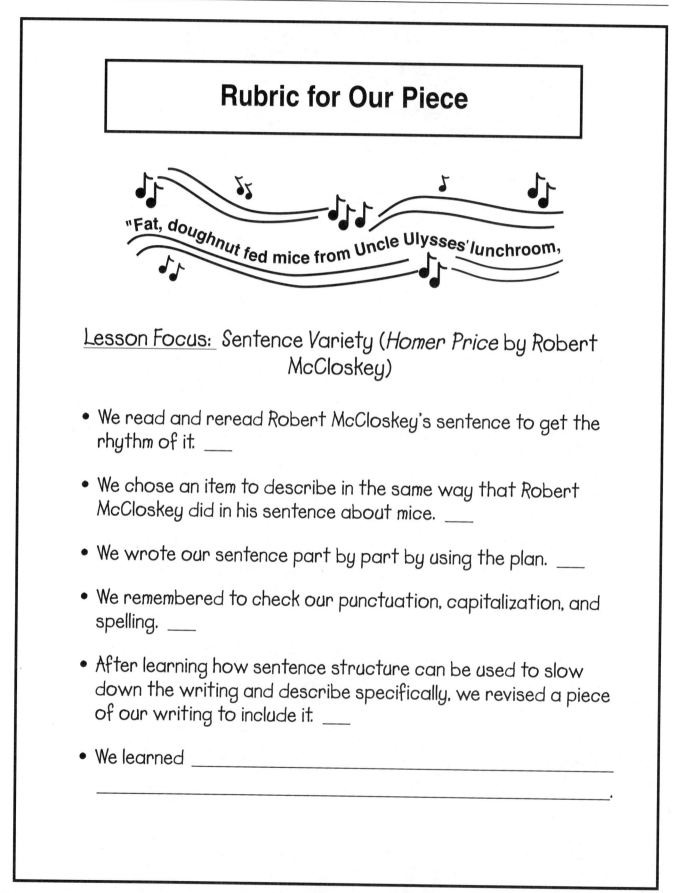

Rubric for Our Piece

"Fat, doughnut fed mice from Uncle Ulysses' lunchroom,

<u>Lesson Focus:</u> Sentence Variety (*Homer Price* by Robert McCloskey)

• We read and reread Robert McCloskey's sentence to get the rhythm of it. ___

• We chose an item to describe in the same way that Robert McCloskey did in his sentence about mice. ___

• We wrote our sentence part by part by using the plan. ___

• We remembered to check our punctuation, capitalization, and spelling. ___

• After learning how sentence structure can be used to slow down the writing and describe specifically, we revised a piece of our writing to include it. ___

• We learned _____

_____.

Sample Student Directions for Writing

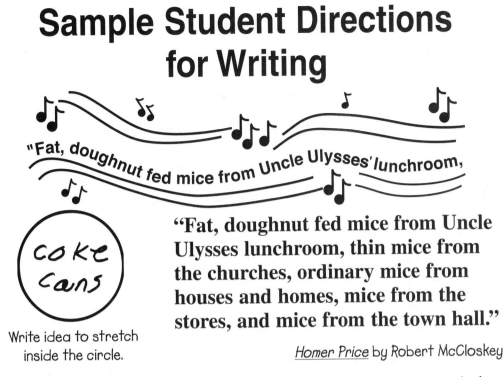

Write idea to stretch inside the circle.

"Fat, doughnut fed mice from Uncle Ulysses lunchroom, thin mice from the churches, ordinary mice from houses and homes, mice from the stores, and mice from the town hall."

Homer Price by Robert McCloskey

comma. Write your *idea word* and then add some more words to describe <u>where</u>. Add a comma.

Opened Squished coke cans dropped on the ground by people,

Think of <u>another word to describe</u> another <u>type</u> of your idea, write it, and then write your <u>idea word</u>. Add some more words to tell <u>where</u> and then add another comma.

Lopsided Cokecans thrown from cars,

Think of <u>another word to describe</u> another type of your <u>idea,</u> write it, and then write your <u>idea word.</u> Add some more words to tell <u>where</u> and then add another comma.

New Coke cans from the 7-11 space store,

Write your <u>idea,</u> add some more words to tell <u>where,</u> and then add another comma.

Coke cans from all over Temple Terres,

Write <u>and</u> repeat your <u>idea,</u> add some more words to tell <u>where,</u> and then end with a period.

and Coke cans from my own house & yours.

Sample Student Writing

Name(s): _____ *Francisco* _____

"Fat, doughnut fed mice from Uncle Ulysses' lunchroom,

On Januray -26-03 my friend Shawn
& I did a good deed. It all started
Whin we saw a church Near
are house on 26th and 50th st. We
got a great Idea. We decided
to ask the paster to hand us
a bag and two pairs of gloves.
Bet your wondering what we
Will do whith those things.
So we went to the side
and I said "Shawn you take
the front and I'll take the
back." Our good deed whas
going to be to clean the church
yard while they wher inside
preaching good things about the
Lord. Shawn and I did the good
deed to show that we care and

Sample Student Writing *(cont.)*

Name(s): **Francisco**

"Fat, doughnut fed mice from Uncle Ulysses' lunchroom,

appreshate them. The church had trash all over the place. Coke cans wher every where. Opened, squished Coke cans droped on the ground by people, Lopsided coke cans thrown from cars, new coke cans from the 7-11 space store, Coke cans from all over temple terres, and coke cans from my own house & yours. Bites of tishu and news pappers flew ever where. We chased down the flying papper and stuffed it in the bag. After an half hour, we sat down on the curb. Shawn said as he rubbed his back "my back is killing me. When we finish heer I am going home to

Sample Student Writing *(cont.)*

Name(s): _____ Francisco _____

"Fat, doughnut fed mice from Uncle Ulysses' lunchroom,

take a bath!" I replied to my
buddy "I'm right behind you shawn."
We worked harder then hard. It
took untile 3 o'clock untile we
where finished and you should have
seen us. Dirt covered my nose and
bites of grass stuck to my shoes.
Shawn didn't look much better. He
had sticky marsh mellow from the
candy rapers giveing his fingers
together. Coke was splattered
all down the front of his Bucs
Jersy and on to his jeans. He
look whorse then me. Just as
the last pease of trash went
into the bag the church doors
flew open and the people rushed
out. They stood on the steps and we

Sample Student Writing *(cont.)*

Name(s): ___Francisco___

"Fat, doughnut fed mice from Uncle Ulysses' lunchroom,

heared them say, "Whooa, Look at
how those two kids cleaned up
five acres of church yard". They
wher so proud of our good
deed that they gave us a bag
of sour cream and onion chips
ered mountain dews to drank. After
we drank and ate our snakes
we went to the park and
thought about what we did.
Shawn and I agread that
people apreshate it when
you do good deeds to show
respect to our elders.

Bibliography

Lesson 1: So Many Memories
Bunting, Eve. *The Memory String.* Houghton Mifflin, 2000. (alternate read-aloud selection: *Dear Levi Letters from the Overland Trail* by Elvira Woodruff. Knopf Books for Young Readers, 1994.)

Lesson 2: Try It Using One
Cleary, Beverly. *Ramona the Pest.* Harper Trophy, 1992.
Wyeth, Sharon Dennis. *Something Beautiful.* Dragonfly, 2002. (alternate read-aloud selection: *House on Mango Street* by Sandra Cisneros. Knopf, 2001

Lesson 3: All in the Mood
Curtis, Jamie Lee. *Today I Feel Silly & Other Moods That Make My Day.* HarperCollins Canada, 2004. (alternate read-aloud selection: *Some Things Are Scary* by Florence Parry Heide. Candlewick Press, 2000.)

Lesson 4: Too Much Worry
Henkes, Kevin. *Wemberly Worried.* Greenwillow, 2000.

Lesson 5: It's Not Too Late, Leo
Kraus, Robert. *Leo the Late Bloomer.* HarperCollins, 1971.

Lesson 6: Write Small to Show
MacLachlan, Patricia. *All the Places to Love.* HarperCollins, 5/30/94.
(alternate read-aloud selection: *Ruby Holler* by Sharon Creech. Harper Trophy, 12/2003, or *The Relatives Came* by Cynthia Rylant. Atheneum, 2/2001.)

Lesson 7: You Gotta Eat!
Palatini, Margie. *Zak's Lunch.* Clarion Books, 1998.

Lesson 8: Be a Maniac About It!
Spinelli, Jerry. *Maniac Magee.* Little, Brown and Company, 1999. (alternate read-aloud selection: *Holes* by Louis Sacher. Yearling Books, 2000, or *Thunder Cake* by Patricia Polacco. Puffin, 2002.)

Lesson 9: Scarecrows That Paint
Rylant, Cynthia. *Scarecrow.* Voyager Books, 2001.

Lesson 10: Lights, Camera and Action
Soto, Gary. *Snapshots from a Wedding.* Puffin, 1998.

Lesson 11: What's It Like?
Fletcher, Ralph. *Fig Pudding.* Yearling Books, 1996.

Lesson 12: Make It Happen
Goble, Roni. *Iktomi and the Boulder.* B.T Bound, 1999.

Lesson 13: Nuttin' Honey
Schotter, Roni. *Nothing Ever Happens on 90th Street.* Orchard Books, 1999.

Lesson 14: Creepy Facts
Collard, Sneed B., III. *Creepy Creatures.* Kidsbooks, 1998. (alternate read-aloud selection: *Cockroach Cooties* by Laurence Yep. Hyperion Press, 2001.)

Lesson 15: Facts, Examples, and Something Personal
Shauf, RuthAnn. "Nutrition."

Lesson 16: Clumping for Detail
Abercrombie, Barbara. *Charlie Anderson.* How Design Books, 2003.

Lesson 17: Some Place Special
Bouchard, David. *If You're Not from the Prairie . . .* B. T. Bound, 1999.

Lesson 18: Using What You've Got
Curtis, Christopher Paul. *Bud, Not Buddy.* Yearling Books, 2002. (alternate read-aloud selection: *But No Candy* by Gloria Houston, Philomel Books, 1992, or *Welcome to the River of Grass* by Jane Yolen, Putnam Pub. Group Juv., 2001.)

Lesson 19: Miss Nelson Said What?
Allard, Harry & James Marshall. *Miss Nelson Is Missing.* Houghton Mifflin, 1985.

Lesson 20: All in the Name
Cisneros, Sandra. *The House on Mango Street,* "My Name." Vintage, 1991. (alternate read-aloud selection: *Williwaw!* by Tom Bodett, Yearling Books, 2000.)

Lesson 21: Characters Come Alive
Rylant, Cynthia. *Missing May.* Yearling Books, 1993.

Lesson 22: Pledging with Our Voices
Martin, Bill Jr. & Michael Sampson. *I Pledge Allegiance.* Candlewick Press, 2000. (alternate read-aloud selection: *America Is . . . .* by Louise Borden. McElderry Books, 2002.)

Lesson 23: Personality Plus
Cisneros, Sandra. *Woman Hollering Creek,* "Eleven." Vintage, 1992.

Lesson 24: Age Matters, So Does Sentence Fluency (same selection as Lesson 23)

Lesson 25: A Show Sentence
Zolotow, Charlotte. *The Seashore Book.* Harper Trophy, 1994.

Lesson 26: Yo! It's All in the Beat
Spinelli, Jerry. *Knots in My Yo-Yo String.* Knopf Books for Young Readers, 1998. (alternate read-aloud selection: *Library Card* by Jerry Spinelli. Apple, 1998.)

Lesson 27: Rhythm That Paints Pictures
McCloskey, Robert. *Homer Price.* Puffin, 1976. (alternate read-aloud selection: *Haunting at Home Plate* by David Patneaude. Albert Whitman & Co., 2003.)